Party image
and electoral behavior

PARTY IMAGE
AND ELECTORAL BEHAVIOR

Richard J. Trilling
Duke University

A Wiley-Interscience Publication

JOHN WILEY & SONS, New York / **London** / **Sydney** / **Toronto**

71602

Library of Congress Cataloging in Publication Data:

Trilling, Richard J
  Party image and electoral behavior.

  "A Wiley-Interscience publication."
  Includes bibliographical references and index.
  1. Political parties—United States. 2. Party
affiliation—United States. 3. Voting—United States.
4. Public opinion—United States. 5. United States—
Politics and government—1945. I. Title.

JK2271.T65   329'.02   76-24794
ISBN 0-471-88935-0

Printed in the United States of America

10 9 8 7 6 5 4 3 2 1

To Faye and the two cuties

Preface

Electoral change has been so swift and monumental in the past 25 years that our sensibilities have been shaken and our understanding undermined. Why did voters forsake the stable, placid politics of the 1950s for the turbulence of the 1960s and the dismay of the 1970s? The study of the party images of Americans offers some clues to the dynamics of the contemporary American political scene.

One of the manifestations of electoral change has been the transformation of Southern politics from the Democratic "Solid South" to its more recent condition in which the Republican Party, prior to the 1974 Congressional elections at least, competed earnestly and frequently victoriously for statewide offices and Presidential electors. With the exception of Donald R. Matthews and James W. Prothro's classic study, *Negroes and the New Southern Politics*, no major work has yet examined the attitudinal basis for this transformation of Southern politics. Matthews and Prothro speculated that changing party images had contributed and would contribute to this transformation.

Originally I wanted to examine, over the 20 years of the present study, the speculative role of party images proposed by Matthews and Prothro. I soon discovered that the concept had implications reaching far beyond the South, beyond the early 1960s studied by Matthews and Prothro, and beyond the 20 years following Eisenhower's first election — the span of time in my own study. This book attempts to document the importance of the concept of party image for electoral behavior and to speculate about the implications of the data for the American electoral-party system.

The study of party image provides a content-based interpretation of party attachment. At a time when scholars are discovering greater volatility in partisan identifications, the bases for such attachments must be examined. Party images, though substantively and operationally different from party identifications, are clearly anchored in traditional political issues yet responsive to contemporary political issues in a manner that promotes our understanding of stability and change in party identifications.

The study of party image also provides a new and useful technique for measuring attachments to party. Not only can scholars in the future continue to ask if a respondent "generally considers" himself or herself a Republican, a Democrat, or an Independent, but scholars can also study partisan attachments by counting the numbers of likes and dislikes an individual has for the party and by analyzing the substantive likes and dislikes the individual holds.

Finally, the study of party image calls into question traditional, structural explanations of political behavior. Class differences in party image have subsided, thus suggesting that scholars may need to reject the use of class distinctions, or reconceptualize what we mean by class differences, or discover which emerging values will influence political behavior and how they are associated with subjective class differences.

The book is organized into several parts. An Introduction presents the concept of party image and relates it to other works in the discipline. In Part I party images are examined over time in three ways. First, in Chapter 2, a general index of party image is developed and compared to the standard index of partisanship employed by political scientists. Second, in Chapter 3, separate indexes are developed for the components of the general index, while the substantive concerns of the voters which constitute their party images are discussed in Chapter 4. Part II examines party images among important political groups in American society. Chapters 5 and 6 analyze party image differences between the working and middle classes, and Chapter 7 compares the party images of blacks and whites, probing the dynamics of Southern political change. Part III deals more specifically with theoretical propositions — Chapter 8 analyzes the ability of party images to transform party identifications, and Chapter 9 relates the properties of the concept of party image to the dynamics of the party system and to contemporary American politics.

In an endeavor such as this the scholar relies on others for assistance and encouragement. My debt begins, as do those of many contemporary political scientists, with benefits from the efforts of the Survey Research Center/Center for Political Studies at the University of Michigan, which conducted the seven surveys that furnished the data for the secondary analysis conducted in this book. I also thank the Inter-University Consortium for Political Research for making these data available to me. Neither the SRC/CPS nor the ICPR is responsible for the analysis or conclusions herein.

I am grateful to the Duke University Research Council and to the Department of Political Science, Duke University, for supporting my research and providing computer time.

Gerald M. Pomper, William Mishler, Donald Freeman, and Samuel Kirkpatrick have read portions of the manuscript and I owe them my gratitude for their time and comments. Remaining errors of omission and comission are of course my own.

For assistance in computer programming and data processing, I thank Jim Musselwhite, Jerry Herbert, Doug Arnett, Greg Mahler, Dan Harkins, and Sharon Poss. For their care and effort in typing portions of the manuscript, I thank Meri-Li Douglas and Barbara Culbertson.

I thank my family for encouragement and respite and assure my children that we can go on our vacation and go swimming now that the manuscript is finished.

RICHARD J. TRILLING

Durham, North Carolina
July 1976

Contents

Party image
and electoral behavior

chapter 1

Introduction — the relevance of party image

Students of American voting behavior have long sought to expand the set of conceptual tools and analytical skills available to them for the study of individual electoral behavior. Recent developments in American electoral politics have provided further impetus to this quest. Traditional patterns of voting behavior were sharply altered in the 1960s; for instance, Republican voting in the South was increased. The typically low levels of political involvement, interest, and participation of the 1950s gave way to the intense and emotional demonstrations of the 1960s. The low levels of conceptualization that also characterized the American voter in the 1950s were apparently replaced by "reasonable" if not "rational" individual electoral decision making in more recent national elections. Finally, the traditional tools of political explanation, particularly party identification, increasingly failed to explain these notable phenomena. If the goal of empirical political science — to develop universal explanations of political behavior — had not been sufficient to stimulate students of electoral behavior to attempt to broaden their set of explanatory variables, the inexplicability of recent phenomena most definitely has done so.

Party image is a concept whose properties have received little attention. This book examines these properties and reports on the relevance of the concept for the study of political behavior generally and for the examination of "issue voting," "party decomposition," and "electoral realignment" specifically — topics of considerable interest to political scientists at the moment. Clearly the concept of party image will not be able to explain all the recent phenomena that have attracted the attention of journalists and scholars alike. Nor will it provide a singularly complete explanation for any one of these phenomena. However, its relevance (its relatedness) to political behavior and to the three topics just mentioned will be demonstrated persuasively by the data to be examined here. These data will also offer the basis for a tentative theory of electoral change and stability which has as its linchpin the concept of party image.

A party image quite simply is a mental picture an individual has about a political party and is apt to be "vague, often confused and contradictory."[1] It is not the same thing as an individual's psychological attachment to a party — his party identification — because two individuals who are equally committed to a party psychologically may "have different mental pictures of it and evaluate these pictures in different ways."[2] An individual's party image not surprisingly is likely to be related to his party identification, but his party image will consist less of purely psychological, affective components and more of substantive components.

For the most part so far scholars have studied the concept of party image empirically, and have operationalized it, by asking individuals what they like and dislike about the Republican and Democratic parties. Responses to such questions have provided a wealth of data from which interesting inferences about individual political motivation can be made. The frequency and variety of these responses permit one to discuss the clarity and salience of party images. The substantive richness of the responses permits one to discuss the long-term and short-term issues in American politics that affect individual electoral behavior. And finally, indexes that count the number of such responses provide powerful tools for predicting voting behavior and partisan stability and change, and for tracing the changing attitudes of significant political groups in American society.

PARTY IMAGE AND CANDIDATE IMAGE

Studies that have asked individuals what they like and dislike about the parties have traditionally also asked individuals what they like and dislike about the Presidential candidates of the Republican and Democratic Parties. These likes and dislikes are said to measure "candidate images." Typically, however, the responses to the party image questionnaire items have been combined for purposes of analysis with the responses to the candidate image items. By combining these two sets of responses, scholars have been able to identify the combination of forces that elect a President,[3] to classify Americans according to their levels of conceptualization,[4] and to locate the sources of electoral change.[5] Kelley and Mirer even constructed a simple rule for combining these two sets of likes and dislikes which has the important virtue of predicting individual voting choice quite successfully.[6]

It can be argued, however, that the now traditional combination of these two sets of likes and dislikes has overlooked one theoretical implication in these data, the meaning of American political parties for the American voter as separate from the candidates nominated by these parties. In other words, the likes and dislikes of Americans for their political parties, that is, the party images of Americans, can be interpreted as evidence of the meaning these parties hold for those who perceive them. Isolating party images from candidate images should let us investigate the substantive and perhaps long-term meanings of parties for voters while minimizing the influence of the short-term candidate component. Candidates and issues are treated theoretically as short-term phenomena precisely because they remain in the political environment for only short durations, soon to be replaced by new candidates and issues.[7]

Furthermore, as we trace these likes and dislikes for the parties over time, we shall discover the long-term and short-term components in the political agenda of Americans. This agenda is not necessarily what parties, politicans, elected officials, political observers, or political events define it to be. Rather, the likes and dislikes Americans articulate about their political parties reveal the imprint that past and present issues, events, and candidates have left in their perceptions of political parties. Obviously the correspondence and discrepency between the agenda defined by the responses of American citizens and the agenda defined by political actors and events is an interesting and crucial subject for investigation, often best undertaken by political journalists commenting on individual campaigns.[8] However, the wealth of data that permits the determination of the meaning of political parties for Americans cannot be mined exhaustively in one study. Therefore, this book quite explicitly restricts its focus to the longitudinal examination of the likes and dislikes Americans have for their parties. These data reveal the impact of those environmental phenomena that compete for the attention of the American voter. Consequently these data will allow us to make inferences about the environmental phenomena without studying them directly.

THE RELEVANCE OF PARTY IMAGE

The concept of party image has great theoretical, and as we shall see empirical, relevance for the study of three topics of current interest to political scientists. First, the frequency and variety of the likes and dislikes Americans have for their parties indicate the extent to which parties continue to have meaning for voters and continue to arouse interest and concern among them. That is, party image data provide information about the alleged decomposition of American parties. The ability of political parties to command the loyalties of individuals, to influence their political behavior through these loyalties, and to link individuals with their government has apparently declined in recent years. This decline has variously been labeled decomposition[9] or dealignment.[10] Evidence of party decomposition includes the growing number of independents,[11] the declining ability of party identification to structure the vote,[12] the increasing incidence of split-ticket voting,[13] and "an increasing longitudinal velocity in aggregate outcomes of presidential elections" in which "the amplitude of partisan swing . . . [has increased] and presidential landslides [have] become common."[14] Burnham warns that "[i]f 'partisan decomposition' continues under . . . conditions of pervasive public discontent, democracy will be progressively emptied of any operational meaning . . . [and] a true crisis of regime will emerge."[15]

Although American political thought has always included an "antiparty" element, perhaps first represented by James Madison in

Federalist No. 10,[16] most political scientists would agree that political parties can perform the crucial functions of helping to keep governmental officials accountable and of mobilizing and informing the public.[17] As Americans find more or fewer things to like and dislike about their parties, we can infer that parties have more or less meaning for Americans. Party image data cannot provide definitive data about party decomposition but they can provide complementary and illuminating information about this normatively important process.

Second, the substance of the likes and dislikes of Americans for their parties offers an indirect measure of the salience of particular political issues. Furthermore, the degree to which political issues penetrate the party images of Americans provides a basis for evaluating the significance of opinions on political issues for electoral choice. The study of issue voting has revealed that individual voting choice has been more strongly correlated with opinions in recent years than in the 1950s.[18] For an individual to engage in issue voting — to vote on the basis of opinions rather than on the basis of traditional partisan loyalties or candidate images — an individual must have an opinion, must care about the issue, and must perceive differences between the parties on the issue.[19] The degree of penetration of specific political issues into the party images of Americans reveals information about individual perceptions of party differences, about individual concerns for the issues, and about the extent of opinion on the issue. The analysis of party image data cannot replace the more complete and sophisticated analysis of issue voting provided by more direct measures of opinion,[20] but party image data do offer a complementary means of examining the significance of issues for electoral choice.

Third, the study of party images has direct relevance for the theory of electoral realignment. According to this theory, American political history has been marked by periods of relative electoral stability punctuated by somewhat regular upheavals in the coalitional bases of American political parties. Social and economic crises prompt these electoral upheavals and eventually transform traditional party loyalties. These social and economic crises provide a set of critical issues that form the political agenda for the ensuing political generation.[21]

Many scholars have contributed to the evolving theory of electoral relignment but the most notable work has been done by Burnham and Sundquist.[22] Sundquist's thorough examination of American political history documents the frequency and periodicity of coalitional upheavals and investigates the realigning potential of such contemporary issues as race and Vietnam.[23] Burnham's analysis places special emphasis on the role of realignments in transforming the American party systems and speculates about a "critical realignment of a kind radically different from all others in American electoral history . . . [in which] critical realignment and party dissolution have uniquely become, in our time, inseparably-linked aspects of the some disruptive change in the flow of our potential history."[24]

Sellers argues that the critical issues that stimulate an electoral realignment do so first by altering the party images of large numbers of voters.[25] By this argument, then, the process of realignment involves two stages. First, critical issues cause changes in party image; second, these new party images cause changes in party identification.

THE THEORETICAL ROLE OF PARTY IMAGE

Sellers' discussion of party image is the most articulate theoretical treatment of the concept. In speculating about the causes of realignment, Sellers suggests:

> The crucial factor would seem to be the gross images of the parties as they are perceived (whether accurately or not) by voters in the process of forming or, to a lesser extent, changing identifications . . . the images that the parties project, the ways in which they do this, and the ways in which the voters perceive the parties seem to be the major determinants of political alignment.[26]

Sellers continues by speculating that the process of realignment involves, first, a few voters with established identifications changing them to the party with the image that is now more appealing because of the circumstances causing realignment; second, the desertion by a large number of voters from a party for an election or two without abandoning their identifications; and third, the formation by a great majority of the new voters of an identification with the newly advantaged party.[27] While Sellers' discussion is most provocative, he provides no empirical data for the evaluation of the critical theoretical role for party image that he describes.

The first major empirical treatment of the concept of party image was undertaken by Matthews and Prothro in their classic study of Southern political behavior. They operationalized party image by asking individuals what they liked and disliked about the political parties. The responses to these questions seemed to provide the basis for an explanation of Southern electoral change. Matthews and Prothro argued that the defections of nominal Southern White Democrats to the Republican Party from 1952 on were not the results of short-term forces such as personalities and issues. Instead, they speculated that the relative importance of two long-lasting issues — the pro-civil-rights position of the national Democratic Party and its support for federal governmental intervention in the economy — "in affecting the votes, images, and loyalties of southern whites may be the key to the puzzling future of southern politics."[28] That is, Matthews and Prothro felt that long-term processes were altering traditional voting patterns in the South, and these scholars were able to demonstrate that in the period 1960–1964, party images played a crucial role in these processes. The Matthews and Prothro study provided the first major empirical data on the concept of party image, data that seemed to convey a critical role for party image in altering traditional patterns of political behavior and partisan loyalties.

Furthermore, at a somewhat more theoretical level, Matthews and Prothro argued that "while party image is not so deeply rooted or so stable as party identification, it is likely to be less ephemeral than voter attitudes toward the issues and candidates of specific campaigns."[29] We know, in fact, that party identification is typically learned at a very early age and persists throughout an individual's lifetime.[30] The Sellers and Matthews and Prothro claim can thus be restated: party identifications are the basic linchpin to stable American politics. They remain generally stable throughout an individual's lifetime. Party images are not so stable as identifications. When crises cause party images to change substantially, these new images can in turn induce change in party identifications.

Few other theoretical treatments of the party image concept can be found in the literature. But a very interesting theoretical role for party image is suggested by John Meisel in his study of Canadian electoral behavior. Meisel argues that party identifications in Canada are typically volatile, unlike the stable identifications that are thought to exist in America. Consequently, the student of electoral behavior is deprived of his traditional tool for examining the long-term component of the vote. If most people vote most of the time in accordance with some underlying psychological attachment they maintain with a party, then in the long-term this attachment is the most accurate factor in predicting individual votes. Deviations from these predicted votes are said to result from the presence of short-term factors in the political environment, such as issues and candidates.[31] In place of party identification, Meisel suggests that party image might provide such a long-term component of electoral behavior, although he does not formalize or test such a model.[32] Recent evidence also questions the stability of party identifications among Americans,[33] lending further urgency to the search for long-term components of the electoral decision.

THE EMPIRICAL INVESTIGATION OF PARTY IMAGE

Until recently party images received greater attention in British electoral studies than in American works. In *Straight Fight,* which first discusses party images, the authors Milne and MacKenzie argue that long-standing political issues that effectively define and distinguish between the parties are "elevated to the status of party images. A party, so to speak, 'annexes' particular issues and assimilates them to its own image."[34] In turn, party images become a frequent reason for the individual's voting choice.[35] In *Marginal Seat* they extend this argument:

> Normally, issues do not develop into party images unless a vital difference of policy is perceived between the parties. A party, by "plugging" a popular issue, "annexes" it, and after a time the issue is identified with the party.[36]

But the connection between issues and images is not necessarily so proximate or direct:

> Party images . . . are symbols; the party is often supported because it is believed to stand for something dear to the elector. It matters little that the "something" may be an issue no longer of topical importance; the attachment to the symbol, and to the party, persists. Indeed, some party images resemble images of distant, disintegrating stars; the image is still clearly perceived by means of light-waves at a moment when the star no longer exists.[37]

In *Floating Voters and the Floating Vote,* Daudt points out two useful distinctions concerning party images. First, survey questions about political issues perceived by respondents elicit opinions on *current* issues, whereas with regard to party image, "the inquiry is into the way in which informants perceived the real or imagined party activities in the present *and the past.*[38] Second, "[i]n determining the party identification one seeks to find out whether and to what extent an informant feels himself drawn to one particular party; in ascertaining what constitutes a party image one investigates, if possible, what informants think of *all the parties.*"[39]

Despite the utility of the concept of party image, Butler and Stokes warn that under certain conditions voters may force their images to fit their preexisting party choices[40] and that the "parties do plainly owe some of their personification in the public's mind to their identification with those who lead them, and a great leader, a Disraeli or a Roosevelt, may impart something of themselves to images of their parties that are held long after they have gone."[41]

It is interesting to speculate that the importance of party image was first noted and discussed in Great Britain because the disciplined, ideological nature of British parties made party images so much more relevant than in the United States. This question is beyond the scope of the present analysis, although we shall return to it briefly in the Conclusion.

At any rate, the American literature on party image is rather scanty. In an early effort, which anticipates much of the analysis in the following chapters, V. O. Key suggests that the individual's "shorthand image of party may encompass a bundle of particular policies about which imformation and opinions may be sparse. . . ."[42] Furthermore, even these ill-informed images can provide a modicum of reason for the voting choice.[43] John Kessel's treatment of the Goldwater candidacy includes an examination of the party images among Americans in 1964, but Kessel despairs that, "The general queries about parties and candidates elicit so much in the way of traditional political views that issue references are a relatively minor theme. A more specific question is needed to tap the voters' thinking on issues."[44] Finally, in two recent investigations, Gerald Pomper and Merle Black and George Rabinowitz have examined the substantive themes contained in the party image data.[45]

Literature less specifically related to party image is somewhat more abundant. Several important pieces have been published that have relied on combinations of the party image and candidate image responses. The Survey Research Center extracted six attitudes from the party and candidate image responses and reported on the relative impact of these attitudes in affecting electoral choice. Also, the impact of these attitudes has been traced over time.[46] This same combination of party and candidate image responses has provided scholars with the raw data for analyzing the levels of conceptualization among Americans — the degree of clarity and the information content of the responses have been classified into several different levels.[47] Finally, many authors have relied on the party image items — those questions eliciting likes and dislikes about the parties — for purposes other than the study of party image.[48]

In all of these studies several different methodologies have been employed to transform the actual responses into meaningful data. Most scholars have been interested in grouping these responses according to content — either into such broad categories as *groups* in society or with regard to more specific content such as economic and welfare issues or Vietnam. In addition to the substantive analysis, indexes of party image have been computed, based solely on the numbers of likes and dislikes for each of the parties. Matthews and Prothro collapsed such an index into five categories, providing a model that will be used extensively in the chapters that follow. Finally, what others have not done so far is to explore extensively party images among critical groups in American society. All of these methodologies will be utilized in this book.

THE PRESENT STUDY

The scope of the analysis is the set of six Presidential election studies conducted by the Survey Research Center/Center for Political Studies (SRC/CPS) from 1952 to 1972. The advantages of using these data sets should be fairly obvious. First, the long-term and presumably more meaningful aspects of the data should be revealed in this 20-year time span. Second, the time span covers approximately half of a "political generation," said to last about 40 years by students of electoral realignment, so it should provide a good deal of information about the present political alignment and about the causes of the present coalitional bases to the parties. Finally, this particular 20-year period has contained a great variety of political scenarios, ranging from the more placid politics of the Eisenhower years, through the turbulent demonstrations of the 1960s, up to (but unfortunately not past) the appearance of Watergate in the political environment. In addition to the six data sets from the Presidential elections of this 20-year period, a panel study of Americans from 1956 to 1960 has also been analyzed. This study, also conducted by the Survey Research Center, interviewed the same sample of Americans in 1956, 1958, and 1960, and should permit us to examine the process of change more intensely.[49]

The remaining chapters separate themselves logically into three divisions. Part I, containing Chapters 2, 3, and 4, provides an empirical overview of party images. Chapter 2 introduces the basic party image index, presents the distributions of Americans along this index, and discusses its utility in the study of electoral behavior. Chapter 3 investigates whether likes and dislikes for the parties have an equal impact on political behavior. Chapter 4 uses the richness of the specific responses to the party image questionnaire items to trace the meaning of parties for Americans over time and to examine key issues in American politics in the past 25 years.

Part II examines party images among societal groups that have produced the basic cleavages in American politics. Chapters 5 and 6 explore the differences between the party images of working class and middle class Americans. As class differences in American politics have subsided generally, status differences have come to the fore, the most relevant being racial differences between blacks and whites, which are discussed in Chapter 7.

Part III investigates the theoretical properties of the concept of party image. Chapter 8 specifically confronts Sellers' claim that party images can induce change in party identification. Chapter 9 (Conclusion) summarizes the evidence about the relevance of party image for party decomposition, issue voting, and electoral realignment, presents a tentative theory of the role of party image in electoral behavior, and draws out the implications of the party image data for the American electoral party system.

NOTES

1. Donald R. Matthews and James W. Prothro, *Negroes and the New Southern Politics* (New York: Harcourt, Brace and World, 1966), p. 378.
2. *Ibid.*
3. Donald E. Stokes, Angus Campbell, and Warren Miller, "Components of Electoral Decision," *American Political Science Review,* **52** (1958), 367–387.
4. Angus Campbell, Philip E. Converse, Warren E. Miller, and Donald E. Stokes, *The American Voter* (New York: Wiley, 1960), pp 216–265.
5. Donald E. Stokes, "Some Dynamic Aspects of Contests for the Presidency," *American Political Science Review,* **60** (1966), 19–28.
6. Stanley Kelley, Jr. and Thad W. Mirer, "The Simple Act of Voting," *American Political Science Review,* **68** (1974), 572–591.
7. The theoretical distinction between long-term and short-term influence on

the electoral decision was first proposed by Philip E. Converse, "The Concept of a Normal Vote," pp. 2–29 in Angus Campbell, Philip E. Converse, Warren E. Miller, and Donald E. Stokes, *Elections and the Political Order* (New York: Wiley, 1966). For a recent application of this model, see Richard W. Boyd, "Popular Control of Political Policy: A Normal Vote Analysis of the 1968 Election," *American Political Science Review*, **66** (1972), 429–449.

8. The insightful but perhaps less systematic research that brings together the activities of political actors with the apparent responses of the electorate is exemplified in the writings of Samuel Lubell and Theodore White and also in the analyses of prominent columnists such as Tom Wicker and Jules Whitcover.

9. See the writings of Walter Dean Burnham, for instance "The Changing Shape of the American Political Universe," *American Political Science Review*, **59** (1965), 7–28, and *Critical Elections and the Mainsprings of American Politics* (New York: Norton, 1970).

10. Ronald Inglehart and Avram Hochstein, "Alignment and Dealignment of the Electorate in France and the United States," *Comparative Political Studies*, 5:3 (October 1972), 343–372.

11. *Ibid.* See also Norval D. Glenn, "Sources of the Shift to Political Independence: Some Evidence From a Cohort Analysis," *Social Science Quarterly*, **53**:3 (December 1972), 494–519.

12. This was most notable in 1968 and 1972. In 1968, Republican or Democratic party identifications did not prevent large numbers of voters from supporting George Wallace, the candidate of the American Independent Party. In 1972, the Democratic Party suffered a massive number of defections of its identifiers.

13. See Walter De Vries and V. Lance Tarrance, *The Ticket-Splitter: A New Force in American Politics* (Grand Rapids, Mich.: William B. Eerdmans, 1972).

14. Walter Dean Burnham, "American Politics in the 1970s: Beyond Party?" in Louis Maisel and Paul M. Sacks, eds., *The Future of Political Parties*, Sage Electoral Studies Yearbook, Vol. 1 (Beverly Hills, Calif.: Sage Publications, 1975), p. 246.

15. *Ibid.*, p. 272.

16. In *Federalist No. 10*, Madison argues that the Republican form of government will minimize the pernicious influence of faction (political party).

17. Proponents of "party government" claim that responsible, disciplined political parties can perform vital tasks in a democracy, especially including those of educating and mobilizing the electorate and of providing the electorate with a mechanism through which to control public policy. See the arguments presented by E. E. Schattschneider in *Party Government* (New York: Holt, Rinehart and Winston, 1942) and by the Committee on Political Parties, American Political Science Association, "Toward a More Responsible Two-Party System," *American Political Science Review*, **54,** Supple-

ment (September 1950). More empirically based appraisals of American political parties, which are also positive but less uniformly so, are contained in Samuel J. Eldersveld, *Poltical Parties* (Chicago: Rand McNally, 1964) and Frank J. Sorauf, *Party Politics in America,* 2nd. ed. (Boston: Little, Brown, 1972).

18. See especially Arthur H. Miller, Warren E. Miller, Alden S. Raine, and Thad A. Brown, "A Majority Party in Disarray: Policy Polarization in the 1972 Election," paper presented at the 1972 Annual Meeting of the American Political Science Association, Jung Hotel, New Orleans, Louisiana, September 4–8, 1973. On mass belief systems and individual attitude structures, also see Norman H. Nie, "Mass Belief Systems Revisited: Political Change and Attitude Structure," *Journal of Politics,* **36** (1974), 540–591.

19. These criteria for issue voting were first enumerated by Angus Campbell et al., in *The American Voter, op. cit.,* p. 170.

20. See for instance the two papers by David E. RePass, "Issue Salience and Party Choice," *American Political Science Review,* **65** (1971), 389–400, and "Levels of Rationality Among the American Electorate," paper presented at the 1974 Annual Meeting of the American Political Science Association, Palmer House Hotel, Chicago, Ill., August 29–September 2, 1974.

21. Burnham, *Critical Elections, op. cit.*

22. Burnham, *Critical Elections, op. cit.,* and James L. Sundquist, *Dynamics of the Party System* (Washington: Brookings, 1973). See also V. O. Key, Jr., "A Theory of Critical Elections," *Journal of Politics,* **17** (1955), 3–18; Key, "Secular Realignment and the Party System," *Journal of Politics,* **21** (1959), 198–210; Angus Campbell, "A Classification of Presidential Elections," pp. 63–77 in Campbell et al., *Elections and the Political Order, op. cit.*; and Gerald M. Pomper, *Elections in America* (New York: Dodd, Mead, 1970), pp. 99–125.

23. See especially Sundquist, *op. cit.,* pp. 308–331.

24. Burnham, "American Politics in the 1970s: Beyond Party?" *op. cit.,* pp. 238–239. See also Burnham, "The End of American Party Politics," *Transaction,* **7**:2 (December 1969), 12–22.

25. Charles Sellers, "The Equilibrium Cycle in Two-Party Politics," *Public Opinion Quarterly,* **29** (1965), 16–38.

26. *Ibid.,* p. 26.

27. *Ibid.,* p. 30.

28. Matthews and Prothro, *op. cit.,* p. 396. Also see the other writings by Matthews and Prothro on party image: "Southern Images of Political Parties: An Analysis of White and Negro Attitudes," pp. 82–111 in Avery Leiserson, ed., *The American South in the 1960s* (New York: Praeger, 1964); and "The Concept of Party Image and Its Importance for the Southern Electorate," pp. 139–174 in M. Kent Jennings and L. Harmon Zeigler, eds., *The Electoral Process* (Englewood Cliffs, N. J.: Prentice-Hall, 1966).

29. Matthews and Prothro, *Negroes and the New Southern Politics, op. cit.,* p. 378.

30. The political socialization literature documents these points thoroughly. See for instance Herbert H. Hyman, *Political Socialization* (Glencoe, Ill.: Free Press, 1959) and Fred I. Greenstein, *Children and Politics* (New Haven: Yale University Press, 1965).

31. Converse, "The Concept of a Normal Vote," *op. cit.*

32. John Meisel, *Working Papers on Canadian Politics,* Enlarged ed. (Montreal: McGill-Queen's University Press, 1973), p. 67.

33. Douglas Dobson and Douglas St. Angelo, "Party Identification and the Floating Vote: Some Dynamics," *American Political Science Review,* **69** (1975), 481–490; Richard A. Brody, "Change and Stability in Partisan Identification: A Note of Caution" (unpublished manuscript: Stanford University, 1975).

34. R. S. Milne and H. C. Mackenzie, *Straight Fight* (London: The Hansard Society, 1954), p. 137.

35. *Ibid.,* p. 129.

36. R. S. Milne and H. C. Mackenzie, *Marginal Seat, 1955* (London: The Hansard Society, 1958), p. 130.

37. *Ibid.*

38. H. Daudt, *Floating Voters and the Floating Vote* (Leiden: H. E. Stenfert Kroese N. V., 1961), p. 140, emphasis added.

39. *Ibid.,* p. 140, emphasis in original.

40. David Butler and Donald Stokes, *Political Change in Britain* (New York: St. Martin's Press, 1969), p. 370.

41. *Ibid.,* pp. 371–372.

42. V. O. Key, Jr., *Public Opinion and American Democracy* (New York: Knopf, 1961), p. 433.

43. *Ibid.,* pp. 460–472.

44. John Kessel, *The Goldwater Coalition* (Indianapolis: Bobbs-Merrill, 1968), p. 276.

45. Gerald M. Pomper, *Voters' Choice* (New York: Dodd, Mead, 1975), Ch. 7; Merle Black and George Rabinowitz, "An Overview of American Electoral Change: 1952–1972," paper prepared for delivery at the annual meeting of the Southern Political Science Association, Braniff Place, New Orleans, La., November 8, 1974. See also Michael R. Kagay and Greg A. Caldeira, " 'I Like the Looks of His Face': Elements of Electoral Choice, 1952–1972," paper prepared for delivery at the Annual Meeting of the American Political Science Association, San Francisco Hilton Hotel, San Francisco, Calif., September 2–5, 1975.

46. In addition to the references cited above in notes 3, 4, and 5, see Angus Campbell, "Interpreting the Presidential Victory," pp. 256–281 in Milton C. Cummings, Jr., ed., *The National Election of 1964* (Washington: Brookings, 1966).

47. See Angus Campbell, et al., *The American Voter*, *op. cit.,* pp. 216–265; John

C. Pierce, "Party Identification and the Changing Role of Ideology in American Politics," *Midwest Journal of Political Science*, **14** (1970), 25–42; and C. Anthony Broh, *Toward a Theory of Issue Voting*, Sage American Politics Series, Vol. 1, series no. 04-011 (Beverly Hills: Sage Publications, 1973).

48. For instance, see Richard W. Boyd, "Presidential Elections: An Explanation of Voting Defection," *American Political Science Review*, **63** (1969), 498–514; Andrew T. Cowart, "Electoral Choice in the American States: Incumbency Effects, Partisan Forces, and Divergent Partisan Majorities," *American Political Science Review*, **67** (1973), 835–853; Carl C. Hetrick, "Policy Issues and the Electoral Process," *Western Political Quarterly*, **25** (1972), 165–182; William R. Shaffer, "Partisan Loyalty and the Perceptions of Party, Candidates and Issues," *Western Political Quarterly*, **25** (1972), 424–433; and Samuel A. Kirkpatrick, "Political Attitudes and Behavior: Some Consequences of Attitudinal Ordering," *Midwest Journal of Political Science*, **14** (1970), 1–24.

49. In each of these seven surveys the actual questionnaire items used to measure party images appeared as follows:

(a) Is there anything in particular that you like about the Democratic Party? What is that?

(b) Is there anything in particular that you don't like about the Democratic Party? What is that?

(c) Is there anything in particular that you like about the Republican Party? What is that?

(d) Is there anything in particular that you don't like about the Republican Party? What is that?

These items appear, *respectively*, as the following variables in the Inter-University Consortium for Political Research codebooks:

1952: $v18, v19, v20, v21$
1956: $v15, v16, v17, v18$
1960: $v20, v21, v22, v23$
1964: $v21, v22, v23, v24$
1968: $v28, v29, v30, v31$
1972: $v31, v33, v35, v37$
Panel: $v15, v16, v17, v18, v313, v314, v315, v316, v586, v587, v588, v589$

To increase the number of cases available for analysis, weighting schemes were used when available. All data reported in this book rely on valid cross-sectional samples of the following sizes:

1952: $N = 1899$ (no weighting)
1954: $N = 1762$ (no weighting)
1960: $N = 1954$ (weighted from 1181)

1964: $N = 4658$ (weighted from 1834)
1968: $N = 3100$ (weighted from 1673)
1972: $N = 1372$ (no weighting)
Panel: $N = 1514$ (no weighting)

Detailed information on the sample designs for each of these studies is available in the codebooks for the studies available from the Inter-University Consortium for Political Research (ICPR).

Finally, all data were made available by the ICPR, which bears no responsibility for the analysis.

part I

An overview of party images
among Americans

chapter 2

The index of party image

In this chapter we develop an index of party image to compare the concept of party image to that of party identification.[1] The similarities in the behavior of the two concepts validate the concept of party image but their differences reveal the interactive role of the two in affecting electoral behavior. The index measures the extent of favorability Americans have for the Republican or Democratic Party. In response to the four party image questions eliciting what Americans like and dislike about the two parties, respondents could offer up to five responses. The index is devised simply by counting as positive each response favorable to the Republican Party or unfavorable to the Democratic Party and as negative each response favorable to the Democratic Party or unfavorable to the Republican Party. "Don't knows" and other missing data categories were coded zero. Except in 1972, this index ranged from +10 for most strongly pro-Republican to −10 for most strongly pro-Democratic. Then, as suggested by Matthews and Prothro, this raw index was collapsed into five categories: strongly pro-Democratic (DD), mildly pro-Democratic (D), neutral (N), mildly pro-Republican (R), and strongly pro-Republican (RR). This index thus captures the extent to which the number of likes and dislikes an individual has for the parties predisposes him toward one party more than toward the other.

Such an index obviously fails to capture the rich variety and substance in the likes and dislikes Americans have for their parties. These likes and dislikes are examined instead in Chapter 4. At this point the index can introduce the concept of party image and can reveal its potential for explaining the dynamics of American politics from 1952 through 1972.

A NOTE ON THE 1972 SRC/CPS STUDY

In 1972 the SRC/CPS recorded no more than three responses to each of the four questions eliciting the individual's likes and dislikes for the parties. Consequently the index can range only from −6 to +6, rather than from −10 to +10. To compare the 1972 data to data from earlier years we must make a choice. We may use only the first three responses for each year, preserving the equivalence of the measure. This procedure, however, would sacrifice valuable information contained in those fourth and fifth responses. Empirically, in earlier studies few people offer more than three responses,[2] so the choice will be less crucial than it might seem. However, individuals who do offer more than three responses are typically more partisan and more likely to vote. Since only one of the seven data sets being employed involves this problem, it would seem preferable to use all five responses wherever possible and to treat the 1972 data carefully.[3] Given this choice, equivalence is then maximized by collapsing the index into five categories, ranging from strongly pro-Democratic to strongly pro-Republican again, by using the same cutting points as in other years.[4]

Because fewer responses were recorded in 1972, it is mathematically possible, even probable, that a larger proportion of individuals will be coded as neutral than in other years. Consequently, the evidence below that party images were less well-defined in the minds of Americans in 1972 than in earlier years must be considered carefully. Fortunately it is possible to demonstrate unambiguously, as we shall in Chapter 3, that the stimuli, "Democratic Party" and "Republican Party," were less likely to provoke responses among Americans in 1972. For the moment, however, the reader should be somewhat cautious in assessing the substantive distinctiveness of the 1972 data.

PARTY IMAGE OVER TIME

We begin the examination of party images by following the distributions of Americans on the index of party image over the 20-year period of our study. Table 2.1 presents these distributions. The data reveal great stability over time in the aggregate measure of party image. In general, 20–25% of all Americans are coded as neutral image-holders during these years, with a little more than 40% of all Americans coded as pro-Democratic and a little less than 40% coded as pro-Republican. Despite the great change in American politics in this period, the index of party image reveals an underlying stability, in the aggregate at least. Such stability resembles that of aggregate distributions of party identification among Americans, also presented in the table.

Party images behave very much but not entirely like party identifications, both in the aggregate, as measured in the table, and at the individual level, as we shall see. Yet the concept of party image is neither identical to that of party identification, nor is it insensitive to change in American politics. We address the latter point first. There is evidence in the table that the aggregate measure of party image responds to short-term political forces. Some shift favoring the Democratic Party can be seen in 1964, reflecting the negative personal image the Republican candidate had among 1964 respondents.[5] In 1968 Democrats suffered in the eyes of the electorate,[6] and the Republican gain in the aggregate measure of party image exceeded what the party had lost in 1964, so the party attained a high for these years at 39.4% in the combined percents with pro-Republican images. In 1972 a significant increase in the proportion of neutral image-holders occurred (to 36%). Thus in 1972 parties seemed relatively unable to project their identities at the same time that they were relatively unable to structure images of candidates, opinions on the issues, or the voting choice of individuals.[7]

We must remember, however, that mathematically fewer people could have been coded in nonneutral categories simply because fewer responses were recorded in 1972. Nevertheless, by 1972 the decline over the years in the proportion of individuals with strongly pro-Democratic images had become striking, indicating, as other studies have,[8] that the

TABLE 2.1 Distributions of Party Image and Party Identification, by Year

Party Image

Year	Strongly Pro-Democratic (-10 to -4)[a]	Mildly Pro-Democratic (-3 to -1)	Neutral (0)	Mildly Pro-Republican (+1 to +3)	Strongly Pro-Republican (+4 to +10)[a]	Total Percent	(N)
1952	16.0%	26.0%	20.8%	20.1%	17.1%	100.0%	(1899)
1956	15.6%	28.4%	22.2%	22.9%	10.9%	100.0%	(1762)
1960	14.0%	30.2%	22.5%	27.7%	10.6%	100.0%	(1954)
1964	14.4%	33.5%	25.6%	18.8%	7.7%	100.0%	(4658)
1968	10.4%	26.4%	23.8%	25.7%	13.7%	100.0%	(3100)
1972	8.4%	26.7%	36.1%	23.0%	5.8%	100.0%	(1372)

Party Identification

Year	Strong Democrat	Weak Democrat	Independent Democrat	Independent	Independent Republican	Weak Republican	Strong Republican	Total Percent	(N)
1952	22.7%	26.0%	10.0%	5.9%	7.3%	14.2%	13.9%	100.0%	(1729)
1956	21.5%	23.8%	6.6%	9.2%	8.6%	14.8%	15.5%	100.0%	(1690)
1960	20.9%	25.5%	6.5%	10.1%	6.9%	14.1%	16.0%	100.0%	(1864)
1964	27.0%	25.3%	9.1%	7.9%	5.8%	13.6%	11.3%	100.0%	(4561)
1968	20.1%	25.6%	10.0%	10.8%	8.8%	15.0%	10.8%	100.0%	(3049)
1972	13.2%	28.2%	10.8%	12.4%	10.8%	13.9%	10.8%	100.1%[b]	(1342)

[a] In 1972 extreme categories range from -6 to -4 and from +4 to +6.
[b] Row does not total 100.0% due to rounding error.

Democratic Party has experienced greater disaffection than the Republican Party in this electoral period. Consequently, the aggregate measure of party image reveals both the basic stability of American politics and the presence of forces for change.

PARTY IMAGE AND PARTY IDENTIFICATION

Of course, distributions of the party identifications of Americans also reflect stability and change in American politics, even though the two concepts are not identical. Party identifications are acquired by the young child and typically retained through the individual's lifetime.[9] The aggregate distributions of party identification in Table 2.1 reflect the stability that one would expect from this process of political socialization. But change is also evident here. Since 1964 the combined proportion of Independent Democrats, Independent Republicans, and Independents has risen from around 23 to 30% or higher.[10] Also since 1964 the proportion of strong Democrats has fallen precipitously, from 27 to 13%. Both these trends tentatively provide evidence of party decomposition similar to the finding that party images in 1972 were not very well-developed.

The degree of interchangeability between party image and party identification can be seen in the fairly stable relationship between the two concepts over time. Cross-tabulations of party identification by party image have been reduced for the purpose of presentation into the one-dimensional arrays of Table 2.2. Within each image category, the difference between the percent identifying with the Democratic Party and the percent identifying with the Republican Party is given in the appropriate cell of the table.[11] As one reads across any row from strongly pro-Democratic to strongly pro-Republican, this difference shifts from strongly favoring the Democrats to strongly favoring the Republicans. What this table confirms for the entire 20-year period is Matthews and Prothro's finding for the early 1960s that extreme images and extreme partisanship go hand in hand.[12] This consistent relationship thus suggests the meaningfulness and validity of the concept of party image.

Yet the relationship between party image and party identification is neither perfect nor immutable. Even among strong image-holders, there is never complete association between image and identification. And the

TABLE 2.2   Relationship Between Party Identification and Party Image, by Year[a]

Year	Party Image[b]						
	DD	D	N	R	RR	Gamma	(N)
1952	93.4	74.0	31.3	−29.6	−62.6	.781	(1729)
	(302)	(482)	(246)	(375)	(324)		
1956	93.4	70.7	4.7	−54.6	−92.2	.834	(1690)
	(273)	(484)	(343)	(398)	(192)		
1960	94.5	72.8	11.1	−57.5	−79.2	.821	(1864)
	(270)	(571)	(376)	(440)	(207)		
1964	92.6	75.2	23.3	−39.5	−83.9	.785	(4561)
	(666)	(1553)	(1118)	(869)	(355)		
1968	90.0	80.4	27.1	−21.8	−66.5	.732	(3049)
	(321)	(810)	(704)	(790)	(424)		
1972	93.1	74.8	7.3	−42.2	−70.8	.724	(1342)
	(115)	(365)	(470)	(313)	(79)		

[a]Entries are the differences between the percent identifying with the Democratic Party and the percent identifying with the Republican Party for the respective categories of party image. Image category n's on which the percents are based are given in parentheses under the entries. Independent Democrats and Independent Republicans are coded as partisans; Independents are excluded.
[b]Key: DD=Strongly pro-Democratic (-10 to -4); D=Mildly pro-Democratic (-3 to -1); N=Neutral (0); R=Mildly pro-Republican (+1 to +3); RR=Strongly pro-Republican (+4 to +10). In 1972 extreme categories range from -6 to -4 and from +4 to +6.

advantage in terms of identifiers which the Democratic Party has possessed among neutral image-holders has been quite volatile. Thus while we should expect the concepts to overlap somewhat in their ability to explain political behavior, the concepts are not completely interchangeable. In fact, there is a meaningful interactive relationship between the two that we can detect as we examine their separate and combined impacts on the vote.

THE SEPARATE IMPACTS ON THE VOTE

Since party images are so closely related to party identifications, it is not surprising that images should also be strongly related to the vote. Table 2.3 documents this strong relationship. Close to 90% or more of the extreme image-holders vote for the party projecting the image. As we read across from the strongly pro-Democratic image column to the

TABLE 2.3   Relationship Between Vote and Party Image, by Year

Year	Vote[a]	Party Image[b]					Gamma
		DD	D	N	R	RR	
1952	Dem.	93.6%	73.8%	41.7%	10.1%	0.7%	.902
	Rep.	6.4%	26.2%	58.3%	89.9%	99.3%	
	Diff.	87.2%	47.6%	16.6%	-79.8%	-98.6%	
	(N)	(203)	(298)	(187)	(278)	(269)	(1235)
1956	Dem.	89.1%	68.4%	22.2%	7.2%	1.2%	.881
	Rep.	10.9%	31.6%	77.8%	92.8%	98.8%	
	Diff.	78.2%	36.8%	-55.6%	-85.6%	-97.6%	
	(N)	(221)	(354)	(216)	(304)	(171)	(1266)
1960	Dem.	93.1%	79.9%	46.3%	11.4%	1.2%	.878
	Rep.	6.9%	20.1%	53.8%	88.6%	98.8%	
	Diff.	86.2%	59.8%	-7.6%	-77.2%	-97.6%	
	(N)	(232)	(407)	(249)	(360)	(173)	(1421)
1964	Dem.	97.7%	90.6%	73.4%	27.4%	3.2%	.873
	Rep.	2.3%	9.4%	26.6%	72.6%	96.8%	
	Diff.	95.4%	81.2%	47.8%	-45.2%	-93.6%	
	(N)	(518)	(1122)	(698)	(654)	(316)	(3308)
1968	Dem.	86.7%	74.3%	31.3%	15.9%	4.0%	.633
	Rep.	6.2%	18.5%	54.7%	69.0%	83.6%	
	AIP	7.1%	7.2%	14.0%	15.1%	12.4%	
	(N)	(226)	(552)	(386)	(516)	(354)	(2034)
1968	Dem.	86.7%	74.3%	31.3%	15.9%	4.0%	.811
	Other	13.3%	25.7%	68.7%	84.1%	96.0%	
	Diff.	73.4%	48.6%	-37.4%	-68.2%	-92.0%	
	(N)	(226)	(552)	(386)	(516)	(354)	(2034)
1972	Dem.	88.8%	60.2%	23.5%	4.5%	1.4%	.840
	Rep.	11.2%	39.8%	76.5%	95.5%	98.6%	
	Diff.	77.6%	20.4%	-53.0%	-91.0%	-97.2%	
	(N)	(89)	(254)	(293)	(267)	(71)	(974)

[a]Key: Dem.=Democratic; Rep.=Republican; AIP (1968 only)=American Independent Party; Other (1968 only)=AIP plus Republican.
[b]Key: DD=Strongly pro-Democratic (-10 to -4); D=Mildly pro-Democratic (-3 to -1); N=Neutral (0); R=Mildly pro-Republican (+1 to +3); RR=Strongly pro-Republican (+4 to +10). In 1972 extreme categories range from -6 to -4 and from +4 to +6.

strongly pro-Republican image column, the proportion of Democratic voters decreases sharply, the proportion of Republican voters increases, and the difference between the Democratic and Republican percentages moves from highly positive to highly negative. These findings are true even for 1968, although the Wallace candidacy reduced the magnitude of the figures in the difference row for the second set of 1968 data, in which the Nixon-Wallace votes are combined. Pro-Republican image-holders are strongly and clearly non-Democratic in their votes.

In Table 2.1 distributions of party image disadvantaged Republicans less than did distributions of party identification. In Table 2.3 we see the Republicans receive larger shares of the votes of their supporters, as measured by party images, than do the Democrats of their supporters (compare column 5 with column 1). In addition, Republicans usually do better among neutral image-holders. Together these facts help to explain why the Republican share of the vote exceeds Republican identification figures.

In terms of the more general phenomenon manifested in these data, we speculate that the party disadvantaged by the partisan distribution of voters which emerged from the most recent realignment (in the 1930s) may nevertheless fail to consistently suffer the full potential opposition within the electorate, either because images somewhat compensate for or override the impact of identifications on the vote, or because the loyalty of the supporters of the minority party exceeds the loyalty of the supporters of the majority party. In fact, that the minority party was able to maintain or win over the partisan commitment of these individuals despite the critical nature of the forces that prompted realignment may account for the greater loyalty of the supporters now. If their commitment could withstand the social and economic forces prompting realignment, it is not so surprising that their commitment can withstand the appeal of weaker forces in more recent years. Similarly, Ennis has also speculated about the importance of party images for buttressing the intense loyalty of minority party supporters:

> The implication, that minority voters have maintained support for their party's candidates by rallying about the symbol of the party, suggests that over time they become more partisan than their counterparts in a majority context. Partisanship in this sense does not mean political hyperactivity but rather a tenacious attachment to the major symbols of one's party, in contrast to the more labile, issue-centered politics of voters in a majority setting who can afford the luxury of disagreeing with the party on political issues.[13]

Short-term forces affect the impact of image on the vote. Even the greater loyalty on the part of minority partisans is not impervious to short-term forces. In 1964 Goldwater did poorly among all except the strongly pro-Republican image-holders, losing drastically among the neutral image-holders, where Republicans apparently need to do well to compensate for their low number of identifiers. In 1972, among mild and neutral image-holders, the Democratic Party attracted relatively low proportions of voters. A mildly pro-Democratic image was apparently not sufficient to withstand the strong issue-oriented motivations that led many otherwise Democratic voters to vote Republican in 1972.[14]

Table 2.4 displays the relationship between party identification and the vote. Both parties have consistently done best among their respective

TABLE 2.4   Relationship Between Vote and Party Identification, by Year

Year	Vote	Party Identification[a]			Gamma
		Democratic	Independent	Republican	
1952	Democratic	70.5%	19.7%	4.3%	.940
	Republican	29.5%	80.3%	95.7%	
	Difference	41.0%	-60.6%	-91.4%	
	(N)	(654)	(61)	(460)	(1175)
1956	Democratic	73.7%	16.5%	4.3%	.939
	Republican	26.3%	83.5%	95.7%	
	Difference	47.4%	-67.0%	-91.4%	
	(N)	(634)	(115)	(511)	(1260)
1960	Democratic	81.8%	46.0%	7.8%	.921
	Republican	18.2%	54.0%	92.2%	
	Difference	63.6%	-8.0%	-84.4%	
	(N)	(719)	(113)	(565)	(1397)
1964	Democratic	89.3%	76.5%	26.5%	.881
	Republican	10.7%	23.5%	73.5%	
	Difference	78.6%	53.0%	-47.0%	
	(N)	(1997)	(179)	(1116)	(3292)
1968	Democratic	67.2%	24.4%	6.1%	.606
	Republican	20.1%	55.1%	86.3%	
	Am. Ind. Party	12.7%	20.5%	7.6%	
	(N)	(1088)	(176)	(768)	(2032)
1968	Democratic	67.2%	24.4%	6.1%	.821
	Non-Democratic	29.8%	75.6%	93.9%	
	Difference	37.4%	-51.2%	-87.8%	
	(N)	(1088)	(176)	(768)	(2032)
1972	Democratic	57.4%	22.0%	2.8%	.903
	Republican	42.6%	78.0%	97.2%	
	Difference	14.8%	-56.0%	-94.4%	
	(N)	(495)	(82)	(394)	(971)

[a]Independent Democrats and Independent Republicans are classified as partisans, not as Independents.

partisans, but the ability of the Democratic Party to hold its supporters wavered in 1972, when only 57.4% of the Democratic identifiers voted Democratic. Except in 1964, Republicans have done better than Democrats among Independents. Furthermore, except in 1964 Republicans have attracted larger vote shares of their own partisans than the Democrats have attracted of their own partisans, perhaps again because the loyalty of minority partisans was forged in the process of realignment.

In Table 2.5 the vote is regressed against party image and party identification, and the linear regression coefficients offer a measure with which to investigate the declining impact of partisan attitudes — what Burnham calls "decomposition."[15] For the entire 20-year period, the standardized regression coefficients for party image, but not for party identification, decline in a statistically significant fashion. The impacts of the two partisan attitudes have both been declining since 1960. Furthermore, the combined impact of these two attitudes, measured by the coefficient of determination (R^2), has declined in a statistically significant fashion for this entire 20-year period. Moreover, both partisan attitudes had greatly reduced impacts in 1972, although the 1972 party image

TABLE 2.5   Multiple Linear Regression of Party Image and Party Identification on the Vote, by Year[a]

Year	Party Image		Party Identification		R^2
	b	Beta	b	Beta	
1952	.251	.733	.143	.653	.584
1956	.249	.670	.148	.678	.525
1960	.266	.692	.154	.699	.565
1964	.254	.658	.131	.625	.493
1968	.232	.608	.140	.608	.453
1972	.165	.386	.073	.330	.409
Serial Regression Coefficient (Unstandardized)		-.056 (p < .05)		-.054 (n.s.)	-.033 (p < .01)

[a]Democratic Vote is scored as 1, non-Democratic vote as 2. Unstandardized regression coefficients express the increase in percent non-Democratic vote associated with an increase in one position on the image or identification scales. Identification is scored from -3 (Strong Democrat) to +3 (Strong Republican); Image is scored from -2 (Strongly pro-Democratic) to +2 (Strongly pro-Republican).

data no doubt reflect the fewer responses recorded in that year. Table 2.5 thus presents a picture of the declining abilities of two similar partisan forces to structure the vote of Americans. This may be the inevitable result of time which makes the realignment of the 1930s less and less salient,[16] or it may reflect a real decaying process in the ability of political parties to motivate voters and to link them with the governmental process.

Burnham warns that party decomposition may have progressed so far that a future realignment-like process will produce the end of American party politics rather than a new, viable party system.[17] To the extent that party images provide a crucial link in the transformation of one party system into a viable successor, then Table 2.5, which reveals that party images have had a declining impact on the vote, seems to support Burnham's pessimistic warning.

The data so far speak to the validity of the concept of party image. This validity is manifested in the similar properties it shares with the party identification construct. The impact of party image on the vote parallels that of party identification, and neutral image-holders are more volatile in the direction of their vote, as are Independents.

THE INTERACTIVE IMPACTS ON THE VOTE

To study the simultaneous impact party image and party identification have on the vote, an analysis of covariance was performed to determine the impact of party identification on the vote within categories of party image.[18] Controlling for party image in this manner is also consistent with Sellers' argument that party images are firmed up or altered before identifications are altered.[19] Table 2.6 presents the unstandardized regression coefficients and intercepts for the party identification variable within categories of party image, for each of the six years.

To understand the figures in Table 2.6 one must first realize that the party identification construct was scored from -3 (strong Democrat) to $+3$ (strong Republican). The left side of Table 2.6 presents five sets of regression coefficients, one for each category of party image. These regression coefficients measure the unit increase in the percent voting Republican which accompanies a unit increase in the 7-point party identification scale, within each of the five party image categories. Thus, for example, among strongly pro-Democratic image-holders in 1952

TABLE 2.6 Linear Regression of Party Identification on the Vote, Within Categories of Party Image, by Year

Year[a]	Regression Coefficient					Intercept				
	Party Image[b]					Party Image[b]				
	DD	D	N	R	RR	DD	D	N	R	RR
1952	3.8%	11.1%	11.2%	5.5%	0.9%	15.3%	45.1%	65.2%	85.9%	97.9%
(N)	(203)	(298)	(130)	(276)	(268)	(203)	(298)	(130)	(276)	(268)
1956	6.4%	13.2%	8.9%	5.6%	2.7%	26.1%	53.3%	78.8%	85.2%	92.8%
(N)	(220)	(352)	(214)	(303)	(171)	(220)	(352)	(214)	(303)	(171)
1960	7.8%	10.3%	12.7%	6.9%	1.8%	25.3%	37.9%	56.1%	78.2%	95.4%
(N)	(228)	(407)	(229)	(360)	(173)	(228)	(407)	(229)	(360)	(173)
1964	3.5%	5.4%	7.2%	8.0%	4.5%	10.9%	19.2%	29.9%	63.5%	86.9%
(N)	(515)	(1122)	(694)	(648)	(313)	(515)	(1122)	(694)	(648)	(313)
1968	4.6%	14.9%	10.0%	7.9%	0.7%	23.6%	53.5%	73.1%	79.1%	95.0%
(N)	(226)	(550)	(386)	(516)	(354)	(226)	(550)	(386)	(516)	(354)
1972	7.4%	11.8%	9.2%	2.8%	2.4%	4.9%	24.3%	48.8%	84.5%	86.7%
(N)	(89)	(254)	(290)	(267)	(71)	(89)	(254)	(293)	(267)	(71)

[a]Impact of Identification on the vote with no controls for party image:

Year	(N)	Regression Coefficient	Intercept
1952	(1175)	14.3%	63.2%
1956	(1260)	14.8%	63.8%
1960	(1397)	15.4%	55.2%
1964	(3292)	13.1%	41.4%
1968	(2032)	14.0%	65.5%
1972	(974)	12.2%	33.9%

[b]Party Image coded as Strongly pro-Democratic (DD) = -2; Mildly pro-Democratic (D) = -1; Neutral (N) = 0; Mildly pro-Republican (R) = +1; Strongly pro-Republican (RR) = +2.

(column 1), a unit increase of one on the party identification scale produces a 3.8% gain in the expected Republican percentage of the vote, so weak Democratic identifiers would be expected to be 3.8% more Republican in their vote than strong Democratic identifiers. The right side of Table 2.6 presents intercepts (columns 6–10), which measure the expected Republican percentage of the vote when party identification equals 0 (Independents), within each of the five party image categories. For instance, among strongly pro-Democratic image-holders in 1952 (column 6), only 15.3% of the Independents would have been expected to vote Republican. Among mildly pro-Republican image-holders in the same year (column 9), 85.9% of the Independents would have been expected to vote Republican. Finally, in a note to Table 2.6, the intercepts and regression coefficients for party identification are presented under no control (i.e., for the entire sample.) A more complete table, Table 2.7, displays the expected Republican percentage of the vote for each and every combination of the five image categories and the seven party identification categories for each of the six election years. Table 2.6 summarizes the more complex display of Table 2.7 and presents highlights that suggest the lawlike relationship between party image and party identification. We shall examine Table 2.7 after analyzing these highlights.

For the regression coefficients within the different categories of party image, notice in Table 2.6 that consistently for each year there is a unimodal pattern.[20] Within the left side, reading across, the values are low for extreme image-holders and higher for mild and neutral image-holders, and these values produce a single peak, typically among neutral image-holders or among mildly pro-Democratic image-holders. In other words, among strongly pro-Democratic or strongly pro-Republican image-holders, party identification has a minimal impact on the vote — in a sense, the vote is determined only by the strong image held by the individual. Specifically, among strongly pro-Republican image-holders, strong Democratic identifiers are *not* much more Democratic in their vote than even strong Republican identifiers. In 1968 for instance, among strongly pro-Republican image-holders (column 5), strong Republican identifiers were only 4.2% (6 × 0.7%) more non-Democratic in their vote than strong Democratic identifiers, who are at the other end of the identification continuum. For these extreme image-holders, party identification only weakly affects the vote. However, among individuals with less extreme party images, the impact of party identification on the

TABLE 2.7 Expected Non-Democratic Vote Percentages for Categories of Party Image and Party Identification, by Year[a]

Party Identification	Year	Party Image[b]				
		DD	D	N	R	RR
Strong	1952	3.9	11.5	31.6	69.4	95.2
Democrat	1956	6.9	13.7	52.1	68.4	84.7
	1960	1.9	7.0	18.0	57.5	90.0
	1964	0.4	3.0	8.3	39.5	73.4
	1968	9.8	18.8	43.1	55.4	92.9
	1972	-17.3	-11.1	21.2	76.1	79.5
Weak	1952	7.7	22.7	42.8	74.9	96.1
Democrat	1956	13.3	26.9	61.0	74.0	87.4
	1960	9.7	17.3	30.7	64.4	91.8
	1964	3.9	8.4	15.5	47.5	77.9
	1968	14.4	33.7	53.1	63.3	93.6
	1972	-9.9	0.7	30.4	78.9	81.9
Independent	1952	11.5	33.9	54.0	80.4	97.0
Democrat	1956	19.7	40.1	69.9	79.6	90.1
	1960	17.5	27.6	43.4	71.3	93.6
	1964	7.4	13.8	22.7	55.5	82.4
	1968	19.0	48.6	63.1	71.2	94.3
	1972	-2.5	12.5	39.6	81.7	84.3
Independent	1952	15.3	45.1	65.2	85.9	97.9
	1956	26.1	53.3	78.8	85.2	92.8
	1960	25.3	37.9	56.1	78.2	95.4
	1964	10.9	19.2	29.9	63.5	86.9
	1968	23.6	53.5	73.1	79.1	95.0
	1972	4.9	24.3	48.8	84.5	86.7
Independent	1952	19.1	56.3	76.4	91.4	98.8
Republican	1956	32.5	66.5	87.7	90.8	95.5
	1960	33.1	48.2	68.8	85.1	97.2
	1964	14.4	24.6	37.1	71.5	91.4
	1968	28.2	68.4	83.1	87.0	95.7
	1972	12.3	36.1	58.0	87.3	91.1
Weak	1952	22.9	67.5	87.6	96.9	99.7
Republican	1956	38.9	79.7	96.6	96.4	98.2
	1960	40.9	58.5	81.5	92.0	99.0
	1964	17.9	30.0	44.3	79.5	95.9
	1968	32.8	83.3	93.1	94.9	96.4
	1972	19.7	47.9	67.2	90.1	91.5
Strong	1952	26.7	78.7	98.8	102.4	100.6
Republican	1956	45.3	92.9	105.5	102.0	100.9
	1960	48.7	68.8	94.2	98.9	100.8
	1964	21.4	35.4	51.5	87.5	100.4
	1968	37.4	98.2	103.1	102.8	97.1
	1972	27.1	59.7	76.4	92.9	93.9

[a]Each cell entry is the non-Democratic percentage of the vote.

[b]Key: DD = Strongly pro-Democratic; D = Mildly pro-Democratic; N = Neutral; R = Mildly pro-Republican; RR = Strongly pro-Republican.

vote is more substantial, especially among mildly pro-Democratic image-holders.

The overall pattern of regression coefficients in Table 2.6 reveals an interactive impact of identification and image on the vote not unlike the kind of attitude conflict situation discussed in *The American Voter*.[21] Among strong partisans, when attitudes conflict with identification, identification is likely to determine the vote. Among weak partisans conflict is more apt to be resolved in accordance with attitudes.[22] When image and identification conflict, two patterns of resolution are also evident. Among strong image-holders, image dominates and identification has very little impact on the vote. Among mild or neutral image-holders, party identification is free to have considerably more impact on the vote. These general findings do not seem to have been deflected in any consistent way from year to year, although year to year idiosyncrasies will be discussed below.

The resolution of conflict can be analyzed further by combining the regression coefficients and intercepts of Table 2.6. The linear regression equations (of the form $Y = a + bX$) give the expected non-Democratic percent of the vote (Y) for different values of party identification (X) within the different party image categories, where the values for a (intercept) and b (regression coefficient) are given in Table 2.6. The expected vote percentages are presented in Table 2.7. The entries in the upper left-hand corner and the lower right-hand corner of Table 2.7 are the expected non-Democratic vote percentages that result from non-conflictual situations in which strong image and strong identification reinforce each other. The vote is strongly one-sided in these cells. As weaker levels of partisanship interact (in the center of Table 2.7) and as one strongly partisan force interacts with one weakly partisan force (in the lower left- and upper right-hand corners of Table 2.7), the vote is more evenly distributed.

Table 2.7 thus reveals the long-term trends and short-term deviations from the trends in the impacts that image and identification have on the vote. The pattern is for image to become more important among weaker identifiers and for identification to become more important among mild and neutral image-holders, but the impacts of both image and identification vary over time, although in no particularly consistent fashion. In 1960, for instance, the impact of party identification on the vote increased. Among strongly pro-Democratic image-holders (DD), 48.7% of the strong Republican identifiers (SR) were expected to vote Republican, compared to an expected Republican vote of only 1.9% of the strong Democratic identifiers (SD), a differential of 46.8%. This differential in the expected Republican percentage of the vote between extreme identification categories varies considerably in Table 2.7 and was as small as 5.4% among strongly pro-Republican image-holders (RR) in 1952 (100.6–95.2%). This variation over time within categories of party image is due primarily to the volatility in intercept values, which are considerably less stable than the regression coefficients for party identification (compare the volatility among values on the left side of the Table). The intercepts, in turn, seem to capture and express the volatility of the impact of short-term forces in the political environment. In any given year, the forces that stimulate voting partisanship and the forces that stimulate voting turnout typically favor one party over the other.[23] These intercepts seem to reflect a similar phenomenon. Apparently they summarize the effects of forces in the environment that predispose the electorate in its voting choice somewhat independently of party images.

A better sense for the substantive meaning of this volatility can be gained by reexamining the data of Table 2.6 for the idiosyncrasies that appear from year to year. The figures for 1952 and 1956 are roughly the same, reflecting the similarity in the Eisenhower elections, which were characterized by a willingness on the part of Democratic identifiers to vote for the Republican candidate, of whom they thought highly.[24] In 1960 we encounter a symmetry in the regression coefficients, seemingly reflecting the closeness of the election. By 1964 the intercepts among nonextreme image-holders had dropped to respective lows for these years, responding apparently to Goldwater's unpopularity. Also in 1964, for the only time in this 20-year period, the regression coefficient among mildly pro-Republican image-holders was greater than among mildly pro-Democratic image-holders, reflecting the uniquely higher voting defection rates of mildly pro-Republican image-holders in this year.

In 1972 the ratio of defections among mildly pro-Democratic image-holders to that among mildly pro-Republican image-holders, as measured by the ratio of the regression coefficients (11.8:2.8), is greater than for any of these other election years, due to the particularly small impact of identification among mildly pro-Republican image-holders. When we combine this small impact ($b = 2.8$) with the intercept for this group ($a = 84.5$, relatively high for these years), we are led to expect strong and fairly uniform Republican voting among mildly pro-Republican image-holders, even those with Democratic identifications. Thus in 1972 a notable asymmetry existed: among mildly pro-Democratic image-holders, Republican identifiers were considerably more Republican in their vote than were Democratic identifiers; but among mildly pro-Republican image-holders, Democratic identifiers were *not* considerably less Republican in their vote. Furthermore, among Independents the expected Democratic vote among strongly pro-Democratic image-holders was lowest for these years in 1972 (compare intercepts), so that even the strong impact of identification for these strongly pro-Democratic image-holders ($b = 7.4$) had very little to build on. We see, then, how decimated were the traditional Democratic ranks in 1972.

Finally, differences in the range of values across rows in Table 2.7 suggest that the importance of image is generally greater for Democratic identifiers than it is for Republican identifiers; that is, defections in the vote from the party one identifies with — defections caused by party image — have favored the Republicans in this electoral period. This is consistent with the argument made earlier that the loyalty of present partisans reflects the process of realignment that forged present patterns of partisanship.

PARTY IMAGES AMONG SRC PANEL MEMBERS

In 1956, 1958, and 1960 the Survey Research Center/Center for Political Studies conducted a three-wave panel study of a sample of Americans. We can truncate the SRC sample from the 1514 individuals interviewed at least once in the study down to the 1132 individuals interviewed in each of the three waves.[25] Each of these 1132 individuals was asked in each wave what he or she liked and disliked about the Republican and Democratic Parties, so the responses permit us to study individual-level stability and change in the party images of Americans.

The panel data document considerably more change among individuals than do the aggregate measures of party image presented in Table 2.1. Although the net distributions of the party images of panel members, presented in Table 2.8, resemble the stable patterns of Table 2.1, only about 36% of the panel maintains its party image index score between two waves, as measured by the Pearsonian correlation coefficient. For the collapsed five-category party image index, the coefficients are not very different. Thus at the individual level relatively few people possess absolutely stable party images. In fact, over the three

TABLE 2.8 Party Images Among SRC Panel Members, by Year

	Distributions Along the Collapsed Party Image Index[a]							Mean[b]
Year	DD	D	N	R	RR	Total	Number of Cases	
1956	15.3%	28.1%	21.9%	23.7%	10.9%	99.9%[c]	1132	-0.38
1958	14.2%	34.9%	24.9%	20.8%	5.2%	100.0%	1132	-0.77
1960	15.7%	30.3%	21.7%	22.3%	9.9%	99.9%[c]	1132	-0.47

Individual-level Pearsonian Correlation Coefficients

	21-point Index		Collapsed Index	
	r	r^2	r	r^2
1956-1958	+.589	+.347	+.608	+.370
1958-1960	+.606	+.367	+.628	+.394
1956-1960	+.608	+.370	+.609	+.371

[a]Key: DD = Strongly pro-Democratic; D = Mildly pro-Democratic; N = Neutral; R = Mildly pro-Republican; RR = Strongly pro-Republican.

[b]Based on 21-point Party Image Index; negative values are pro-Democratic.

[c]Row does not total 100.0% due to rounding errors.

waves of the panel, only 23% possess the same collapsed party image index score in each of the three waves.

Yet party images are not so unstable as this picture appears to paint them. Individuals do not stray very far from the party images they once possessed. Of all individuals with pro-Democratic images in 1956, 64% (317 of 492) possessed pro-Democratic images in 1958 *and* in 1960. Of all individuals with pro-Republican images in 1956, 46% (181 of 392) possessed pro-Republican images in 1958 *and* in 1960. Less than one-quarter (24%, or 59 of 248) of the 1956 neutral image-holders maintained their neutrality over all three waves, however. Together, 49% [(317 + 181 + 59)/(492 + 392 + 238)] of the 1956 panel members remained through 1960 in the same "general neighborhood" they had been in in 1956. Furthermore, about 42% of the panel remains in the same collapsed party image category in any two year comparison.

To evaluate the relative stability of individual party images requires comparison with the stability of other political attitudes measured on similarly constructed scales. Such comparisons reveal that party images are moderately stable (or unstable, depending on one's perspective). Comparing three-point scales, 79% of the 1132 panel members remained in the same party identification scale category (Democratic, Independent, or Republican) between any two waves,[26] whereas only 42% remained in the same party image scale category (pro-Democratic, Neutral, pro-Republican). Comparing seven-point scales, party images seem as stable as party identifications; between 39% and 42% remain in the same category between any two waves[27] compared to figures of about 38% for the party identification scale. Finally, images seem definitely more stable than do opinions on issues, which for most people fluctuate randomly.[28]

How do we explain this moderate stability? The stability of party identification results from the long-term process of political socialization that produced it. Opinions on issues are unstable because the short-term nature of issues minimizes (reduces) their salience. Party images seem to draw more evenly than identifications or opinions on long-term and short-term stimuli for their creation and alteration. The party image index has been constructed by counting the number of likes and dislikes an individual has for the two parties. The specific likes and dislikes, to be analyzed in Chapter 4, reveal long-term continuities and short-term responsiveness in the party images of Americans. Presumably the long-term continuities are transmitted by the process of socialization (though less steadfastly than are party identifications). The short-term responsiveness reveals the susceptibility of party image to influences other than long-term ones, some no doubt random. Thus as Matthews and Prothro reason, "party image is not so deeply rooted or so stable as party identification, [and] it is likely to be less ephemeral than voter attitudes toward the issues and candidates of specific campaigns."[29]

CONCLUSION

The long-term trends in the data we have just examined convincingly demonstrate the relevance of the concept of party image for the study of electoral behavior and provide progressively more information about the meaning of political parties for Americans. The data to be presented in the remainder of the book will amplify this relevance and specify this meaning. In the aggregate, distributions of party image have remained relatively stable since 1952, yet this stability, like the relative stability of measures of party identification, obscures a significant trend — the continuing process of the parties' failure to link voters with their government. We find further evidence of party decomposition in later chapters, and hints in Chapter 4 that this decomposition results in part from the growing irrelevancy of the themes that prompted the last realignment or from the failure of parties to take polarizing stands on those issues that have emerged in recent years as potentially realigning. Whatever its cause, decomposition threatens to preclude the future ability of parties to structure politics and to influence policy.

If this first trend reveals the relative meaningfulness of parties to Americans, specifically a declining meaningfulness, a second trend reveals the potential for electoral change inherent in the party images of Americans. We anticipate the discussion of Chapter 7, for instance, by noting that party images can sensitively trace preferences of blacks and whites, which manifests the power in the concept. Party images document the transformation of American politics from a politics of region to a politics of race, reveal the responsiveness of blacks to events of the 1960s and the mobilization of blacks into the Democratic camp in 1964, and testify to the perceptiveness of Americans after 1964 that parties would fail to realign around the racial issue.

The third trend, tracing the significant and consistent interactive influence of party image and party identification on the vote, resembles the pattern of influence that attitudes have traditionally had on electoral behavior, and consequently offers strong evidence of the validity of the concept of party image. This interactive pattern points out how the influence of party image is restricted by the presence of competing attitudes, and how attitudinal forces are sensitive to the political environment.

In fact all of these trends are sensitive and responsive to short-term forces, which becomes even more obvious when we examine the substantive concerns of the voters revealed by their party images (see Chapter 4). The deviations we have already encountered can be reasonably interpreted on the basis of our knowledge of the particular election under question. Consequently, the trends we have found in no way tightly constrain the electoral behavior of Americans. The role of party image in influencing that behavior seems clear, but images themselves can respond to what transpires in the political environment. In other words, party images effectively play an intermediary role, translating what transpires in the political environment into meaningful terms for the voter, a process we discuss further in the concluding chapter. In sum, the likes and dislikes Americans have for their political parties do constitute the meaning of American political parties for American voters, a proposition for which we accumulate further evidence as we proceed through the remainder of our analysis.

NOTES

1. This chapter is a revision of my "Party Image and Electoral Behavior," *American Politics Quarterly*, **3**:3 (July 1975), 284–314.

2. The mean percents offering more than three responses to each of the four party image items are: like about the Democrats, 6.98%; dislike about the Democrats, 5.52%; like about the Republicans, 4.54%; dislike about the Republicans, 3.34%. In general the percents have decreased since high values in 1952, respectively, of 9.2%, 9.7%, 8.6%, and 5.6%.

3. The alternative strategy of using only the first three responses is chosen by Bruce A. Campbell. See his "Patterns of Change in the Partisan Loyalties of Native Southerners: 1952-1972," paper prepared for delivery at the Annual Meeting of the Midwest Political Science Association, Pick-Congress Hotel, Chicago, Ill., May 1–3, 1975.

4. The collapsed index combines original scores in the following manner: -10 to -4, -3 to -1, 0, $+1$ to $+3$, and $+4$ to $+10$. In 1972 the extreme categories range from -6 to -4 and from $+4$ to $+6$.

5. Philip E. Converse, Aage R. Clausen, and Warren E. Miller, "Electoral Myth and Reality: The 1964 Election," *American Political Science Review*, **59** (1965), 321–336.

6. Philip E. Converse, Warren E. Miller, Jerrold C. Rusk, and Arthur C. Wolfe, "Continuity and Change in American Politics: Parties and Issues in the 1968 Election," *American Political Science Review*, **63** (1969), 1083–1105.

7. In 1972 party identification was not strongly related to images of the candidates, to opinions on the issues, or to voting preference. See Arthur H. Miller, Warren E. Miller, Alden S. Raine, and Thad A. Brown, "A Majority Party in Disarray: Policy Polarization in the 1972 Election," paper prepared for delivery at the Annual Meeting of the American Political Science Association, Jung Hotel, New Orleans, La., September 4–8, 1973.

8. Walter Dean Burnham, *Critical Elections and the Mainsprings of American Politics* (New York: Norton, 1970), pp. 120–121; Norval D. Glenn, "Sources of the Shift to Political Independence: Some Evidence from a Cohort Analysis," *Social Science Quarterly*, **53**:3 (1972), 494–519; Miller et al., "A Majority Party in Disarray," *op. cit.*, p. 86.

9. Herbert H. Hyman, *Political Socialization* (Glencoe, Ill.: Free Press, 1959); Fred I. Greenstein, *Children and Politics* (New Haven: Yale University Press, 1965).

10. According to Glenn, *op. cit.*, the proportion rose as high as 49% in 1969, only to subside to 34% in 1972.

11. Independent Democrats and independent Republicans are classified throughout this book as partisans, not as Independents.

12. Donald R. Matthews and James W. Prothro, *Negroes and the New Southern Politics* (New York: Harcourt, Brace and World, 1966), p. 395.

13. Philip H. Ennis, "The Contextual Dimension in Voting," in William N. McPhee and William N. Glaser, eds., *Public Opinion and Congressional Elections* (New York: Free Press, 1962), p. 209.

14. There were sharp issue differences between Democrats who voted for McGovern and Democrats who voted for Nixon. See Miller, et al., "A Majority Party in Disarray," *op. cit.*, pp. 9–27. These authors also state that McGovern lost "numerically significant and ideologically distinct" Democratic Party supporters to an opponent "whose policy positions were sufficiently more attractive to outweigh normal considerations of party loyalty and candidate preference at the polls" (p.1). Finally, the authors claim (p. 25) that Democrats of all preference positions except liberal defected in large numbers.

15. Burnham, *Critical Elections*, *op. cit.*; Burnham, "The Changing Shape of the American Political Universe," *American Political Science Review*, **59** (1965), 7–28.

16. Paul R. Abramson, "Generational Change in the American Electorate," *American Political Science Review*, **68** (1974), 93–105.

17. Burnham, "The End of American Party Politics," *Trans-action*, **7**:2 (1969), 12–22.

18. On analysis of covariance, see Hubert M. Blalock, Jr., *Social Statistics*, 2nd ed. (New York: McGraw-Hill, 1960), pp. 474–491.

19. Charles Sellers, "The Equilibrium Cycle in Two-Party Politics," *Public Opinion Quarterly*, **29** (1965), 16–38.

20. This finding of consistency is substantively more important than the actual values, so statistical significance tests were not performed on the often small differences in values.

21. Angus Campbell, Philip E. Converse, Warren E. Miller, and Donald E. Stokes, *The American Voter* (New York: Wiley, 1960), pp. 128–142.

22. A similar conflictual situation, between identification and issue partisanship, is analyzed by David E. RePass. See his "Issue Salience and Party Choice," *American Political Science Review*, **65** (1971), 388–400. RePass states: "It is among . . . identifiers whose current evaluations of political objects contradict their traditional party loyalties, that we can look for voting change . . . when issue partisanship conflicted with party identification, the issues often overcame the long-term party loyalties; the stronger the issue partisanship, the greater its electoral effect."

23. Angus Campbell, "Surge and Decline: A Study of Electoral Change," pp. 40–62 in Angus Campbell, Philip E. Converse, Warren E. Miller, and Donald E. Stokes, *Elections and the Political Order* (New York: Wiley, 1966).

24. See Campbell et al., *The American Voter*, *op cit.*, pp. 54–56, 141–142.

25. For details on the panel study, see Chapter 1, note 46, and also the ICPR *American Panel Study Codebook*.

26. In this collapsed party identification scale, strong Democrats, weak Democrats, and independent Democrats are grouped together as Democrats; strong Republicans, weak Republicans and independent Republicans are grouped together as Republicans; and Independents are kept separate.

27. The seven-point party image scale collapses the original 21-point party image scale in the following manner: -10 to -7, -6 to -4, -3 to -1, 0, $+1$ to $+3$, $+4$ to $+6$, and $+7$ to $+10$.

28. For an analysis of the instability of opinions of issues among SRC panel members, see Philip E. Converse, "The Nature of Belief Systems in Mass Publics," pp. 206–261 in David E. Apter, ed., *Ideology and Discontent* (New York: Free Press, 1964). For debate over this instability, see Converse, "Attitudes and Non-attitudes: Continuation of a Dialogue," pp. 168–189 in Edward R. Tufte, ed., *The Quantitative Analysis of Social Problems* (Reading, Mass.: Addison-Wesley, 1970); John C. Pierce and Douglas D. Rose, "Nonattitudes and American Public Opinion: The Examination of a Thesis," *American Political Science Review*, **68** (1974), 629–649; Converse, "Comment: The Status of Nonattitudes," *American Political Science Review*, **68** (1974), 650–660; Pierce and Rose, "Rejoinder to 'Comment' by Philip E.

Converse," *American Political Science Review*, **68** (1974), 661–666; and Robert S. Erikson, "The SRC Panel Data and Mass Political Attitudes," paper prepared for delivery at the Annual Meeting of the American Political Science Association, San Francisco Hilton Hotel, San Francisco, Calif., September 1–5, 1975.

29. Matthews and Prothro, *Negroes and the New Southern Politics*, *op. cit.*, p. 378.

chapter 3
The relative strength
of likes and dislikes

The index of party image examined in the preceding chapter combines likes and dislikes to measure the individual's overall predisposition toward the two political parties. In this procedure likes and dislikes are weighted equally. Similarly, Kelley and Mirer developed an index (combining candidate images with party images) that weights equally the likes an individual has with his or her dislikes.[1] Such a balancing procedure seems reasonable, at least in the effort to develop a single measure of the individual's net affect toward the parties, and the validity of the overall index has been demonstrated in Chapter 2.

Yet combining likes and dislikes necessarily obscures the relative importance of these two cognitive elements. At first it might seem that an individual's like should in fact balance his or her dislike. Attitude measurement rather routinely utilizes instruments, for instance, items whose response categories range from "strongly dislike" through "neutral" to "strongly like", which presume the universality of symmetry.[2] Some experimental data reveal, however, that ". . . a 'positive attitude' or 'positive affect' does not have an effect upon 'measured behavior' oppositely equivalent to the effect of a 'negative attitude' or 'negative affect.' "[3] In fact, the same experimental data suggest an "asymmetry" in the effects of liking and disliking on behavior — in the particular experiment, behavior was more likely to respond to disliking than to liking.[4]

Such a finding compels us to examine the relative impact of the likes and dislikes Americans have for their political parties on their ensuing political behavior. In this chapter, then, we separate these likes and dislikes to evaluate them both individually and in comparison with one another. We shall consider two kinds of evidence. First, we treat separately each set of likes and dislikes offered by Americans in response to the party image questionnaire items, recording respectively the number of likes for the Democratic Party, the number of dislikes for the Democratic Party, the number of likes for the Republican Party, and the number of dislikes for the Republican Party. This approach will allow us to develop an index for each set of preferences, to investigate the distributions of individuals along each of these four indexes over time, and to make comparisons among the four indexes. We deal here only with the *number* of different response categories rather than with their substantive content, the subject of Chapter 4.

THE DISTRIBUTION OF LIKES AND DISLIKES OVER TIME

The distributions over time of these four indexes are presented in Table 3.1, which also contains the means for each index as well as the total proportion offering at least one response to the questionnaire item. The means reveal that positive affect toward the Democratic Party has declined fairly steadily and fairly sharply over this 20-year period and that positive affect toward the Republican Party has also declined fairly steadily but not nearly so sharply. On the other hand, negative affect toward either party has been relatively low and considerably more stable, especially negative affect toward the Republican Party. Exceptions to this generalization are the violent increase in negative affect toward the Democratic Party in 1952 and again in 1968. Throughout this time period more people have things to say about the Democratic Party than about the Republican Party. The proportion offering at least one reason

TABLE 3.1   Distributions of the Number of Likes and Dislikes Americans Have for Their Political Parties, by Year[a]

Year	Like or Dislike[b]	0	1	2	3	4	5	3 Or More	Mean
1952	LD	39.1	23.2	18.6	10.0	5.5	3.6	19.1	1.31
	DLD	46.9	21.4	13.4	8.7	4.5	5.1	18.3	1.18
	LR	53.0	18.7	12.4	7.3	4.6	4.1	16.0	1.04
	DLR	51.6	23.8	13.4	5.6	3.3	2.3	11.2	0.92
1956	LD	41.1	23.8	18.2	9.6	4.6	2.7	16.9	1.21
	DLD	56.5	25.1	11.8	4.3	1.2	1.2	6.7	0.72
	LR	47.6	27.2	13.3	7.7	2.9	1.2	11.8	0.95
	DLR	52.8	23.3	13.3	6.4	2.3	1.9	10.6	0.88
1960	LD	42.9	26.5	15.8	8.9	4.0	1.9	14.8	1.10
	DLD	63.4	20.6	7.9	5.4	1.7	1.1	8.2	0.65
	LR	53.0	22.3	14.3	6.6	2.5	1.3	10.4	0.87
	DLR	55.6	22.4	13.7	5.7	1.7	1.0	8.4	0.79
1964	LD	40.2	27.6	16.9	9.3	4.0	2.0	15.3	1.15
	DLD	59.0	22.2	10.8	4.5	2.3	1.4	8.2	0.73
	LR	62.9	19.9	11.0	4.1	1.3	0.8	6.2	0.63
	DLR	50.4	27.9	13.9	5.3	1.8	0.6	7.7	0.82
1968	LD	48.2	21.7	15.2	8.5	4.1	2.3	14.9	1.06
	DLD	41.3	23.5	17.1	9.1	5.0	4.1	18.2	1.25
	LR	55.2	22.1	12.2	6.4	2.5	1.7	11.6	0.84
	DLR	51.9	24.0	14.0	6.4	2.2	1.6	10.2	0.88
1972	LD	56.4	21.1	12.7	9.8	c	c	9.8	c
	DLD	59.3	20.6	11.4	8.7	c	c	8.7	c
	LR	63.8	16.9	10.9	8.3	c	c	8.3	c
	DLR	56.0	20.3	12.8	10.9	c	c	10.9	c

[a]Except for the right-hand column, entries are the percent of respondents with the given number of likes or dislikes.
[b]Key: LD = Likes Democrats; DLD = Dislikes Democrats; LR = Likes Republicans; DLR = Dislikes Republicans.
[c]No more than 3 responses were recorded in 1972; means are not computed because they are not comparable with other years.

for liking the Democratic Party is always greater than the proportion offering at least one reason for liking the Republican Party, and the proportion offering at least one reason for disliking the Democratic Party is also greater than the proportion offering at least one reason for disliking the Republican Party. Of course, in this time period the Democratic Party has been the majority party whose majority was formed in the Depression and in the realignment of the 1930s. The data thus suggest that the majority party has a greater number of defining characteristics than the minority party. Table 3.1 reveals that the "Democratic Party" is a symbol that triggers images in the minds of more individuals than does the symbol, "Republican Party." We found evidence in Chapter 2 that the process of realignment, in forging the partisan identifications of Americans, makes its force felt long after the resolution of the social and economic crisis that prompted the realignment. We encounter even stronger evidence in Chapter 4 of the ongoing influence of the process of realignment. In Table 3.1, we find another, although quite different, manifestation of this influence.

Yet the data suggest more than simply the ongoing influence of the process of realignment. There is preliminary evidence of party decomposition — of the loosening ties between party and voter. If the majority status of the Democratic Party were the only relevant stimulus to motivate likes and dislikes, why do we find that the Republican Party is also less able to evoke positive affect over this 20-year period? In other words, some process seems to be operating on both parties; the fact that fewer people like the Republican Party at the same time that fewer people like the Democratic Party suggests that the process may be that of party decomposition. These remarks must be regarded as preliminary, however. For one thing, the decline in the proportion liking the Democratic Party has been notable only since 1964, so the candidates, issues, and events of the last two Presidential elections may very well account for the decrease in positive Democratic affect in these years.

The data also reveal the idiosyncratic nature of the 1952 and 1968 elections in increasing the proportion of individuals disliking the Democratic Party and of the 1964 and 1972 elections in decreasing the proportion of individuals liking the Republican Party.

A NOTE ON THE 1972 STUDY

As was discussed in Chapter 2, in 1972 the Survey Research Center/ Center for Political Studies recorded only up to three responses to each of the four party image items, a procedure that threatens the comparability of the 1972 data. In Chapter 2 it was also pointed out that in 1972 a significantly large proportion of Americans were coded zero (neutral) on the party image index (both the original index and the collapsed index discussed in Chapter 2). Table 3.1 now permits us to separate some of the real significance of 1972 from the potential influence of the methodological difficulty alluded to. Notice that the proportion offering *no* reason for liking or disliking the two parties, with one exception, is higher for 1972 than for any other year, respectively. Thus the 1972 sample manifests a real disinterest in parties relative to other years. Furthermore, in 1972 the proportion offering three reasons for liking the Democratic Party (strictly equivalent to the "three or more" category of previous years) was far below the norm for this comparable category for earlier years. The disinterest in politics was felt particularly, then, by the Democratic Party. More generally, evidence in Chapter 2 of party decomposition in 1972 or of other forms of the distinctiveness of the 1972 election seems to reflect a real political phenomenon, whatever the possible effect of lack of methodological equivalence.

In addition, in computing the means in Table 3.1, were we to rely on the proportion offering "three or more" responses, our analysis in the previous section would in no way be affected. The decline is virtually identical, for all four indexes, especially between 1956 and 1968, whether we use the "three or more" category or the more complete data of the table. Using the "three or more" category would permit us to include 1972 means, whose values only reenforce if not exaggerate the 1952–1968 trends. Furthermore, relying on the "three or more" category underestimates the decline between 1952 and 1956 in the number of likes for the Democrats and the number of likes for the Republicans.

PARTY IDENTIFICATION AND THE NUMBER OF LIKES AND DISLIKES

We pursue our analysis of the number of likes and dislikes by investigating the impact on party identification. Table 3.2 presents the separate relationships between the number of likes and dislikes and the party identification of the respondent. The number of likes and dislikes has been collapsed into three categories (none, one or two, three or more), and the data in the table constitute the difference, for the respective category of likes and dislikes, between the proportion identifying with the Democratic Party and the proportion identifying with the Republican Party. In addition, gamma values, measuring the relationships for the tables from which these data were drawn, are also presented as summary statistics. The difference between the proportion identifying with the Democratic Party and the proportion identifying with the Republican Party should increase from negative to strongly positive as

TABLE 3.2 Difference Between the Percent Identifying with the Democratic Party and the Percent Identifying with the Republican Party by the Number of Likes or Dislikes for the Parties, by Year

Year	Number	Likes Democrats		Dislikes Democrats		Likes Republicans		Dislikes Republicans	
		Differ-ence	N	Differ-ence	N	Differ-ence	N	Differ-ence	N
1952	0	-31.8	591	+58.6	733	+71.7	844	-7.9	820
	1-2	+42.2	777	+12.9	651	-5.0	584	+41.3	697
	3-5	+74.6	361	-32.5	345	-57.8	301	+84.4	212
	Gamma	-.641	1729	+.542	1729	+.743	1729	-.565	1729
1956	0	-43.1	671	+38.6	927	+60.4	779	-16.1	866
	1-2	+38.0	722	-8.5	646	-14.5	702	+34.6	637
	3-5	+78.7	297	-71.8	117	-71.3	209	+73.8	187
	Gamma	-.711	1690	+.515	1690	+.705	1690	-.534	1690
1960	0	-54.9	768	+42.5	1153	+58.9	959	-7.5	1012
	1-2	+48.8	810	-17.2	551	-17.8	701	+34.1	692
	3-5	+79.7	286	-61.2	160	-70.6	204	+85.0	160
	Gamma	-.739	1864	+.584	1864	+.698	1864	-.490	1864
1964	0	-19.0	1792	+53.3	2667	+63.3	2847	+16.2	2259
	1-2	+49.7	2062	+13.3	1522	-13.5	1430	+40.0	1947
	3-5	+86.8	707	-58.9	372	-71.9	284	+72.6	355
	Gamma	-.697	4561	+.523	4561	+.713	4561	-.324	4561
1968	0	-19.1	1454	+53.7	1241	+59.2	1666	+4.8	1568
	1-2	+54.8	1134	+9.9	1249	-10.9	1057	+37.7	1169
	3-5	+72.0	461	-20.4	559	-59.8	326	+51.9	312
	Gamma	-.640	3049	+.443	3049	+.660	3049	-.329	3049
1972	0	-13.9	746	+33.5	786	+41.0	848	-0.4	741
	1-2	+48.5	462	-1.2	437	-12.3	437	+30.6	451
	3-5	+75.4	134	-29.7	119	-65.8	114	+60.6	150
	Gamma	-.597	1342	+.352	1342	+.561	1342	-.366	1342

the number of likes for the Democratic Party or the number of dislikes for the Republican Party increases. The difference between the proportion identifying with the Democratic Party and the proportion identifying with the Republican Party should decrease from strongly positive to negative as the number of dislikes for the Democratic Party or the number of likes for the Republican Party increases. These patterns are observed in Table 3.2 and are readily detected in the signs of the gamma coefficients, which are negative for the likes for the Democrats and dislikes for the Republican sections of the table and positive for the two other relationships.[5]

Since the proportion of Independents in the electorate has increased since 1952, the difference between the proportion identifying with the Democratic Party and the proportion identifying with the Republican Party necessarily will have decreased. Furthermore, gamma coefficients measuring the relationships between party identification and the numbers of likes and dislikes for the parties will reflect the growing proportion of Independents. Consequently, in the discussion to follow, trends in the gamma values do not provide independent evidence of party decomposition but merely reenforce previous evidence of this process.

For our purposes in this chapter the most important finding in Table 3.2 is that the relationship between identification and the number of likes or dislikes is consistently stronger for likes than for dislikes. Examining the absolute values of the gamma coefficients reveals that likes for the Democratic Party are more closely associated with party identification than are dislikes for the Democratic Party; similarly, for the Republican data, party identification is more closely associated with likes than with dislikes. Consequently there is in fact an asymmetry, but it is just the opposite of what the experimental data alluded to at the beginning of the chapter led us to expect. Likes do not balance dislikes and likes outweigh dislikes at least in terms of their relationships with party identification. Shortly we shall investigate this phenomenon in relation to voting behavior.

Interestingly the difference in absolute values of the gamma coefficients depends somewhat on which party data we are examining. With regard to Democratic likes and dislikes, the difference increased fairly steadily from 1952 to 1972, indicating that the asymmetry increased fairly steadily, and likes were relatively more important vis-à-vis party identification in 1972 than they had been in 1952. However, the gamma coefficients also reveal that both Democratic likes and dislikes have been less and less important in structuring party identification since 1960, attesting to the decaying relationship between party image and party identification which was also evident in Table 2.2. Thus Democratic likes were relatively more important vis-à-vis party identification in 1972 than they had been in 1952 because the relationship between Democratic likes and party identification had decayed less over this time span than had the relationship between Democratic dislikes and party identification.

Examining the Republican data reveals a more confusing pattern. The difference in absolute values of the gamma coefficients indicates two periods within this 20-year span. Through 1960 the differential impact of likes and dislikes on party identification was fairly constant and moderate. Since 1960, however, it has been much greater, although decreasing from the high watermark of 1964. The ability of likes for the Republican Party to structure party identification decayed only in the past two Presidential election years. For Republican dislikes, however, the decay occurred from 1952 through 1964, but has leveled off since then. In fact, the 1964 election is notable among these data. Without the 1964 values the patterns for the Republican gamma values suggest a steady decay since 1952, for both likes and dislikes, and an increase in the ability of likes to structure party identification relative to the ability of the dislikes to do so, which resulted from the sharper decay in the ability of dislikes to affect party identification. Thus the decaying ability of party images to affect party identification is found among Republican likes and dislikes, also.

Perhaps more interesting, however, is the relative distinctiveness of the 1964 data. Particularly noteworthy is the ability in 1964 of Republican likes to affect party identification. Between 1960 and 1964, or in the 1964 campaign, likes for the Republican Party became much more strongly, yet temporarily, related to party identification. That is, individuals with no likes for the Republican Party were more likely than in other years to be Democratic identifiers and individuals with three or more likes for the Republican Party were more likely than in other years to be Republican identifiers. Let us postpone for a moment the investigation of the causes of this distinctiveness, since the unique 1964 pattern will emerge again shortly.

In the aggregate at least, likes for the Democratic Party parallel likes for the Republican Party in their abilities to affect party identification. Similarly, dislikes for the Democratic Party and dislikes for the Republican Party parallel each other, as can be seen by comparing the appropriate gamma values. Furthermore, these patterns indicate a declining relationship between likes and dislikes and party identification, as we have already noted.

Having examined the summary measures for the relationships in Table 3.2, we can now probe the impact of likes and dislikes a bit further by discussing the values themselves in the table. Each figure is itself the difference between the proportion identifying with the Democratic Party and the proportion identifying with the Republican Party for the respective category of number of likes or dislikes. For any year there are three figures within each section of the table. For instance, with regard to likes for the Democratic Party in 1952, the difference in the proportion identifying with the Democratic Party and the proportion identifying with the Republican Party ranges from -31.8 (for individuals with no reasons for liking the Democratic Party) to $+74.6$ (for individuals with three or more reasons for liking the Democratic Party). The *range* of difference is thus 106.4 (the absolute difference between the figures -31.8 and $+74.6$). This range can be compared over time and across likes and dislikes in order to determine whether likes or dislikes have a larger impact on party identification.

With only one exception we find that the range of difference is greater for likes than for dislikes, which is further evidence that likes for the parties affect party identification more than do dislikes. For the Democratic data, the range is exceptionally large for likes in 1960 and for dislikes in 1964, producing differences between the range for likes and the range for dislikes that reach a high in 1960 and a low in 1964. In other words, in 1960 likes about the Democratic Party were more closely related to party identification than at any other time in this 20-year period, and were more closely related to party identification than were dislikes about the Democratic Party throughout this 20-year period. Dislikes, on the other hand, were more closely related to party identification in 1964 than at any other time in this 20-year period, and so were able for the only time in these 20 years to make party identification more responsive to dislikes than to likes.

At the same time, in 1964, likes about the Republican Party were also more closely related to party identification than at any other point in this time span, as evidenced by the range in differences associated with categories of the dislike index. These strange patterns in the data must be viewed against the norm of Table 3.2. In American politics it is not at all unusual for individuals to have good and bad things to say about both parties at the same time. Thus, for instance, Americans can like the Democratic Party at the same time that they like the Republican Party, although probably for very different reasons. And Table 3.2 has revealed so far that these likes seem to carry greater impact than do dislikes, at least in regard to party identification. But in 1964 likes about the Republican Party acted similarly to dislikes about the Democratic Party, so American politics seemed temporarily, at least, to have become polarized.

How polarized was American politics in 1964? Do these data permit us to begin to answer this question? Pomper has noted how, apparently beginning in 1964, issue preference and party identification among Americans have come more in line with one another.[6] Others have discussed the ideological nature of the 1964 election.[7] Later in this book we shall encounter additional evidence of the apparently criticial nature of the 1964 election. The gamma values in Table 3.2 should already have alerted us to its uniqueness.

In an ideologically constrained, polarized party system, attributes that an individual likes about one party will be attributes that an individual dislikes about the other party. For instance, if one party is supportive of welfare policies and is perceived favorably by an individual as being supportive, then the other party, which is not supportive, will be perceived unfavorably by this same individual. Of course in this chapter we are dealing only with the number of likes and dislikes Americans have for their parties, not with the substance of their likes and dislikes, so the hypothetical argument is that for each like for one party an individual has, the individual will have a dislike for the other party.

If American politics became more polarized in 1964, and if the argument in the preceding paragraph makes sense, then correlations between likes and dislikes should show a marked difference in 1964 compared to other years. Specifically, we would expect the correlation between the number of likes for the Democratic Party and the number of dislikes for the Republican Party to be noticeably stronger in 1964 than in earlier years. Table 3.3 presents the relevant correlation coefficients.

In fact, the correlation coefficients show no such marked increase in polarization in 1964. Moreover, throughout the 20 years there have been moderately strong correlations between the number of likes for the Democrats and the number of dislikes for the Republicans and between the number of dislikes for the Democrats and the number of likes for the Republicans. The number of reasons an individual offers for liking one party is related to the number of reasons the individual offers for disliking the other party. Furthermore, individuals who offer reasons for liking one party are not even somewhat likely to offer reasons for liking the other party. These data paint a picture of a somewhat more constrained party system than one would have expected. Finally, the only significant additional point in the data is the increase in 1972 in the correlation between the number of dislikes for the Democratic Party and the number of dislikes for the Republican. Thus in 1972 there was evidence of a growing generalized alienation from the party system.

TABLE 3.3 Correlations Between Number of Likes and Number of Dislikes Americans Have for Their Parties, by Party and Year (Pearson Coefficients)[a]

	LD	DLD	LR	DLR		LD	DLD	LR	DLR
		1952					**1956**		
LD	+1.000	---	---	---		+1.000	---	---	---
DLD	-.059	+1.000	---	---		-.121	+1.000	---	---
LR	-.119	+.641	+1.000	---		-.138	+.518	+1.000	---
DLR	+.594	-.002	-.125	---		+.543	+.057	-.063	+1.000
		1960					**1964**		
LD	+1.000	---	---	---		+1.000	---	---	---
DLD	-.152	+1.000	---	---		-.097	+1.000	---	---
LR	-.163	+.552	+1.000	---		-.130	+.557	+1.000	---
DLR	+.513	+.028	-.111	+1.000		+.448	+.096	-.019	+1.000
		1968					**1972**		
LD	+1.000	---	---	---		+1.000	---	---	---
DLD	-.036	+1.000	---	---		+.063	+1.000	---	---
LR	-.032	+.532	+1.000	---		+.044	+.490	+1.000	---
DLR	+.417	+.151	-.003	+1.000		+.479	+.298	+.088	+1.000

[a]Key: LD = Likes Democrats; DLD = Dislikes Democrats; LR = Likes Republicans; DLR = Dislikes Republicans.

If we find no evidence here of increased polarization in 1964, how do we explain the unique data patterns for this year? The answer, somewhat simplistically, is that significantly fewer individuals had good things to say about the Republican Party in 1964. The distributions of party identifiers among the three categories for each of the likes or dislikes indexes reveals that in 1964 a substantially smaller proportion (37.6%) of all identifiers had at least one reason for liking the Republican Party. What seems to have happened is that individuals whose party identification had not been related to the number of reasons for liking the Republican Party, but who had had at least one reason for liking the Republican Party, no longer had a reason, in 1964, for liking the Republican Party. Of all party identifiers 62.4% had no reason for liking the Republican Party, a proportion that corresponded well with the 61.4% of all identifiers who identified themselves as Democratic (78.0% of these 61.4% had no reason for liking the Republican Party).

Compare this correspondence to the correspondence in 1972. In 1972 an even larger proportion (36.8%) failed to offer at least one reason for liking the Republican Party, but the gamma value (.561) was considerably below what it had been in 1964 (.713). Of the 52.2% of all identifiers who considered themselves Democrats in 1972, 75.9% had no reason for liking the Republican Party, and this figure of 75.9% certainly differs very little from the analogous figure of 78.0% in 1972. The two years seem to differ, then, in the 9% or so who were willing to consider themselves Democrats in 1964, who normally have at least one reason to like the Republican Party, but who did not have such a reason in 1964.

This 9% or so adds flexibility to American politics, not just with regard to the relative size of groups of party identifiers, but also in the extent to which a certain kind of polarization exists. Consider these four possibilities. (1) Some or most of these 9% will normally have at least one thing to like about the Republican Party and will be Democratic identifiers. Thus the overall relationship between the number of likes for the Republican Party and party identification will be weakened, as it seems to be normally. (2) When these individuals have nothing to like about the Republican Party but consider themselves Republican, the relationship will also be weakened, but there is no apparent example of this in the six data sets we have examined. (3) When these individuals have nothing to like about the Republican Party at the same time that they consider themselves Democratic, then the relationship between the number of likes for the Republican Party and party identification will be strengthened, as it was in 1964. (4) When these individuals have at least one reason for liking the Republican Party and consider themselves Republican identifiers, the relationship will also be strengthened, as perhaps it had been in 1952.

This is clearly a simplified analysis of one aspect of the dynamics of American politics. For instance, it ignores the crucial question of why individuals might change their party identification, whether randomly,[8] in response to short-term issues,[9] or as a consequence of changing party images.[10] But in a sense the reasons for changing identifications are temporarily not important once the relationship between identification and the number of likes for the Republican Party has been established. By then the political system will or will not possess a certain degree of constraint that may either facilitate programmatic policy implementation or inhibit pluralistic coalition making. But flexibility is a two-edged sword; the relative polarization created today is likely to be undone tomorrow.

After this excursion into the possible dynamics of the American electoral system, let us return briefly to the data of Table 3.2. The range of differences in this table drops sharply for all four indexes between 1964 and 1968, even for those indexes for which 1964 did not mark a high point. The relatively small range of differences for 1968 continues in 1972. In other words, following the critical or at least distinctive election of 1964, the likes and dislikes of Americans have been less and less related to the party identifications of Americans. In Chapter 4 we encounter evidence that critical issues of a realigning potential that fail to realign the party system may lead to further party decomposition because the very issues that voters are most concerned about are not debated in the terms voters want and are not translated into meaningful political alternatives for the voters by the parties. This failure on the part of the parties to polarize around critical issues seems to turn people away from the party system as voters realize that the parties are either unwilling or unable to deal with the issues most salient to them. The simple count of the number of likes and dislikes, reported in Table 3.2, reveals a similar process. The critical nature of the 1964 election led to further party decomposition, although in this table evidence for this phenomenon is very preliminary and the substantive basis for the phenomenon, if it is a real one, is clearly lacking and must await the analysis found in Chapter 4.

LIKES AND DISLIKES AND THE VOTE

We have attempted to determine whether there is an asymmetry in the impact likes and dislikes have on political behavior. If we define political behavior broadly to include attitudes, then the previous section reveals an asymmetry, although not the one we anticipated. Likes rather than dislikes affect party identification more strongly. In this section we shall focus on political behavior defined more narrowly, specifically on the individual's vote.[11] Table 3.4 presents reduced forms of the cross-tabulations of vote by likes and dislikes, including gamma coefficients to summarize the relationships. As in Chapter 2, the data are non-Democratic percentages of the vote.

TABLE 3.4   Percent Voting Democratic By the Number of Likes or Dislikes for the Parties, by Year

Year	Number	Likes Democrats		Dislikes Democrats		Likes Republicans		Dislikes Republicans	
		%	N	%	N	%	N	%	N
1952	0	8.6	430	74.7	462	80.7	549	19.2	588
	1-2	55.4	578	37.4	514	25.5	458	57.7	520
	3-5	76.8	276	10.4	308	3.2	277	88.6	176
	Gamma	-.781	1284	+.753	1284	+.897	1284	-.767	1284
1956	0	7.9	484	57.9	644	72.4	537	21.4	612
	1-2	53.6	550	31.3	537	27.2	559	54.5	512
	3-5	85.0	254	7.5	107	4.2	192	84.8	164
	Gamma	-.854	1288	+.581	1288	+.811	1288	-.703	1288
1960	0	12.4	566	63.8	804	72.4	651	26.9	680
	1-2	58.8	588	24.5	449	28.4	566	56.8	579
	3-5	89.0	245	7.5	146	1.1	182	87.1	140
	Gamma	-.844	1399	+.738	1399	+.820	1399	-.645	1399
1964	0	50.0	1507	88.5	2416	91.2	2565	63.9	1968
	1-2	83.4	1896	58.9	1344	47.9	1244	78.9	1764
	3-5	95.6	675	16.0	318	17.1	269	95.7	346
	Gamma	-.720	4078	+.764	4078	+.850	4078	-.453	4078
1968	0	10.9	1016	61.6	837	57.7	1120	26.1	1114
	1-2	56.8	840	31.1	931	23.0	823	47.0	881
	3-5	73.4	368	11.4	456	8.2	281	66.8	229
	Gamma	-.775	2224	+.642	2224	+.689	2224	-.479	2224
1972	0	15.6	531	41.8	529	45.5	574	17.0	513
	1-2	46.1	345	22.9	354	15.9	308	42.8	360
	3-5	66.7	108	11.9	101	3.9	102	65.8	111
	Gamma	-.658	984	+.464	984	+.695	984	-.610	984

Again we find, by examining the gamma coefficients, that likes have a greater impact than dislikes. Reasons for liking the Democratic Party structure the vote more than do reasons for disliking the Democratic Party; similarly, reasons for liking the Republican Party structure the vote more than reasons for disliking the Republican Party. However there are no clear patterns over time to the gamma coefficients, unlike the data for party identifications.

We do find again that the 1964 election data behave differently from the data of other years. The difference in the absolute values of the gamma coefficients for the Democratic data reveal that in 1964, for the only time in the 20-year period, dislikes structured the vote more than likes. For the Republican data, on the other hand, the difference in the structuring ability of likes and dislikes was greatest for the 20-year span, and favored the likes. Gamma values attained or approached relative lows for Democratic likes and Republican dislikes and relative highs for Democratic dislikes and Republican likes. Thus we find the unusual occurrence of relative polarization, in the aggregate at least, for the likes and dislikes of Americans, despite the lack of individual-level polarization.

If we examine the range of differences again, we also find evidence of the distinctiveness of the 1964 election. The range of difference simply measures, in this case, the proportion of non-Democratic voters among individuals with no reasons for liking or disliking the party minus the proportion of non-Democratic voters among individuals with three or more reasons for liking or disliking the party. The number of reasons for liking the Democratic Party or for disliking the Republican Party affected voting behavior relatively little in 1964, whereas the number of reasons for disliking the Democratic Party was particularly important for the voting decision in that year.

This range of differences also reiterates the greater impact of likes over dislikes. Of all comparisons, likes produce a greater range of differences than dislikes 10 out of 12 times. Of the two exceptions, one occurred in 1964, resulting, as was mentioned, from the high range in Democratic dislikes. The other exception occurred in 1972, when Republican dislikes structured voting more than Republican likes. In 1972 likes and dislikes structured the vote relatively little; party-related themes simply failed to stir the electorate or to provide logical means for the voters to make their electoral choice and influence government.[12]

CONCLUSION

In this chapter we sought to determine if likes and dislikes affected political behavior differently. Although we anticipated that negative affect — dislikes — might carry the greater weight, we have found consistently that positive affect — likes — have been more strongly related to party identification and to the vote. This finding is somewhat surprising, since a strong American political tradition is to "throw the rascals out," that is, to act on negative evaluations of politicians and parties. Perhaps this is a healthy finding for the future of democracy, for it suggests that citizens can be constructive in their criticisms of government and can appreciate and respond to the positive achievements of parties.

It must be remembered, of course, that likes and dislikes in the real world rarely have the opportunity to act independently of each other, that some cumulative process is employed by the voter to put together the various sentiments he possesses in order to bring these sentiments to bear upon his vote. As Kelley and Mirer argue, a simple process is more likely to be employed than a complicated process, and the simple linear model they propose has remarkable abilities in predicting the vote, suggesting that voters act as if they (unconsciously) employ the very model Kelley and Mirer propose.[13] A similar linear model is the one proposed in Chapter 2, which differs from the Kelley-Mirer model, of course, in excplicitly not using the candidate image data.

The data in this chapter also demonstrate the relevance of the concept of party image for the study of party decomposition and electoral realignment. We have encountered preliminary evidence that parties are becoming less salient to voters, and we have found striking evidence of the distinctive, if not critical nature, of the 1964 election. A critical election is inherent to the process of critical electoral realignment, for if realignment occurs in a sudden fashion, it does so at the time of a critical election.[14] The strange behavior of the 1964 election in the data of this chapter requires that we examine further the possibility of realignment before or during the 1964 election.

Having thus examined the number of likes and dislikes Americans have for their parties, we proceed to an examination of the substance of those likes and dislikes in the next chapter. These substantive likes and dislikes not only trace the issues and themes that have appeared on the political scene since 1952, but they permit us to discuss more specifically the possibility of electoral realignment and the process of party decomposition, and they introduce us to the process by which political issues intrude upon the awareness of the voters.

NOTES

1. Stanley Kelley, Jr. and Thad W. Mirer, "The Simple Act of Voting," *American Political Science Review*, **68** (1974), 572–591.

2. Nehemiah Jordan, "The 'Asymmetry' of 'Liking' and 'Disliking': A Phenomenon Meriting Further Reflection and Research," *Public Opinion Quarterly*, **29** (1965), p. 320.

3. *Ibid.*, p. 315.

4. *Ibid., passim.* For an interesting application of this "asymmetry" proposition, see Samuel Kernell, "Presidential Popularity and Negative Voting: An Alternative Explanation of the Mid-Term Electoral Decline of the President's Party," paper prepared for delivery at the 1974 Annual Meeting of the American Political Science Association, Palmer House Hotel, Chicago, Ill., August 29–September 2, 1974.

5. Republican voting is positively associated with disliking the Democrats and liking the Republicans, so these gammas are positive. Republican voting is negatively associated with liking the Democrats and disliking the Republicans, so these gammas are negative.

6. Gerald M. Pomper, "From Confusion to Clarity: Issues and American Voters, 1956–1968," *American Political Science Review,* **66** (1972), 415–428.

7. See, for instance, John O. Field and Ronald E. Anderson, "Ideology in the Public's Conceptualization of the 1964 Election," *Public Opinion Quarterly,* **33** (1969), 380–398.

8. Edward C. Dreyer, "Change and Stability in Party Identifications," *Journal of Politics,* **35** (1973), 712–722.

9. Douglas Dobson and Douglas St. Angelo, "Party Identification and the Floating Vote: Some Dynamics," *American Political Science Review,* **69** (1975), 481–490; and Richard A. Brody, "Change and Stability in Partisan Identification: A Note of Caution" (unpublished manuscript: Stanford University, 1975).

10. This particular hypothesis will be explored in Chapter 8.

11. Throughout the book the vote will be dichotomized (Democratic/non-Democratic) to handle more easily the 1968 Wallace voters. The vote variable is the voter's expected vote (his preference), taken from the preelection interview schedules. Definite choices and preferred choices where indefinite were combined for the respective parties.

12. On the 1972 election, see Arthur H. Miller, Warren E. Miller, Alden S. Raine, and Thad A. Brown, "A Majority Party in Disarray: Policy Polarization in the 1972 Election," paper prepared for delivery at the Annual Meeting of the American Political Science Association, Jung Hotel, New Orleans, La., September 4–8, 1973.

13. Kelley and Mirer, *op. cit.*

14. Substantial electoral change stretched across a series of elections constitutes a "secular realignment." When this change is focused in one (or perhaps two) elections, the election is referred to as a critical election. For the seminal works for this terminology, see V. O. Key, Jr., "A Theory of Critical Elections," *Journal of Politics,* **17** (1955), 3–18; and Key, "Secular Realignment and the Party System," *Journal of Politics,* **21** (1959), 198–210.

chapter 4

The substantive likes and dislikes of Americans

We have seen, in Chapter 2, that an index of the number of likes and dislikes an individual has for the two major American political parties is a useful tool in the study of voting behavior and, in Chapter 3, that these likes and dislikes affect the individual's political behavior differently. We have found preliminary evidence of party decomposition and of a distinctiveness in the 1964 data. So far, however, we have not examined the opinions that cause the affective ties we have measured. In this chapter we turn to these specific substantive concerns.

The Survey Research Center/Center for Political Studies developed a set of Master Codes for coding responses to the party image questionnaire items.[1] These Master Codes have permitted investigators to examine the levels of conceptualization among Americans[2] and the broad substantive concerns citizens have for parties and candidates.[3] For the present analysis two procedures were followed. First, the hundreds of possible response categories were collapsed into seven broad, substantive classifications.[4] These classifications are: (1) responses about PEOPLE in the parties, either candidates in the present election or prominent figures generally, (2) responses about the parties as MANAGERS of government, (3) responses about the PHILOSOPHY of the parties, (4) responses about the DOMESTIC POLICIES favored by the parties, (5) responses about the FOREIGN POLICIES favored by the two parties, (6) responses about the GROUPS in society that are seen to benefit or lose from the actions of the parties, and (7) responses, typically vague, about the PARTY itself.[5] Each of the seven sets of responses was then combined into an index of favorability toward the parties by counting each reason for liking the Republican Party or for disliking the Democratic Party as +1 and each reason for liking the Democratic Party or for disliking the Republican Party as −1 and by adding these responses together. In forming any one of these seven indexes, responses that did not fall in the given category were coded 0 for the given index. Missing data categories were coded 0 for all seven of the indexes. As with the generalized party image index discussed in Chapter 2, any one of these indexes could possibly range from −10 (most pro-Democratic) to +10 (most pro-Republican), except in 1972. This procedure creates seven broad *substantive indexes* that resemble the original index in counting the number of likes and dislikes but that differ from it because each of them counts only those likes and dislikes that refer to a single broad substantive category.

The second procedure was to isolate from the Master Codes those categories that dealt specifically with issues of particular concern over these 20 years (economic and welfare matters, race, corruption, Vietnam, law and order, and other "social" issues from the 1972 campaign). For any one of these topics, each reason offered for liking the Democratic Party or for disliking the Republican Party was coded −1, each reason for liking the Republican Party and disliking the Democratic Party was coded +1, and these responses were then added together. Missing data categories and responses dealing with any topic other than the one of specific interest were coded 0. These indexes could also range from −10 to +10, since any respondent was free to offer up to 20 responses dealing with one of these specific topics, but no respondent did.

For both of these sets of indexes we shall examine distributions over time, mean index scores over time, and the abilities over time of these indexes to affect the voting decision. In all three analyses the lack of complete equivalence between the 1972 data and the other sets of data should be kept in mind. In general we shall discover trends in the data that are not due primarily to the possible nonequivalence of the 1972 data and that should not present a serious problem. However, we should be alert to the possibility that any distinctiveness we find in the 1972 data may in part result from the smaller set of responses in that year.

THE MEANING OF SUBSTANTIVE PREFERENCES

What can we expect these broad and specific indexes to tell us? The substantive likes and dislikes Americans have for their parties reveal the substantive concerns that voters associate with their parties — the "meaning" of parties in their minds. The party image questionnaire items tap the substantive concerns that have come to define the political parties, not as journalists, party leaders, or candidates define them, but as voters themselves define them. In other words, the likes and dislikes Americans have for their political parties, that is, their party images, can be interpreted to demonstrate the perceived meaning of these parties.

Such an argument actually is implicit in some of the literature on electoral realignment, in which critical social issues are said to cause massive and durable alterations in political identifications.[6] Sellers argues that the critical issues that stimulate an electoral realignment do so first by altering the party images of large numbers of voters, and it is these new party images that in turn transform party identifications.[7] Burnham argues that the issues which prompt realignment structure the political agenda for the ensuing party system.[8] Thus it is not surprising that the Survey Research Center has consistently found references to the Depression in the responses to the party image items.[9]

Of course voters partially define parties in terms of candidates and leaders, and references to individuals within the parties show up even when one examines only the party image items. But such references are different than the responses obtained by asking people directly what they like and dislike about the candidates. Candidate references that appear within the party image responses presumably reflect a process by which candidates have been incorporated by the individual into the individual's mental picture of the party. Tracing candidate responses within the party image items would in turn permit us to determine to what extent parties are defined by voters primarily as collections of leaders and also to what extent parties are conceptualized by voters as personifications rather than as ideology-transmitting institutions.[10]

Isolating party image responses from candidate image responses permits us to address more directly the substantive meaning of parties for Americans — what parties "stand for" in the people's minds when they are not asked this directly but are permitted in a sense to "freely associate."[11] More importantly, this free association is apt to reveal highly salient images because respondents are directed to think in terms of likes and dislikes (i.e., in nonneutral, affective terms).

Furthermore, the richness of the responses will reveal not only the associations an individual offers in response to the stimuli, "Democratic Party" and "Republican Party," but will also permit us to trace the possible variability in this richness over time. To the extent that responses become less rich, less complete, less explicit, or less frequent, we may infer that parties have become less meaningful for Americans, that party decomposition has occurred.

Finally, interpreting party images as the meanings voters attach to parties is not really a new concept but is implicit in Milne and Mackenzie's treatment of the subject. Issues are "annexed" by parties, incorporated by parties into their images, and are added to the vote-structuring abilities that derive from their names-as-symbols when such issues effectively distinguish between the parties and do not involve ubiquitous traits such as honesty and integrity (perhaps not so ubiquitous as was once thought).[12]

THE BROAD SUBSTANTIVE INDEXES OVER TIME

It is illuminating to begin the investigation of the meaning of parties for Americans by discussing the distributions of the electorate along these broad substantive indexes over time. Table 4.1 presents these distributions in collapsed form.

These seven classifications sort themselves out into three categories. First, two themes have consistently favored the Democratic Party — the GROUPS index especially but also the DOMESTIC POLICIES index. As we shall see later, the GROUPS classification includes references to the common person and the poor. In other words, there is a good deal of overlap in the empirical referents of the responses used for these two indexes,[13] and this overlap defines the substance of the favorability that

TABLE 4.1 Distributions of the Substantive Party Image Indexes, by Year[a]

Index	Year	Party Image[b]					Mean[c]
		DD	D	N	R	RR	
PEOPLE	1952	0.1	8.5	75.7	15.6	0.1	+0.10
	1956	0.1	10.9	67.6	21.2	0.2	+0.14
	1960	0.0	5.1	85.1	9.8	0.0	+0.06
	1964	0.1	12.8	79.4	7.7	0.1	-0.07
	1968	0.1	11.4	76.7	11.6	0.2	0.00
	1972	0.0	5.0	81.6	13.1	0.1	+0.10
MANAGERS	1952	0.0	3.2	67.5	28.2	1.1	+0.44
	1956	0.0	2.2	84.8	12.9	0.1	+0.16
	1960	0.0	5.4	79.7	14.7	0.3	+0.14
	1964	0.0	5.8	81.0	12.9	0.3	+0.11
	1968	0.0	5.0	75.6	19.2	0.2	+0.22
	1972	0.0	8.4	80.7	10.9	0.1	+0.04
PHILOSOPHY	1952	0.1	10.5	76.9	12.0	0.4	+0.05
	1956	0.1	7.5	81.9	9.4	0.2	+0.03
	1960	0.2	9.2	78.7	11.3	0.6	+0.08
	1964	0.0	9.9	72.9	16.7	0.6	+0.17
	1968	0.4	9.3	72.2	17.6	0.5	+0.14
	1972	0.0	7.3	77.6	14.9	0.1	+0.10
DOMESTIC	1952	3.2	33.2	45.4	17.4	0.7	-0.41
POLICIES	1956	1.8	25.2	59.8	13.2	0.0	-0.28
	1960	1.1	24.4	61.0	13.2	0.4	-0.20
	1964	0.8	21.5	67.9	9.6	0.1	-0.22
	1968	0.7	18.1	67.3	12.6	0.4	-0.09
	1972	0.6	15.6	72.6	11.0	0.1	-0.09
FOREIGN	1952	0.2	4.5	74.0	21.1	0.3	+0.24
POLICIES	1956	0.0	4.2	77.2	18.3	0.3	+0.19
	1960	0.0	7.6	77.2	15.2	0.1	+0.10
	1964	0.0	5.8	84.2	10.0	0.1	+0.07
	1968	0.0	2.6	75.2	16.8	0.3	+0.25
	1972	0.0	5.3	83.1	11.5	0.0	+0.08

the Democratic Party has enjoyed among the party images of Americans from 1952 to 1972. This substance concerns, of course, matters related to the Depression and to the issues that have defined the political agenda for America since the Depression.

At the same time, the one index that would seem to measure the salience of this substance best is the DOMESTIC POLICIES index, whose favorability for the Democrats has declined steadily over this 20-year period. This decline would seem to offer evidence for the proposition that the themes that prompted the realignment of the 1930s have less and less meaning for Americans. We can see this further in

TABLE 4.1 Cont.

Index	Year	Party Image[b]					Mean[c]
		DD	D	N	R	RR	
GROUPS	1952	2.3	31.5	61.6	4.5	0.1	-0.56
	1956	3.4	34.1	57.3	5.1	0.2	-0.68
	1960	2.0	29.9	62.2	6.0	0.0	-0.53
	1964	1.3	21.6	62.0	5.0	0.1	-0.48
	1968	2.1	27.2	65.0	5.6	0.1	-0.45
	1972	2.0	29.1	63.8	4.9	0.0	-0.50
PARTY	1952	0.0	12.8	77.6	9.7	0.0	-0.02
	1956	0.0	14.6	70.0	15.2	0.1	+0.04
	1960	0.1	15.7	67.7	16.4	0.2	+0.03
	1964	0.0	23.5	65.5	11.0	0.1	-0.14
	1968	0.0	18.2	65.1	16.5	0.2	+0.01
	1972	0.0	11.1	76.5	12.5	0.0	+0.03

[a]Operational definitions of substantive party image indexes can be found in the text and in note 4 to this chapter. Each entry is the percent in the respective party image category for the respective substantive issue. These percents, added across each row, should total 100.0% for each year, except for rounding errors. Numbers of cases on which percents are based, respectively for each year, are: 1952 = (1899); 1956 = (1762); 1960 = (1954); 1964 = (4658); 1968 = (3100); 1972 = (1372).

[b]Key: DD = Strongly pro-Democratic (-10 to -4, except for 1972); D = Mildly pro-Democratic (-3 to -1); N = Neutral (0); R = Mildly pro-Republican (+1 to +3); RR = Strongly pro-Republican (+4 to +10, except for 1972).

[c]Based on the 21-point substantive party image index; positive values favor the Republican Party; negative values favor the Democratic Party.

Table 4.1 by noting for the DOMESTIC POLICIES index that the proportion of the electorate coded as Neutral has increased fairly steadily since 1952. In other words, not only do themes related to the Depression fail to provide the Democratic Party with the overwhelming advantage these themes once provided, but these themes also fail to stir the entire electorate, as much as they once did, to favor either party.

That the GROUPS index persists in its pro-Democratic bias can be attributed, no doubt, to the ability of the Democratic Party to project itself as the party of the downtrodden. In contemporary American politics this has meant that the Democratic Party has maintained a special appeal for blacks. Among the party images of Americans, it was not always the case that blacks perceived the Democratic Party more favorably than did whites. As we shall see in Chapter 7, regional differences in the party images of Americans in the 1950s gave way in the 1960s to racial differences. The 1964 election, particularly, mobilized the sentiments of blacks to strongly favor the Democratic Party.

Throughout this 20-year period no theme has defined favorability to the Republican Party the way the DOMESTIC POLICIES and GROUPS themes have defined favorability toward the Democratic Party. Four of these themes, however, have provided the Republicans with a small net advantage: FOREIGN POLICIES, MANAGERS of government, PEOPLE within the party, and PHILOSOPHY of the parties. The advantage provided by the FOREIGN POLICIES and MANAGERS of government themes has apparently been declining, despite the temporary increased advantage the Republicans enjoyed from both of these themes in 1968.

These increases and the increased advantage enjoyed by the Republicans from the MANAGERS of government theme in 1952 manifest greater volatility than that which occurs within the Democratic themes of DOMESTIC POLICIES and GROUPS. It may be that such volatility occurs because the Republican Party has no theme defining it, in the voters' collective eyes, the way the Democratic Party does. That is, the long-term defining nature of the Democratic Party — its positive association with the Depression — is fairly constant, or perhaps erodes at a slow, constant pace. The Republican Party, on the other hand, lacks a defining theme in the voter's eyes and its images are therefore more responsive to the short-term influences that appear from election to election. In 1952 voters were persuaded that the Republican Party would offer a more reliable set of governmental managers.[14] In 1968 voters disapproved of Johnson's performance as President, and this disapproval involved doubts about Democratic FOREIGN POLICY and about Democrats as MANAGERS of government.[15]

The PEOPLE index suggests that leaders within the party have been more important to Americans' images of the Republican Party than to their images of the Democratic Party. What seems to be the case is that leaders within the Democratic Party are important because of the ideological or substantive accomplishments with which they are associated. It is these issue-related themes, especially the Depression, which emerge, then, in those party images of Americans that define Democratic favorability. Traditional Democratic heroes are favorably cited in response to the candidate image items apparently because of the

GROUPS and DOMESTIC POLICIES themes with which they are related. For Republicans, on the other hand, perhaps because they have no consistent defining theme in the voters' eyes, personalities and the attributes of candidates become more important.[16]

References to traditional, vague party themes, such as "I've always voted Republican (Democratic)," which are used to form the PARTY index, have advantaged neither party over this time period, except in 1964. The neutrality of this theme might have been expected, since it basically includes content-free responses. The Goldwater candidacy, however, provided a significant net Democratic advantage, as it tended to do on all but the PHILOSOPHY index. Goldwater's desire to articulate a conservative philosophy[17] increased citizen perceptions of the Republican Party as conservative, as we shall see below, and produced a gain for the Republicans in the PHILOSOPHY index. And in 1964 the PEOPLE index produced a Democratic advantage for the only time in this 20-year electoral period. Finally, the declining salience of the DOMESTIC POLICIES theme was slightly, though temporarily, reversed in 1964.

Some concluding remarks about the data in Table 4.1 are in order. The extreme partisanship provided by some of the indexes in 1952 (MANAGERS favored the Republicans; GROUPS and DOMESTIC POLICIES favored the Democrats) is not found in the late 1960s or in 1972, with the exception of GROUPS. Even the partisanship of the GROUPS index has declined, however, in comparison to where it stood in the 1950s. The movement of the means for each of these seven indexes seems to be producing stability and neutrality in the present and near future of American politics — the mean values of these indexes seem to be levelling off near or perhaps slightly above zero (that is, slightly favoring the Republican Party).[18] This overall trend suggests that political parties in the present party system have less and less meaning for Americans. The seven categories are sufficiently broad to incorporate both position and valence issues[19] as well as candidates. Whatever the issues, events, or candidates of the day, political parties seem less able to translate these stimuli into political terms. The danger posed by this inability has been well-articulated by Burnham:

> . . . So far as is known, the blunt alternative to party government is the concentration of political power, locally or nationally, in the hands of those who already possess concentrated economic power. If no adequate substitute for party as a means for mobilizing non-elite influence on the governing

process has yet been discovered, the obvious growth of [candidate] "image" and "personality" voting in recent decades should be a matter of some concern to those who would like to see a more complete restoration of the democratic process in the United States.[20]

STRUCTURING THE VOTE

We find further evidence of party decomposition when we investigate the ability of these seven indexes to structure the vote of the American electorate. If these substantive indexes of party image can structure the vote, then individuals with pro-Democratic images should vote Democratic and individuals with pro-Republican images should vote Republican. Of course the ability of these indexes to structure the vote will be limited, since the data of Table 4.1 reveal that a varying but consistently large proportion of the electorate is classified as neutral on any one of the indexes for any year. In addition, on the combined overall index discussed in Chapter 2, from one-quarter to one-third of the electorate is coded as neutral throughout this 20-year period.

Nevertheless, when we examine the ability of these seven substantive indexes to structure the vote, we find varying abilities among the indexes but also an apparent overall decline from 1952 to 1972.[21] The rank order of these seven indexes in their ability to structure the vote resembles their partisanship rankings discussed above. That is, those image indexes on which the electorate's attitudes have been more politicized are also the indexes that have caused greater differences in voting behavior. The DOMESTIC POLICIES and GROUPS indexes, both of which have favored the Democratic Party in attitude, translate that favorability into votes better than those indexes that do not favor either party as much as these do. However, especially for the DOMESTIC POLICIES index, the ability to structure the vote has declined. These conclusions emerge from the data of Table 4.2.

Table 4.2 presents the proportion of the electorate that has had its vote structured by these seven party image indexes for each year. The percents are computed by adding the number of pro-Democratic image-holders voting Democratic to the number of pro-Republican image-holders voting Republican and dividing by the total number of image-holders, including neutral image-holders. We notice immediately that the mean for the seven indexes has declined over this 20-year

TABLE 4.2 Proportion of the Vote Structured by Each of the Seven Substantive Party Image Indexes, by Year[a]

Party Image Index	Year						Mean[b]
	1952	1956	1960	1964	1968	1972	
PEOPLE	22.5	27.2	13.0	16.4	15.8	16.5	18.6
MANAGERS	34.6	15.7	20.5	13.9	22.9	16.5	20.7
PHILOSOPHY	24.7	17.8	21.3	22.3	24.6	21.1	22.0
DOMESTIC POLICIES	50.5	34.1	34.4	27.5	27.1	22.0	32.6
FOREIGN POLICIES	24.8	21.2	21.8	12.3	20.8	15.2	18.6
GROUPS	33.7	35.7	34.8	35.3	27.7	24.7	32.0
PARTY	21.3	28.0	30.9	28.9	27.0	17.2	25.6
Mean[c]	33.2	25.9	25.2	22.4	23.7	19.0	----
Standard Deviation[c]	10.0	7.2	6.8	8.0	4.0	3.3	----
(N)	(1284)	(1288)	(1399)	(4078)	(2224)	(984)	

[a]Entries are the sum of the number of pro-Democratic image-holders voting Democratic and the number of pro-Republican image-holders voting Republican divided by the total number of image-holders.

[b]Computed for the entries in the respective row.

[c]Computed for the entries in the respective column.

period, from 33.2% in 1952 to 19.0% in 1972, with a significant but temporary reversal in 1964. In general, in other words, these seven indexes are less and less capable of influencing the vote. Furthermore, the standard deviation of the scores for the seven indexes has also declined, so that these seven indexes are behaving more and more alike — in this case, are failing more and more to determine voting behavior.

The decline has not been uniform, however. The DOMESTIC POLICIES index in 1952 greatly affected the vote but now does so only slightly more than most of the indexes and less so than the GROUPS index. The GROUPS index itself has declined in influence in the past

TABLE 4.3 Democratic Percent of the Vote for Categories of the Collapsed Substantive Party Image Indexes, by Year[a]

Index	Year	Party Image			Gamma
		Pro-Democratic	Neutral	Pro-Republican	
PEOPLE	1952	68.4 (114)	48.7 (258)	18.2 (258)	.754
	1956	73.2 (157)	43.6 (818)	24.6 (313)	.507
	1960	72.0 (82)	46.4 (1155)	24.1 (162)	.492
	1964	87.7 (543)	73.9 (3217)	39.6 (318)	.552
	1968	56.8 (250)	37.7 (1686)	27.8 (288)	.317
	1972	61.1 (54)	33.6 (783)	12.2 (147)	.568
MANAGERS	1952	77.8 (45)	60.3 (744)	17.2 (495)	.746
	1956	72.7 (33)	47.8 (1057)	10.1 (198)	.744
	1960	71.1 (76)	51.7 (1059)	12.1 (264)	.704
	1964	89.7 (261)	77.5 (3273)	38.6 (544)	.655
	1968	60.0 (125)	45.0 (1604)	12.5 (495)	.628
	1972	54.7 (86)	33.1 (771)	9.4 (127)	.561
PHILOSOPHY	1952	73.3 (161)	47.8 (906)	8.3 (217)	.711
	1956	67.9 (131)	44.3 (999)	10.8 (158)	.625
	1960	70.4 (152)	48.7 (1032)	11.2 (215)	.652
	1964	90.8 (455)	81.0 (2937)	27.4 (686)	.768
	1968	66.8 (235)	41.6 (1538)	13.5 (451)	.610
	1972	59.5 (74)	34.4 (727)	10.9 (183)	.592
DOMESTIC POLICIES	1952	77.0 (505)	30.9 (492)	9.8 (287)	.799
	1956	71.3 (362)	37.7 (729)	8.1 (197)	.701
	1960	70.9 (405)	41.7 (775)	11.0 (219)	.655
	1964	92.1 (967)	70.7 (2703)	43.4 (408)	.638
	1968	64.0 (447)	37.5 (1423)	10.7 (354)	.606
	1972	59.3 (162)	29.8 (689)	9.8 (133)	.599

TABLE 4.3 Cont.

Index	Year	Party Image			Gamma
		Pro-Democratic	Neutral	Pro-Republican	
FOREIGN POLICIES	1952	69.9 (73)	51.4 (876)	20.3 (335)	.588
	1956	70.3 (64)	48.2 (950)	16.8 (274)	.619
	1960	75.6 (123)	48.8 (1019)	17.1 (257)	.633
	1964	96.4 (253)	75.6 (3411)	37.7 (414)	.716
	1968	56.8 (88)	43.7 (1624)	19.3 (512)	.495
	1972	61.0 (59)	33.0 (797)	11.7 (128)	.573
GROUPS	1952	73.3 (499)	27.9 (714)	5.6 (71)	.772
	1956	73.1 (527)	23.6 (683)	3.8 (78)	.814
	1960	78.5 (497)	29.7 (798)	6.7 (104)	.806
	1964	91.0 (1436)	65.7 (2443)	33.7 (199)	.689
	1968	69.8 (679)	26.9 (1393)	5.9 (152)	.746
	1972	57.0 (330)	20.8 (597)	3.5 (57)	.698
PARTY	1952	72.4 (181)	44.6 (942)	11.2 (161)	.649
	1956	75.9 (212)	41.4 (835)	17.4 (241)	.633
	1960	78.8 (236)	47.4 (892)	9.2 (271)	.748
	1964	84.1 (1001)	77.0 (2618)	26.6 (459)	.561
	1968	65.4 (431)	35.9 (1403)	18.5 (390)	.540
	1972	45.5 (121)	31.6 (716)	22.4 (147)	.279

[a]Entries are the percent of the party image category voting Democratic and are based on the n's listed below each percent in parentheses. In 1968 the vote is dichotomized into Democratic and non-Democratic. Total N's for each year, on which the gammas are based, are: 1952 = (1284); 1956 = (1288); 1960 = (1399); 1964 = (4078); 1968 = (2224); 1972 = (984).

two elections, although it was fairly stable from 1952 through 1964. The significance of the GROUPS index deserved special attention, so we return it to below. The PARTY index dropped significantly in 1972, which would seem to reflect the relative impotency of political party in the 1972 election.[22]

The data of Table 4.2 only summarize the abilities of the indexes to structure the vote. The more complete data are presented in Table 4.3, which also contains gamma values to measure structuring abilities. These gamma values reaffirm the declining abilities of the indexes to structure the vote, although the steepness of the declines differs considerably from index to index. The steepest decline has been in the PARTY index, falling from near .750 in 1960 to below .300 in 1972. Since the PARTY index measures only vague, almost content-free responses to the parties, it is not as interesting as the less steep decline in the impact the DOMESTIC POLICIES index has had on the vote, since, as we saw earlier, this index politicized attitudes more than any other index and aroused larger proportions of the electorate than the other indexes. Significant jumps occur for some of the indexes, but not one of these indexes has maintained the impact it had in the 1950s.

The proportion of the electorate that has its vote structured by any one of these seven indexes is the number of pro-Democratic image-holders voting Democratic plus the number of pro-Republican image-holders voting Republican divided by the total number of image-holders. We have noted the decreases in these proportions. What is interesting, however, is the relative stability in the ability of these indexes to structure the vote of nonneutral image-holders. That is, if we compute the number of pro-Democratic image-holders voting Democratic plus the number of pro-Republican image-holders voting Republican as a function of the total number of pro-Democratic and pro-Republican image-holders, rather than as a function of all image-holders, we do not encounter the great variation of decline we have just encountered, with one significant exception. The relevant figures are presented in Table 4.4. Between 75 and 80% of nonneutral image-holders have voted for the party projecting the nonneutral image, with the exception of the GROUPS index since 1964. In fact, in 1964 the GROUPS index was able to influence the vote of nonneutral image-holders more strongly than any other index for any year (88.0%), yet the impact of this index fell precipitously to a value 25 percentage points lower by 1972. This drop is the most notable variation in Table 4.4.

TABLE 4.4 Percent of the Vote Structured by Each of the Seven Substantive Party Image Indexes, Nonneutral Image-Holders Only, by Year[a]

Party Image Index	Year						Mean[b]
	1952	1956	1960	1964	1968	1972	
PEOPLE	77.7	74.7	74.6	77.6	63.9	80.6	74.8
	(372)	(470)	(244)	(861)	(538)	(201)	
MANAGERS	82.4	87.4	84.1	70.6	81.9	76.1	80.4
	(540)	(231)	(340)	(805)	(620)	(213)	
PHILOSOPHY	83.9	80.6	81.2	79.8	79.7	80.5	81.0
	(378)	(289)	(367)	(1141)	(686)	(257)	
DOMESTIC POLICIES	81.8	78.0	77.2	81.6	74.2	73.2	77.7
	(792)	(559)	(624)	(1375)	(811)	(245)	
FOREIGN POLICIES	77.9	80.8	72.6	75.2	77.2	79.7	72.2
	(408)	(338)	(380)	(667)	(600)	(187)	
GROUPS	75.9	76.0	81.0	88.0	74.2	62.8	76.3
	(570)	(605)	(601)	(1635)	(831)	(387)	
PARTY	80.1	79.5	85.2	86.6	73.1	63.1	77.9
	(342)	(453)	(507)	(1460)	(821)	(268)	
Mean[c]	80.0	79.6	79.4	79.9	74.9	73.7	----
Standard Deviation[c]	2.7	3.8	4.4	5.8	5.4	7.2	----

[a]Entries are the sum of the number of pro-Democratic image-holders voting Democratic and the number of pro-Republican image-holders voting Republican (non-Democratic) divided by the total number of pro-Democratic plus pro-Republican image-holders. This total is given in parentheses under the percent.

[b]Computed for the entries in the respective row.

[c]Computed for the entries in the respective column.

At this point we can only speculate about the meaning of this drop, but our speculation can be informed by the findings of others. The race issue had its greatest impact on the *party images* of Americans in 1964. Based on data gathered in the early 1960s, Matthews and Prothro argued that perceptions of the Democratic Party as favorable to blacks and to integration — perceptions elicited through the party image items — were causing many Southern whites to foresake the Democratic Party.[23] The salience of this issue in 1964 cannot be doubted, especially for Southerners.[24] Surprisingly, however, party image references to the racial issue dropped substantially between 1968 and 1972. Among Southern white Democratic identifiers, for instance, 16.5% offered references to the racial issue as reasons for disliking the Democratic Party in 1964, compared to only 5.0% in 1968, as we shall see in Chapter 7. Since references to Negroes are included in the GROUPS index, the precipitous drop between 1964 and 1972 seems to reflect the declining salience of this potentially politicizing issue. As Sundquist has argued, the race issue did have realigning potential in the 1960s, but because the parties refused to take opposite, polarizing stands on the issue, its realigning potential soon dissipated.[25] These data seem to display how abruptly even controversial and salient issues such as race can lose their critical nature. Notwithstanding the continuing interest on the part of Americans in issues such as race, the ability of such issues to define the meaning of parties of Americans also depends on the willingness of the parties to define politics in terms of these issues.

THE SPECIFIC SUBSTANTIVE INDEXES

We complete our examination by focusing on the specific responses offered by the electorate to the questions asking their likes and dislikes about the two parties. In general the data reaffirm our earlier conclusions. The frequencies of the modal responses are given in Table 4.5. To be included in this table responses had to be offered by at least 3.0% of the respondents. This figure reveals the long-term trends in the data but is sufficiently high to permit inclusion only of the most prominent short-term trends. Yet it is clearly not so high that it prevents the discovery of these short-term trends.

The dominating theme in the data of Table 4.5 is the persistence of the New Deal issues that prompted realignment. The crisis of the 1930s politicized the electorate in such a way as to produce the "fifth party system."[26] More importantly for our purposes, as Table 4.5 reveals, the issues that prompted realignment have continued to define political parties for Americans. The Democratic Party is liked because it is seen as the party of the common person and because it is perceived as having helped people in the Depression. The Republican image suffers from the perceived association of the Republicans with the Depression and

TABLE 4.5 Most Frequent Reasons for Liking and Disliking the Democratic and Republican Parties, First Responses Only, by Year*

	Year					
	1952	1956	1960	1964	1968	1972
Responses Favoring the Democratic Party						
Like the Democratic Party because:						
1. It promotes good times for average people.[a]	25.8%	18.6%	20.7%	14.6%	13.0%	17.1%
2. It stands for higher wages.[b]	4.6	---	---	---	---	---
3. It's my traditional preference.[c]	3.7	6.0	6.5	8.5	9.0	3.4
4. I just like it.	---	---	---	3.3	---	---
Dislike the Republican Party because:						
1. It causes bad times for average people and stands for business interests.[e]	19.0%	12.1%	10.2%	10.4%	6.6%	13.1%
2. Of Goldwater.[f]	---	---	---	6.2	---	---
3. I just don't like them.[g]	---	---	---	3.3	---	---
4. It's too much like the Democratic Party.[h]	---	---	---	---	5.0	---

75

TABLE 4.5 Cont.

	Year					
	1952	1956	1960	1964	1968	1972

Responses Favoring the Republican Party

Like the Republican Party because:

	1952	1956	1960	1964	1968	1972
1. Of Eisenhower.[i]	4.7%	13.2%	---	---	---	---
2. It's time for a change.[j]	4.8	---	---	---	3.3	---
3. It's the party of peace.[k]	---	4.7	5.2	---	---	---
4. It's conservative.[l]	---	---	4.0	8.7	5.2	4.3
5. It's my traditional[n] preference.[m]	---	---	3.9	4.0	3.1	---
6. It will spend less.[o]	---	---	---	---	3.9	---
7. Of Nixon.	---	---	---	---	---	3.5

Dislike the Democratic Party because:

	1952	1956	1960	1964	1968	1972
1. Of corruption.[p]	7.5%	---	---	---	---	---
2. It will spend too much.[q]	6.4	---	4.7	3.4	5.0	---
3. Taxes are too high.[r]	5.4	---	---	---	---	---
4. Of Stevenson.[s]	---	3.1	3.4	---	---	---
5. It's the war party.[t]	---	4.0	---	---	---	---
6. Of its campaign.[u]	---	5.6	---	---	---	---
7. Of its civil rights stand.[v]	---	---	---	3.4	---	---
8. It's too much like the Republican Party.[w]	---	---	---	---	4.0	---
9. Of Vietnam.[x]	---	---	---	---	4.5	---
10. Of McGovern.[y]	---	---	---	---	---	5.8
11. It's too liberal.[z]	---	---	---	---	---	3.7
(N)	(1899)	(1762)	(1954)	(4658)	(3100)	(1372)

*Entries are the percent offering the respective responses. ICPR Codebook response category Master Codes are given in notes a through z. Where more than one response category is combined to compute table entries, the frequencies for individual response categories are also given in parentheses in notes a through z. To be included in the table, at least 3.0% of the sample had to be coded in the ICPR Master Code category.

a_{1952}: 353 (7.2%), 711 (6.2%), 712 (11.4%); 1956: 353 (3.0%), 711 (8.5%), 712 (9.1%); 1960: 350 (4.0%), 710 (16.7%); 1964: 713; 1968: 711 (7.1%), 712 (5.9%); 1972: 1205 (14.0%), 1233 (3.1%).

b_{1952}: 370. $c_{1952-1968}$: 800; 1972: 101. d_{1964}: 900.

e_{1952}: 351 (5.0%), 355 (4.9%), 633 (9.1%); 1956, 1960: 633; 1964: 633 (7.3%), 713 (3.1%); 1968: 633; 1972: 1209.

f_{1964}: 40. g_{1964}: 900. h_{1968}: 204. i_{1952}, 1956: 10. j_{1952}, 1968: 913.

k_{1956}, 1960: 581. l_{1960}: 282; 1964: 231 (3.0%), 380 (5.7%); 1968: 280; 1972: 816.

$m_{1960-1968}$: 800. n_{1968}: 120. o_{1972}: 32. p_{1952}: 111. q_{1952}, 1960-1968: 130.

r_{1952}: 348. s_{1956}: 50. t_{1956}, 1960: 581. u_{1956}: 841. v_{1964}: 410. w_{1968}: 204.

x_{1968}: 582. y_{1972}: 8. z_{1972}: 815.

with business and the upper class. At the same time we see again that no single theme has defined favorability toward the Republican Party.

It is not unreasonable to suppose that the party that "loses" during a period of electoral realignment suffers from a lack of identity throughout the duration of the emergent party system. Consider a realignment that transforms a majority party to minority status. Before the realignment, this soon-to-be minority party begins to suffer as the basis of its identity becomes less and less salient for the electorate. The realigning crisis places this party in a defensive position in which its identifying characteristics are probably even less salient. Finally, once the crisis has been resolved electorally in favor of the other party, this now-a-minority party can hope only to convince the electorate that it can implement the new political agenda better than can the new majority party. So, while the defining characteristics of the majority party thus reflect the substantive issues that prompted realignment, the minority party is defined less clearly than the majority party is defined and is defined in terms of managerial and statesmanlike attributes rather than in partisan terms.[27] Thus we find that the Republican Party benefits in the recent 20-year period from the MANAGERS theme and from the FOREIGN POLICY theme.

This also suggests a possible explanation for why Watergate failed to become a salient election issue in 1972 but did eventually become so devastating to the Republican Party. The inertia of public reaction toward the parties resisted McGovern's and the Democratic Party's accusations in 1972 of the corruption within the Republican Administration. When facts and events overcame the inertia of the Republican party image as an effective manager of government, the Republican Party, as minority party without a defining theme (except perhaps foreign policy), had little image to fall back on. This, too, explains why the Nixon Administration's defenders relied so heavily on the foreign policy theme in their efforts to save the incumbent President; there was nothing else to fall back on.[28]

The dearth of issues and the dominant theme that does appear in Table 4.5 together suggest that normal politics penetrates very few party images at a time. This is not to say that the party images of Americans are impervious to the presence of political issues. Issues such as Vietnam and civil rights do in fact penetrate the party images of Americans, but it is clear from the data of Table 4.5 that issues must be highly salient to do so, and even then will not fit into the images of many

Americans at the same time. None of the substantive short-term issues that do appear in Table 4.5 is mentioned by as many as one-tenth of the electorate, with the exception of Eisenhower in 1956.

That Vietnam and civil rights did penetrate the images of as many Americans as they did, both to the disadvantage of the Democrats, suggests that these issues had realigning potential. However, these issues quickly dropped out of the images of Americans as Americans perceived that the parties had failed or would fail to take distinguishable stands on them.

The declining salience of the economic theme suggests again that the basis of the last realignment has less and less salience for Americans, either because the issues that were salient to some Americans then are no longer salient to these same Americans, or because younger Americans have replaced those individuals in the electorate for whom the New Deal issues were most salient.[29] What is especialy interesting, however, is that the economic theme had become more important for Americans in 1972, so the Democrtic victories in 1974, that pundits and politicians attributed to inflation and Watergate, are not at all surprising. It may be that Americans, even after Watergate, are willing to believe that parties are capable of translating public demands into public policy.

Unfortunately, such an optimistic picture cannot be gleaned when we examine this economic theme in more detail. In Table 4.5 we find frequency distributions for this economic theme as well as for other issues, mean scores for the indexes, and evidence of the impact of these indexes on voting behavior. The mean score for the economic index has decreased fairly steadily since 1952, moving from highly negative (-0.35) to a point near zero (-0.07). While it is possible that this trend will continue into the range of positive values, by 1972 at least it had reached essentially a neutral position. Moreover, the proportion of individuals in the neutral category has increased steadily, with the exception again of 1964, so the electorate is not really becoming more positive on this scale but is simply becoming more neutral and less aroused by the economic theme. Finally, as the mean has moved toward zero, the ability of the economic theme to structure the vote has also declined steadily, as indicated by the declining proportions of pro-Democratic image-holders voting Democratic and of pro-Republican image-holders voting non-Democratic, and by the declining gamma values. There was a real possibility, then, that by 1974 voters would not perceive either party as likely to act on economic conditions. So, if the pundits and politicians are correct that inflation did in fact motivate voters it is all the more remarkable in the post-Watergate days of cynicism and distrust.

The economic issue was examined because it specifies the theme of the Depression that has manifested itself so consistently in data discussed earlier in this chapter. It is, however, only one of numerous issues that potentially might motivate voters and that potentially might penetrate the party images of voters. We have already found that other specific issues do not occupy important or permanent positions within the party images of Americans (see Table 4.5), and the remaining data will continue to reaffirm this finding.

In Table 4.6 we also find data concerning the frequency and impact of Race, Law and Order, and Vietnam, the critical issues of the 1960s. It is important to remember that the data we are dealing with are the responses to questions about the likes and dislikes of Americans, so the data speak only to the salience of these issues for the *party images* of Americans. The rather limited significance for all three of these issues in Table 4.6 is nevertheless consistent with the findings of other scholars.[30] Finally, Table 4.6 also presents data for other issues thought to be important in the issue-oriented 1972 election,[31] but the data reveal that these other issues also failed to penetrate the party images of Americans.

There is no denying that the issues of race (civil rights), Vietnam, and law and order were highly salient issues in the 1960s. What is perhaps surprising is that other issues, such as the social issue,[32] have failed to penetrate the party images of Americans. This lack of penetration again seems to reveal that party images basically convey the defining attributes of parties for the electorate. Furthermore, the absence of issues in these party images not only demonstrates that issues failed to penetrate party images, but also reflects the frequent pattern of once-present issues disappearing from these images. For instance, the issue of civil rights and integration, which became so salient in the early 1960s that it emerged within the party images of Americans as a highly critical issue, quickly seems to have lost the impact it once had had.[33]

Law and Order and Vietnam both attained sufficiently high levels of salience that relatively large segments of the electorate adopted non-neutral party image positions on these issues in 1968 and 1972. The Law and Order image of almost 6% of the electorate favored the Republican Party in 1968, and 11.8% of the electorate had adopted a pro-Republican image on Vietnam in the same year. The salience of Vietnam dissipated somewhat by 1972, reflecting Nixon's policy of slow disengagement, but 5.8% still favored the Republicans on this issue in 1972 while the pro-Democratic group had grown to 3.7%. These issues were indeed able to enter the party images of Americans.

This is not to say, however, that these issues were necessarily able to structure the vote through their effects on the party images of Americans. In 1968 Law and Order seemed to influence the voting choice of Americans (γ = .667), but Vietnam, which had aroused so many more people (see the left side of Table 4.6), had a much smaller impact on the vote (γ = .336). The impact of issues, then, is not simply proportional to their salience. The minimal impact of Vietnam in 1968 no doubt resulted from the obfuscation of the issue by Nixon and Humphrey.[34] In 1972, however, when differences between the candidates were more easily discerned,[35] the issue structured the vote almost as much as Law and Order had in 1968 (γ = .619).

The impact of race is another story. Its salience developed in the early 1960s, when Matthews and Prothro were studying Southern electoral change. In the first major empirical work on party images, Matthews and Prothro found that large numbers of Southern whites disliked the national Democratic Party because of its prointergration efforts. On the basis of their significant findings, they concluded that party images would continue to play a crucial role in the transformation of party allegiances in the South.[36]

Surprisingly, however, race dropped out of the party images of Americans. Almost 14% of the 1964 respondents held nonneutral images on this issue, but this figure declined to under 9% in 1968 and to under 3% in 1972. As we shall see in Chapter 7, this declining salience of the racial issue also occurred within the party images of Southern white Democratic identifiers.

It is not quite clear how or why this decline happened, since race clearly remains the most significant voting issue in the South. As Sundquist suggests, however, the national parties refused to take opposite stands on the racial issue, and without parties offering clear and opposite cues about the issue, *the ability of the racial issue to define the parties for Americans declined*. This is quite different from saying that race no longer motivates voters, which in fact is not the case. Simply, race is no longer a major component of the party images of Americans, despite its once high salience and despite its past ability through the party images of Americans to structure their vote.

One might wonder whether the apparent evidence of party decompo-

TABLE 4.6 Frequency Distributions and Vote-Structuring Abilities of Selected Specific Party Image Indexes, by Year*

Party Image Index	Year	Frequency Distribution				% Voting Democratic			
		Pro-Democratic	Neutral	Pro-Republican	Mean+	Pro-Democratic	Neutral	Pro-Republican	Gamma#
Economics[a]	1952	32.9	52.0	16.2	-0.35	77.8 (451)	32.3 (595)	10.9 (238)	.777
	1956	18.8	72.1	9.0	-0.18	74.7 (249)	39.6 (904)	3.7 (135)	.741
	1960	20.1	69.0	11.0	-0.14	76.4 (318)	41.5 (896)	10.3 (185)	.708
	1964	19.7	76.3	4.0	-0.23	90.5 (849)	70.0 (3062)	40.7 (167)	.609
	1968	17.2	74.1	8.7	-0.15	62.7 (399)	36.4 (1597)	11.4 (228)	.566
	1972	15.0	75.5	9.4	-0.10	58.4 (149)	30.1 (722)	8.8 (113)	.595
Race[b]	1952	2.8	95.1	2.1	-0.01	78.4 (37)	43.4 (1217)	40.0 (30)	.409
	1956	3.2	94.0	2.7	-0.01	56.5 (46)	42.0 (1202)	45.0 (40)	.129
	1960	3.6	94.5	1.9	-0.02	52.6 (57)	45.6 (1312)	20.0 (30)	.279
	1964	6.9	86.3	6.8	-0.01	94.8 (310)	73.0 (3486)	50.0 (282)	.588
	1968	5.5	91.1	3.4	-0.03	74.8 (135)	37.0 (2014)	14.7 (75)	.642
	1972	2.0	97.2	0.9	-0.01	73.7 (19)	31.2 (958)	14.3 (7)	.674

TABLE 4.6 Cont.

Party Image Index	Year	Frequency Distribution				% Voting Democratic			Gamma #
		Pro-Democratic	Neutral	Pro-Republican	Mean+	Pro-Democratic	Neutral	Pro-Republican	
Law and Order[c]	1968	0.5	93.6	5.9	+0.07	71.4 (14)	40.3 (2061)	11.6 (147)	.667
	1972	0.4	99.3	0.3	0.00	60.0 (5)	31.8 (975)	25.0 (4)	.390
Vietnam[d]	1968	2.2	86.1	11.8	+0.11	51.0 (49)	40.4 (1883)	24.4 (287)	.336
	1972	3.7	90.5	5.8	+0.02	65.9 (41)	32.0 (875)	10.3 (68)	.619
Corruption[e]	1952	0.9	82.1	17.1	+0.21	69.2 (13)	52.7 (978)	15.4 (293)	.706
	1956	0.5	95.6	3.9	+0.04	57.1 (7)	44.1 (1219)	12.9 (62)	.637
	1960	0.2	97.7	2.1	+0.02	100.0 (3)	45.7 (1364)	25.0 (32)	.488
	1964	0.9	93.9	5.2	+0.05	82.4 (34)	75.2 (3814)	35.7 (230)	.654
	1968	0.3	98.1	1.6	+0.02	33.3 (9)	39.2 (2167)	12.5 (48)	.506
	1972	3.6	95.6	0.7	-0.03	59.5 (42)	30.1 (934)	0.0 (8)	.583
Pollution[f]	1968	---	100.0	---	0.00				
	1972	0.2	99.8	---	0.00				

TABLE 4.6 Cont.

Party Image Index	Year	Frequency Distribution				% Voting Democratic			
		Pro-Democratic	Neutral	Pro-Republican	Mean+	Pro-Democratic	Neutral	Pro-Republican	Gamma#
Morality[g]	1972	---	100.0	---	0.00				
Drugs[h]	1972	0.2	99.6	0.2	0.00				
Abortion[i]	1972	---	99.8	0.2	0.00				
Busing[j]	1972	0.1	99.1	0.8	+0.01				
Amnesty[k]	1972	0.1	99.4	0.5	0.00				
POW/MIA[l]	1972	---	99.9	0.1	0.00				
"Social Issue"[m]	1972	0.3	99.0	0.7	0.00				

*Entries in the left-hand table are the percent in the respective party image category. Entries in the right-hand table are the percent in the respective party image category voting Democratic. ICPR Master Codes for the specific indexes are given in notes a through m. In 1968 the vote was dichotomized into Democratic and non-Democratic. For indexes listed below Corruption, so few respondents held non-neutral images that data on the vote-structuring abilities of these indexes would be meaningless and have been omitted.

+Based on 21-point specific party image index; negative values favor the Democratic Party; positive values favor the Republican Party.

TABLE 4.6 Cont.

#Based on cross-tabulations of the dichotomized vote by the collapsed specific party image index. N's for each year respectively are: 1952 = (1284); 1956 = (1288); 1960 = (1399); 1964 = (4078); 1968 = (2224); 1972 = (984).

[a]1952-1968: 300-399; 1972: 900-945.

[b]1952, 1956: 410, 420, 421, 422, 670, 770; 1960, 1964: 400, 410, 420, 421, 670, 770; 1968: 400, 410, 420, 670, 770; 1972: 946, 947, 948, 1217, 1218.

[c]1968: 470-474, 480-484; 1972: 968-978.   [d]1968: 582-589; 1972: 1157-1163.

[e]1952: 111, 112; 1956-1968: 110; 1972: 603-604, 720 (Watergate).

[f]1968: 461; 1972: 962-964.   [g]1972: 979-981.   [h]1972: 982-984.   [i]1972: 985-987.

[j]1972: 991-993.   [k]1972: 1170-1174, 1178.   [l]1972: 1175-1177.

[m]1972: 979-981, 982-984, 1170-1174, 1178.

85

sition that we have found results from the disillusionment some Americans may feel as a consequence of the inability or unwillingness on the part of parties to take opposite, polarizing, realigning stands on those issues that are so important to the voters. Furthermore, if issues such as race still motivate voters and influence their electoral choice,[37] then it seems inevitable that party images devoid of such issues will decline in their ability to structure the vote.

Finally, if we examine the remaining issues in Table 4.6, we note that with the exception of the Corruption issue in 1952, none of these issues penetrated the party images of Americans. Given the rather ideological basis of the 1972 election, this is somewhat surprising, although this finding has also been reported by Pomper.[38] These data simply suggest that the issues of the 1972 campaign were not interpreted by the voters as issues that defined the parties. Because virtually no respondent formed nonneutral images on the basis of the issues (Pollution, Morality, Drugs, Abortion, Busing, Amnesty, POW/MIA, and the Social issue), these issues could not structure the vote and so the right side of Table 4.6 remains empty.

Corruption can in fact become a salient component of party images, as it had in 1952 (17.1% had pro-Republican images). In 1952 alleged corruption in the incumbent Democratic administration had been an effective critical theme in the Republican campaign. McGovern's protestations about Watergate were either ignored or disbelieved, and the issue failed to make a large impression on Americans in 1972. If our earlier specualtion is correct, Americans were unwilling at first to perceive corruption in a party that had traditionally been regarded as an effective manager of government and only 20 years earlier had itself complained of Democratic corruption and been believed.

CONCLUSION

In conclusion, four basic points require summary and discussion. First, party images do seem to convey the meaning of political parties for Americans. The defining attributes of the parties are revealed in the likes and dislikes Americans have for them. In general these attributes reflect the electoral winners and losers in the realignment of the Depression — Democratic favorability derives from perceptions of the Democratic Party as an effective and interested actor in times of economic

hardship. The Republican Party has lacked a positively defining attrib-
ute but has benefitted, somewhat irregularly, from perceptions of it as
an effective manager of government and agent in foreign policy.

Second, party images reveal more than just the defining attributes of
parties; their responsiveness and lack of responsiveness to significant
short-term political issues also reveal a good deal about the American
political process. Most issues have not penetrated the party images of
Americans, so, by implication, those that do can be interpreted to be
highly salient, apparently occasionally possessing realigning potential.
Furthermore, those issues that fail to penetrate the party images of
Americans have apparently failed to define the political parties for
Americans.

Third, the responsiveness and lack of responsiveness of the party
images to short-term issues also reflect the critical role parties can play in
defining their own meaning for the voters. On Vietnam and race, voters
were unable to perceive meaningful differences — defining differences
— between parties. Furthermore, even when critical issues have penetrated the party images of Americans, the ability of these issues to
structure the vote apparently depends on the willingness of parties to
take opposite stands on the issues. Finally, when parties fail to take
opposite stands on critical issues, these issues in turn seem to drop out of
the party images of Americans, because Americans no longer see these
issues as (potentially) defining the parties.

To the extent that issues that remain salient to the voters at the same
time fail to emerge or persist in their party images, we can infer that
these issues fail to define the parties for the voters. The predictive
success scholars have achieved by combining the party image and candidate image items derives from the ability of these combinations to
exhaust the set of relevant political stimuli that exist at any one moment
in time. The set obviously includes the personal attributes of the candidates, but it presumably also includes the association of these candidates
with the presently important issues, including those that do not appear
in the party images of Americans. Thus, race still motivates many voters
and this issue directed many of them to prefer George Wallace for
President in 1968; a time when racial issue responses were dropping out
of the party images of Americans.

We might speculate, then, that the *candidate image* responses would
convey four kinds of information. First, of course, is the set of perceived
attributes of the candidates. Second is the set of associations voters make

between candidates and the long-term substantive issues that have defined the political parties for them. Third is the set of issues that once emerged in the party images of Americans and possessed realigning potential, but failed to realign because the parties never took opposite sides. Wallace's association with the racial issue in 1968 seems the best example. Finally is that set of valence issues that candidates can advocate strongly or not so strongly.

The last basic point involves the dynamics of party images. The responsiveness and lack of responsiveness of these images to critical short-term issues and the evolution, development, and disintegration of long-term defining attributes are threatened by the apparent party decomposition evident in many of the data that have been analyzed. Time serves to make the basis of the present party system less relevant for Americans, at least until the recent economic crisis renewed interest in the traditional themes of the Depression. Whether party decomposition is somewhat inevitable as the salience of the past realignment wanes is an interesting theoretical proposition worthy of investigation. As Burnham has noted, times of realignment are punctuated by increased electoral participation,[39] and the critical issues that can prompt a new realignment do so in part by mobilizing peripheral or new voters. The heightened but short-lived salience of such issues as race and Vietnam, *in the party images of Americans,* suggests that the failure of political parties to help polarize the electorate around these issues may contribute to party decomposition. This should in no way be interpreted as an appeal to these parties to polarize the electorate around such critical issues. Rather, it is merely an observation that suggests a new complexity in the dynamics of the American electoral process.

NOTES

1. See the Appendices to the ICPR (Inter-University Consortium for Political Research) codebooks for each of the voting studies.
2. See, for instance, Angus Campbell, Philip E. Converse, Warren E. Miller, and Donald E. Stokes, *The American Voter* (New York: Wiley, 1960), pp. 216–265; John C. Pierce, "Party Identification and the Changing Role of Ideology in American Politics," *Midwest Journal of Political Science,* **14** (1970), 25–42; and C. Anthony Broh, *Toward a Theory of Issue Voting,* Sage American Politics Series, Vol. 1, series no. 04-011 (Beverly Hills: Sage Publications, 1973).

3. Donald E. Stokes, Angus Campbell, and Warren Miller, "Components of Electoral Decision," *American Political Science Review*, **52** (1958), 367–387; Campbell et al., *The American Voter, op. cit.,* pp. 216–265; Donald E. Stokes, "Some Dynamic Aspects of Contests for the Presidency," *American Political Science Review*, **68** (1974), 572–591; Merle Black and George Rabinowitz, "An Overview of American Electoral Change: 1952–1972," paper prepared for delivery at the Annual Meeting of the Southern Political Science Association, Braniff Place, New Orleans, La., November 8, 1974; and Gerald M. Pomper, *Voters' Choice* (New York: Dodd, Mead, 1975), Ch. 7.

4. The following Master Code categories are utilized for the seven broad substantive party image indexes discussed below.

INDEXES	Year	
	1952–1968	1972
PEOPLE	000–099	0000–0099
MANAGERS	100–199	0600–0699
PHILOSOPHY	200–299	0800–0899
DOMESTIC POLICIES	300–499	0900–0999
FOREIGN POLICIES	500–599	1100–1199
GROUPS	600–799	1200–1299
PARTY	800–899	0100–0199

5. See Stokes et al., "Components of Electoral Decision," *op. cit.;* Campbell et al., *The American Voter, op. cit.;* Stokes, "Some Dynamic Aspects of Contests for the Presidency," *op. cit.* In these earlier classifications of the responses (to the combined candidate and party image items), six categories were created, rather than the seven employed in this chapter. See also Pomper, *Voters' Choice, op. cit.*

6. On electoral realignment, see V. O. Key, Jr., "A Theory of Critical Elections," *Journal of Politics,* **17** (1955), 3–18; Key, "Secular Realignment and the Party System," *Journal of Politics,* **21** (1959), 198–210; Angus Campbell, "A Classification of the Presidential Elections," pp. 63–77 in Angus Campbell, Philip E. Converse, Warren E. Miller, and Donald E. Stokes, *Elections and the Political Order* (New York: Wiley, 1966); Walter Dean Burnham, *Critical Elections and the Mainsprings of American Politics* (New York: Norton, 1970); and James L. Sundquist, *The Dynamics of the Party System* (Washington: Brookings, 1973).

7. Charles Sellers, "The Equilibrium Cycle in Two-Party Politics," *Public Opinion Quarterly,* **29** (1965), 16–38.

8. Burnham, *Critical Elections, op. cit.*

9. Campbell, et al., *The American Voter, op. cit.*

10. I do not mean to imply that political parties must be either programmatic, ideology conveying institutions, or personifications of leaders. I mean to suggest merely that voters' perceptions of parties may reveal to what extent

voters characterize parties in either of these two ways, among the many ways that voters might characterize parties.

11. Such "free associations" seem especially suited for determining if party labels suggest anything to citizens, and if so, exactly what. Consequently, the open-ended nature of the party image items constitutes a real advantage for party image research, even if some scholars have found these questions to be disadvantageous for other kinds of research. For instance, David RePass claims "that the question which asks for likes and dislikes of parties is not a good measure of political cognitions." See p. 50 of his "Levels of Rationality Among the American Electorate," paper prepared for delivery at the Annual Meeting of the American Political Science Association, Palmer House Hotel, Chicago, Ill., August 29–September 2, 1975. RePass continues (in n. 33): ". . . The likes and dislikes about the parties question is one of the first to confront the respondent in the interview, and is a poorly stated question. Most people seem to interpret this question as asking, 'Why are you a Democrat?' or 'Why are you a Republican?' . . . Many respondents can think of nothing to say and many of the others find it difficult to collect their thoughts and articulate meaningful answers."

12. R. S. Milne and H. C. Mackenzie, *Straight Fight* (London: The Hansard Society, 1954); Milne and Mackenzie, *Marginal Seat, 1955* (London: The Hansard Society, 1958).

13. Even though the empirical referents for these two indexes may overlap, the response categories used in the construction of the two indexes do not overlap. On similar findings for these indexes, see Stokes et al., "Components of Electoral Decision," *op. cit.;* Campbell et al., *The American Voter, op. cit.,* pp. 216–265; and Stokes, "Some Dynamic Aspects of Contests for the Presidency," *op. cit.*

14. Campbell et al., *The American Voter, op. cit.*

15. Philip E. Converse, Warren E. Miller, Jerrold Rusk, and Arthur C. Wolfe, "Continuity and Change in American Political Parties: Parties and Issues in the 1968 Election," *American Political Science Review,* **63** (1969), 1083–1105; Benjamin I. Page and Richard A. Brody, "Policy Voting and the Electoral Process: The Vietnam War Issue," *American Political Science Review,* **66** (1972), 979–995.

16. Stokes et al., "Components of Electoral Decision," *op. cit.;* Campbell et al., *The American Voter, op. cit.;* Stokes, "Some Dynamic Aspects of Contests for the Presidency," *op. cit.;* and Philip E. Converse and George Dupeux, "De-Gaulle and Eisenhower: The Public Image of the Victorious General," pp. 292–346 in Campbell et al., *Elections and the Political Order, op. cit.*

17. On the Goldwater campaign see Kessel, *The Goldwater Coalition, op. cit.* See also Philip E. Converse, Aage R. Clausen, and Warren E. Miller, "Electoral Myth and Reality: The 1964 Election," *American Political Science Review,* **59** (1965), 321–336.

18. Averaging these seven means for each year and plotting these averages reveals no significant pattern, however.

19. On position and valence issues see Donald E. Stokes, "Spatial Models of Party Competition," pp. 161–179 in Campbell et al., *Elections and the Political Order, op. cit.*

20. Walter Dean Burnham, "The Changing Shape of the American Political Universe," *American Political Science Review,* **59** (1965), 7–28.

21. For a more sophisticated analysis that standardizes the issue indexes and computes "estimates of the effect of each attitude factor on the two-party division of the vote" in order to "compare the influence of each on the vote in a given year or compare the influence of the same factor on the vote in different years," see Stokes et al., "Components of Electoral Decision," *op. cit.,* esp. pp. 386–387.

22. Arthur H. Miller, Warren E. Miller, Alden S. Raine, and Thad A. Brown, "A Majority Party in Disarray: Policy Polarization in the 1972 Election," paper prepared for delivery at the Annual Meeting of the American Political Science Association, Jung Hotel, New Orleans, La., September 4–8, 1973.

23. Donald R. Matthews and James W. Prothro, *Negroes and the New Southern Politics* (New York: Harcourt, Brace and World, 1966), pp. 396–400; Matthews and Prothro, "Southern Images of Political Parties: An Analysis of White and Negro Attitudes," in Avery Leiserson, ed., *The American South in the 1960's* (New York: Praeger, 1964), pp. 82–111; and Matthews and Prothro, "The Concept of Party Image and Its Importance for the Southern Electorate," in M. Kent Jennings and L. Harmon Zeigler, eds., *The Electoral Process* (Englewood Cliffs, N.J.: Prentice-Hall, 1966), pp. 139–174. See also F. Glenn Abney, "Partisan Realignment in a One-Party System: The Case of Mississippi," *Journal of Politics,* **31** (1969), 1102–1106.

24. Kessel, *The Goldwater Coalition, op. cit.;* Bernard Cosman, *Five States for Goldwater* (University, Ala.: University of Alabama Press, 1966); and Walter Dean Burnham, "American Voting Behavior and the 1964 Election," *Midwest Journal of Political Science,* **12** (1968), 1–40.

25. Sundquist, *The Dynamics of the Party System, op. cit.*

26. Walter Dean Burnham, "Party Systems and the Political Process," pp. 277–307, in William Nisbet Chambers and Walter Dean Burnham, eds., *The American Party Systems* (New York: Oxford University Press, 1967).

27. Samuel Lubell developed a similar theory of American politics in his analysis of post-1930 American presidential elections. See *The Future of American Politics,* 2nd ed. (Garden City, N.Y.: Doubleday-Anchor Books, 1956), especially Chs. 10 and 11.

28. Even on the foreign policy theme, however, the Republicans had done better in 1968, before coming to office, than in 1972, after being in office and after Nixon's trips to Russia and China. That the Republican image as performers in government has generally been more positive when the

party has been in opposition than when it has been in power is also noted by Pomper, *Voters' Choice, op. cit.,* p. 154.

29. On generational replacement and class consciousness among Americans, see Paul R. Abramson, "Generational Change in the American Electorate," *American Political Science Review,* **68** (1974), 93–105.

30. See for instance Miller et al., "A Majority Party in Disarray," *op. cit.*

31. For analysis of the impact of these issues, see *ibid.* The virtually total absence of these issues from the party images of Americans in 1972 cannot reasonably be explained in terms of the distinctively smaller set of responses recorded in 1972. Table 4.5 revealed that these issues were absent from the first responses offered by members of the sample.

32. Richard M. Scammon and Ben J. Wattenberg, *The Real Majority* (New York: Coward-McCann, 1970), *passim.*

33. Miller et al., "A Majority Party in Disarray," *op. cit.,* also note that the salience of race declined after 1968.

34. Page and Brody, "Policy Voting and the Electoral Process," *op. cit.*

35. Miller et al., "A Majority Party in Disarray," *op. cit.*

36. Matthews and Prothro, *Negroes and the New Southern Politics, op. cit.,* esp. pp. 396–400.

37. Even Sundquist, *Dynamics of the Party System, op. cit.,* argues that voters motivated by the issue will move back and forth between the parties in their voting support in search of individual candidates more supportive of the voter's position on the racial issue. On the importance of racial attitudes in the 1968 Presidential race, see Converse et al., "Continuity and Change," *op. cit.;* and Seymour Martin Lipset and Earl Raab, *The Politics of Unreason* (New York: Harper and Row, 1970), Ch. 10.

38. Gerald M. Pomper, *Voters' Choice* (New York: Dodd, Mead, 1975), Ch. 10.

39. Walter Dean Burnham, "Theory and Voting Research: Some Reflections on Converse's 'Change in the American Electorate'," *American Political Science Review,* **68** (1974), p. 1011.

part II

Party images among groups
in American society

chapter 5

Class polarization in the party images of Americans

In Chapter 4 we identified certain themes contained in the party images of Americans since 1952. The theme that has defined the Democratic Party in the voter's mind is the party's favorability toward the common person and its effort to correct the ills of the Depression. In this and the succeeding chapter we examine in some detail the party images of those groups in society we would expect to be most concerned with this theme. In this chapter we examine polarization between classes in the diffuse images they hold for the two parties. In the next chapter we examine in detail the images these classes had concerning domestic policy (defined broadly) the groups in society that are seen to benefit or suffer from the activities of parties, and specific economic matters. Finally, in the next chapter we determine to what extent class differences in party image structure American voting patterns. For now, though, we turn to the question of class polarization in the party images of Americans.

CLASS POLARIZATION AND PARTY IMAGES

By "class polarization" we mean very simply the extent to which party images differ between the two classes — middle class and working class. We define class in subjective terms as the free choice response of the individual to a survey question asking to which class the respondent thinks of himself or herself as belonging. Individuals reluctant to choose between the two classes were asked a follow-up question forcing them to choose. Individuals who still resisted a choice or who were otherwise unclassifiable were excluded from the analysis. Because so few Americans classify themselves in terms other than working or middle class, this dichotomy will be used in the analysis that follows.[1]

Class differences among Americans supposedly have been altered over the past 40 years, in response to several factors. First, the "generation of the Depression," whose political attitudes and patterns of behavior were so strongly influenced by the economic crisis of the 1930s, has slowly been moving out of the electorate, as these individuals have aged and died. Thus the salience of the Depression for the electorate as a whole has ebbed, because of generational replacement, as Abramson has argued,[2] and as the data in Chapter 4 have suggested. Second, the electorate has become younger as the American population has become younger, because of the high birthrates that followed World War II. Third, the new young generation has been better educated than any other generation in American history and this education has not only created a set of individuals with liberal attitudes,[3] but has also undermined the salience of the traditional class basis to politics. The generation of the 1930s saw politics in class terms because economic and class factors were so important in the 1930s, but the process of education has presented the younger generation with a different set of concerns, consisting largely of matters dealing with the quality of life rather than the quantity of material possessions.[4] Fourth, rising affluence throughout all sectors of the population has made less relevant many of the political questions of the 1930s. Finally, America has evolved from an industrial society into a postindustrial society, from a product-oriented economy into a service-oriented economy in which the new professional elite — the core of the new middle class — looks favorably on the service-oriented programs and activities of the Federal Government. It therefore forms the vanguard of contemporary liberalism in contradistinction to its traditional role of safeguarding free enterprise and opposing "big government." The group basis of traditional class politics has been subverted and inverted by the educational, technological, and demographic changes that have transformed American society over the past 40 years.[5]

Consequently, to examine the changing nature of class polarization among Americans, we have to consider the changing distributions of age and educational attainment. Class polarization may have decreased because of generational replacement and/or because class issues are no longer salient to members of the generation of the Depression. If education has transformed American politics, then college-educated individuals in the 1930s should resemble college-educated individuals in the 1960s, except that they were fewer in number. On the other hand, class differences within the contemporary college-educated stratum may not differ from those within the contemporary noncollege-educated stratum, in which case we shall conclude that education has not affected the party images of Americans.

We employ conventional classifications for our control variables, sorting individuals into three educational levels: those who have not graduated from high school, those who have graduated from high school but have not had any post-high-school education, and those who have had at least some post-high-school education. The age categories used in the cross-sectional analyses group together individuals 21 through 30, 31 through 40, 41 through 50, 51 through 60, and 61 through 70. These classifications will be complemented by an analysis that traces the party images of successive birth cohorts.[6]

Finally, in controlling for age, three different processes must be kept in mind. The aging process itself refers to change over the life cycle, including "start up," or the slow assimilation of young adults into their social and political environments, and "slow down," the disengagement of elderly individuals from their social and political environments. If there is a true aging process, then most individuals should change over the life cycle and any cross-sectional or cohort analysis should reveal differences in attitudes or behavior associated with different age groups in the population.

On the other hand, generational phenomena may affect a particularly susceptible cohort, typically at the time when the cohort reaches political maturity (from 21 to 30 years of age), in such a manner as to leave a discernible imprint throughout the lifetime of most individuals in the cohort. For instance, we might well expect the political beliefs of individuals coming to maturity at the time of the Depression to reflect the critical nature of the 1930s environment many years after the Depression had actually passed. Such generational phenomena may overcome or simply deflect traditional aging processes (if the latter exist).

The third factor that tends to interfere with the theoretical study of aging and generational phenomena is "period effects." An entire population may have its political attitudes and behavior deflected by the events and conditions of the moment. If these leave no lasting imprint they can be regarded as theoretically unimportant but must nevertheless be controlled for before aging and generational effects are to be accurately measured.[7]

PARTY IMAGES BY CLASS OVER TIME

Table 5.1 presents mean party image scores for working class and middle class individuals in original and "corrected" form, over time. Original mean scores are the actual values on the generalized party image index developed in Chapter 2. Negative values indicate pro-Democratic images and positive values indicate pro-Republican images. "Corrected" means reflect the movement of the population as a whole and indicate the distance of each of the classes from the population mean. Original means thus permit us to determine the actual tendency of the class in a given year and over time. Corrected means, on the other hand, indicate how much more or less pro-Democratic (or pro-Republican) one of the classes is compared to the population as a whole. As an example, in a year in which the working class has a mean image score of −0.40 and the middle class has a mean image score of −0.05, both classes are pro-Democratic in their images although the working class is more so. If at the same time the population mean is −0.25 (a weighted average of the two class means), then the corrected means would be −0.15 for the working class and +0.20 for the middle class. In this case even though the middle class has a slightly pro-Democratic mean image score, it is nevertheless 0.20 units more pro-Republican than the population as a whole, and the working class is 0.15 units more pro-Democratic than the population as a whole. Finally, we employ a distance measure, defined as our Index of Class Polarization, which is simply the difference between the means of the middle class and the working class (using either the original or the corrected values will give the same difference). This

TABLE 5.1 Mean Party Image Scores by Class and Year

| | Distribution of Population | | | | Mean Party Image Scores | | | | |
| | | | | | Original | | Corrected | | |
	Working Class	Middle Class	N	Population	Working Class	Middle Class	Working Class	Middle Class	Index of Class Polarization
1952	62.2%	37.8%	1735	-0.01	-0.83	+1.33	-0.82	+1.34	2.16
1956	62.9%	37.1%	1694	-0.43	-0.83	+0.26	-0.40	+0.69	1.09
1960	66.9%	33.1%	1863	-0.32	-0.72	+0.50	-0.40	+0.82	1.22
1964	57.9%	42.1%	4472	-0.66	-1.23	+0.13	-0.57	+0.79	1.36
1968	55.3%	44.7%	2988	+0.17	-0.25	+0.69	-0.42	+0.52	0.94
1972	55.6%	44.4%	1325	-0.22	-0.42	+0.04	-0.20	+0.26	0.46

index is always computed by subtracting the mean for the working class from the mean for the middle class. Normally, the index will be positive since the middle class is generally more pro-Republican than the working class. Instances in which the index is negative indicate that the middle class is more pro-Democratic than the working class.

Throughout the 20-year period of our study, working class individuals have had pro-Democratic mean party images and middle class individuals have had pro-Republican mean party images. Through 1960 the working class mean remained fairly stable, only to drop in 1964, rise sharply in 1968, and drop again slightly in 1972. The middle class mean fell sharply between 1952 and 1956, then fluctuated through 1972 attaining a relative high in 1968 and a relative low in 1972. Over this same period of time the Index of Class Polarization has declined, although not steadily, providing less than striking evidence of the declining class basis to American politics.[8] The 1964 election marks a slight reversal in these data, suggesting, as Hamilton has,[9] that class became more salient in that campaign.

Class differences have dissipated somewhat because the middle class has increased in size, as Table 5.1 also reveals. Through 1964 the working class' party image outweighed that of the middle class' image because of the greater size of the former and the greater political concern it evidenced. In 1968, however, its concern diminished just at a time when the middle class became more partisan (its mean party image score rose to +0.69). Recently the working class and middle class have contributed equally to the total partisan direction of the American public, because the size of the middle class has increased and because the partisanship of the working class has decreased. In 1972 working class but not middle class partisanship was revived somewhat, no doubt due to the economic crisis that had already begun.

Consequently, these data reveal two important points. First, we note the declining salience of class, and we shall continue our analysis by trying to find out why this decline has occurred. Second, class polarization, or partisanship, is not necessarily a symmetric process. One class may respond to political stimuli at a time that the other class does not, or both classes may respond at the same time. Through 1964 class polarization existed primarily because the working class was more extreme in its party images than was the middle class. In 1968 the middle class was temporarily more extreme, and in 1972 working class partisanship was revived.

In the aggregate, then, we see that class differences are not so great as they once were. Why? Are class-related matters no longer salient to those individuals for whom they once were, or, as Abramson has suggested, are the people for whom class-related matters were salient becoming fewer in number and being replaced in the electorate with younger individuals who were never very interested in class matters? In turn, has educational change caused this decline? To answer these questions we need to introduce age and education controls.

PARTY IMAGES AMONG AGE GROUPS

Table 5.2 traces original mean party image scores for each of the five age groups for each of the six election years. The extent of the influence of

TABLE 5.2   Mean Party Image Scores for Age Groups, by Year

Year	Age				
	21 to 30	31 to 40	41 to 50	51 to 60	Over 60
			Original Means		
1952	-0.29	-0.63	-0.03	+0.61	+0.55
1956	-0.43	-0.61	-0.43	-0.43	-0.07
1960	-0.61	-0.58	-0.20	-0.49	+0.01
1964	-0.68	-0.56	-0.63	-0.72	-0.49
1968	+0.29	+0.06	+0.17	+0.02	+0.22
1972	-0.34	-0.23	-0.21	-0.33	+0.03
			Corrected Means		
1952	-0.27	-0.61	-0.01	+0.63	+0.57
1956	-0.01	-0.19	-0.01	-0.01	+0.35
1960	-0.24	-0.21	+0.17	-0.12	+0.38
1964	-0.07	+0.05	-0.02	-0.11	+0.12
1968	+0.13	-0.10	+0.01	-0.14	+0.06
1972	-0.12	-0.01	+0.01	-0.11	+0.25

age can be determined by reading across any row. In general no such influence can be found. Instead, there is sharp, distinctive pro-Republicanism in 1952 among individuals over 50 years of age. While the over 60 age group persistently is the most pro-Republican age group, this pro-Republicanism sets in abruptly after age 60, so certainly no linear relationship between age and party image can be found.

Instead we have to determine whether the distinctive pro-Republicanism of the oldest age group is a generational phenomenon or a period effect. A cohort analysis, presented in Table 5.3, reveals that individuals born between 1892 and 1901, who form the 51- to 60-year-old group in 1952, have strongly pro-Republican mean images in 1952 (−0.61) but not in 1956 (−0.28) or in 1960 (−0.44). It would seem then that the 1952 pro-Republicanism of this cohort was a unique occurrence, possibly a response to Eisenhower's first candidacy (but why not his second, four years later?), and not evidence of a persistent generational factor. In fact, none of the birth cohorts in Table 5.3 reveals evidence of consistent, meaningful change associated with the life cycle, and since patterns do not differ appreciably among cohorts, the search for possible evidence of generational factors does not withstand close scrutiny. Only for the data for 1952 is there much variation among cohorts in mean party images. Each cohort seems to respond as each other cohort does to the peculiar effects of each presidential year, especially the pro-Democratic movement in 1964, the pro-Republican movement in 1968, and the movement toward neutrality in 1972. So we must conclude that period effects, rather than the aging process or generational phenomena, account for the variation that can be found in Tables 5.2 and 5.3. Thus we must search elsewhere for an explanation of the declining class differences we observed in Table 5.1.

CLASS DIFFERENCES IN THE PARTY IMAGES OF AGE GROUPS

When we combine age and class in examining party images, we should expect to find evidence of the Depression within the cohort that came to political maturity in the 1930s. Specifically, since economic and class tensions were increased by the Depression, we would expect class differences, measured by the Index of Class Polarization, to be greatest among the Depression generation. In addition, younger Americans today are just as likely to be middle class as to be working class, whereas in 1952

TABLE 5.3 Mean Party Image Scores for Birth Cohorts, by Year

Year	Birth Years of Cohort						
	1942–1951	1932–1941	1922–1931	1912–1921	1902–1911	1892–1901	1882–1891
1952			-0.27	-0.63	-0.03	+0.61	+0.56
1956			-0.44	-0.51	-0.43	-0.28	
1960			-0.56	-0.27	-0.15	-0.44	
1964		-0.59	-0.55	-0.63	-0.89		
1968		+0.19	+0.05	+0.20	+0.06		
1972	-0.32	-0.23	-0.21	-0.35	-0.09		

only one in three young Americans was middle class. The survey data reveal that 32% of the 21 to 30 year olds were middle class in 1952 but 46% of the 21 to 30 year olds were middle class in 1972. On the other hand, the age distributions of the working and middle classes have not differed very much over this 20-year period — the working class has simply contained a majority of Americans.

Table 5.4 presents original mean party image scores for each age group for each year by class. There is preliminary evidence that the reduction of class salience is due to generational replacement. The 61 to 70 year olds in 1952 and 1956 are more extreme in their party images than are the 21 to 30 year olds in 1968 and 1972 who have replaced the former in the electorate. The extent of generational replacement is

TABLE 5.4 Mean Party Image Scores for Age Groups, by Class and Year

Year	Age				
	21 to 30	31 to 40	41 to 50	51 to 60	61 to 70
			Working Class		
1952	−0.77	−1.26	−1.12	−0.13	−0.65
1956	−0.68	−1.07	−0.84	−0.93	−0.47
1960	−0.74	−0.96	−0.69	−1.00	−0.40
1964	−1.33	−1.13	−1.20	−1.22	−1.43
1968	0.00	−0.33	−0.31	−0.50	−0.34
1972	−0.41	−0.40	−0.54	−0.61	−0.25
			Middle Class		
1952	+0.85	+0.63	+1.90	+1.50	+2.06
1956	+0.11	+0.09	+0.08	+0.58	+0.57
1960	+0.77	−0.06	+0.65	+0.53	+1.35
1964	+0.16	+0.06	+0.14	−0.20	+0.17
1968	+0.56	+0.56	+0.69	+0.77	+1.02
1972	−0.22	−0.03	+0.17	+0.19	+0.03

likely exaggerated, however, since 1952 and 1972 both manifested idiosyncratic period effects.

In fact, the process of generational replacement is much less evident when we examine relevant cohort data (see Table 5.5). At first glance new members of the working class seem less extreme in their party images than members of earlier cohorts whom they have replaced (compare 1968 and 1972 data for working class individuals born after 1931 with 1952, 1956, and 1960 data for working class individuals born prior to 1901). When period effects for the population as a whole are removed (by computing differences between class means and population means), the evidence for generational replacement is less striking. Finally, when period effects peculiar to the working or middle class are removed (by computing means corrected respectively by working class or middle class means), not only do the effects of generational replacement within the working class seem to disappear, but these effects seem to emerge rather distinctively within the middle class.[10] Mean party images for new members of the working class do not differ from those for the working class as a whole, but means for new members of the middle class seem slightly more pro-Democratic than means for members of the middle class who have left the electorate. Thus, even after removing the substantive distinctiveness of the 1972 data to which we have alluded throughout the book, we see that younger more pro-Democratic middle class individuals have transformed the electorate somewhat by replacing older individuals who manifested traditional class cleavages.

Since traditional matters of class were relatively unimportant in 1972, it is reasonable that working class identification should have had little effect on party images. Furthermore, as traditional matters of class have lost their significance, the new middle class — more and more composed of educated professionals — has more often come to favor political and social change and the perceived agent for this change, the Democratic Party. Firmer evidence of the changing images of the middle class awaits future election studies.

The data of Tables 5.4 and 5.5 reveal no general process of aging. In the cross-sectional data of Table 5.4, no consistent pattern of the impact of age on party images can be found either within the working class or within the middle class. In the cohort data of Table 5.5, mean party images for each cohort do not respond to the aging process, for either the working or middle class, even correcting for population means or class means.

TABLE 5.5   Mean Party Image Scores for Birth Cohorts, by Class and Year

Year	Birth Years of Cohort						
	1942–1951	1932–1941	1922–1931	1912–1921	1902–1911	1892–1901	1882–1891
			Working Class				
1952			-0.77	-1.26	-1.12	-0.13	-0.65
1956			-0.71	-1.00	-0.88	-0.83	
1960			-0.88	-0.87	-0.61	-0.82	
1964		-1.23	-1.18	-1.12	-1.37		
1968		-0.23	-0.35	-0.29	-0.35		
1972	-0.41	-0.40	-0.54	-0.61	-0.25		
			Middle Class				
1952			+0.85	+0.63	+1.90	+1.50	+2.06
1956			+0.01	+0.21	+0.34	+0.55	
1960			-0.03	+0.78	+0.84	+0.25	
1964		+0.22	+0.14	+0.08	-0.26		
1968		+0.67	+0.60	+0.78	+0.83		
1972	-0.21	-0.03	+0.16	+0.19	+0.03		
		Index of Class Polarization					
1952			+1.62	+1.89	+3.02	+1.63	+2.71
1956			+0.72	+1.21	+1.22	+1.38	
1960			+0.85	+1.65	+1.45	+1.07	
1964		+1.45	+1.32	+1.20	+1.11		
1968		+0.90	+0.95	+1.07	+1.18		
1972	+0.20	+0.37	+0.70	+0.80	+0.28		

If aging does not seem to influence mean party images, generational factors do. After correcting for population and class means (and both population and class means together), we see that working class individuals who came to political maturity at the time of the Depression (age 11 to 30) show a distinctive pro-Democratic tendency in 1952 and 1956. What is notable is that they are more pro-Democratic than both those birth cohorts born earlier and after they were born. Quite reasonably we can infer that the experience of the Depression affected these individuals more strongly than any others, even more strongly than other working class individuals for whom the issues raised by the Depression no doubt were highly salient.

What is interesting about these two Depression cohorts is that the impact of the Depression was not permanent — already by 1956 and 1960 their distinctiveness had dissipated somewhat. These inferences are made after having removed period effects for the population as a whole or for the working class particularly, so the distinctiveness in 1952 reasonably seems to be the last remnants of the impact of the Depression. Thus class salience has declined not just because of generational replacement, but also because matters of class have lost some of their salience for those who were once most aroused by them. What remains to be determined is the role of education in this decline.

CLASS DIFFERENCES AMONG EDUCATION GROUPS

A college education is no longer the rather rare achievement among Americans that it was as recently as 1952. As the educational level of Americans has risen, so too has politics been transformed from a politics of class issues to one dealing with quality of life issues. To determine the role of education in this latter transformation, we must examine class differences within the various strata of educational achievement.

The transformation of the educational levels of Americans is immediately obvious in the survey data in which respondents report their highest level of schooling. The proportion reporting less than a high school education has declined steadily since 1952 from 51.5 to 38.1% in 1972. While the proportion reporting high school graduation but no post-high-school education has grown slightly (from about 24 to almost 33%), the proportion attending classes after high school has doubled from 14.6 to 29.2%.

The transformation of the educational level of Americans may have altered the class basis of American politics and may have contributed to the declining importance of class-related matters. For instance, it may be that working class individuals with more than a high school education have always been less partisan than working class individuals with no more than a high school education. An increase in the number of working class individuals with more than a high school education would produce a decline in the salience of class. In addition, education beyond high school may also have prompted upward social mobility and re-moved from the working class many individuals who otherwise would have shared the party images of the working class. We have already seen that the middle class is relatively less mobilized around class-related matters than is the working class, so the declining size of the working class, brought about by increasing educational achievement, might ac-count for the declining prominence of class-related matters. This is especially so because individuals with more than a high school education, through 1968, were always pro-Republican in their party images, as Table 5.6 demonstrates.

The impact of educational attainment on party images dropped sud-denly in 1972, the year in which individuals with more than a high school education gave up their traditional pro-Republican images. The sudden change in 1972 cannot be attributed to the growing numbers of young and better-educated individuals, for the emergence of these indi-viduals on the political scene would have been gradual and discernible much earlier. Instead, the drop in 1972 would seem to reflect the responsiveness of all educational groupings to the 1972 campaign. In general citizens were more apathetic in 1972, and a disproportionately large number were neutral in their party images, as we saw in Chapter 2. The drop here may be related to this apathy. Yet the apathy explanation is not completely satisfactory, since Table 5.3 revealed that working class individuals were more partisan in party image terms in 1972 than they had been in 1968.

So we are led to examine more carefully the relationship among party image, class, and educational level, and Table 5.7 presents the data. It is clear that class differences have always had a greater impact on party images than have educational differences. Even working class individu-als with more than a high school education have held pro-Democratic party images (except in 1968), and middle class individuals with less than a high school education have nevertheless held pro-Republican party

TABLE 5.6 Mean Party Image Scores for and Distribution of Educational Groups, by Year

Year	Less Than High School Education	High School Education But No More	More Than High School Education
	Mean Party Image Scores		
1952	-0.55	+0.47	+1.46
1956	-0.67	-0.09	+0.30
1960	-0.54	-0.62	+0.37
1964	-1.02	-0.58	+0.14
1968	-0.35	+0.21	+0.86
1972	-0.37	-0.22	-0.01
	Distribution of Educational Groups		
1952	61.5%	23.9%	14.6%
1956	69.2%	12.0%	18.8%
1960	49.0%	29.0%	22.0%
1964	44.6%	31.6%	23.8%
1968	40.6%	32.1%	27.3%
1972	38.1%	32.7%	29.2%

images for the most part. Furthermore, within the working class at least, educational achievement has not affected mean party image scores in any consistent fashion, although perhaps individuals with more than a high school education have been somewhat less strongly pro-Democratic than other working class individuals.

Within the middle class, educational differences have had a greater impact than they have within the working class. Educational attainment is generally associated positively with mean party image scores. Individuals with more than a high school education have been especially pro-Republican, despite the argument that many former working class individuals with Democratic identifications (and presumably pro-Democratic party images) are entering this group. It may be that the

TABLE 5.7 Mean Party Image Scores by Class and Educational Grouping, by Year

Year	Working Class			Middle Class		
	Less Than High School Education	High School Education But No More	More Than High School Education	Less Than High School Education	High School Education But No More	More Than High School Education
1952	-1.03	-0.55	-0.55	+0.75	+1.64	+1.72
1956	-0.86	-0.94	-0.25	-0.07	+0.55	+0.49
1960	-0.63	-1.05	-0.30	+0.05	+0.40	+0.79
1964	-1.23	-1.22	-1.25	-0.40	+0.04	+0.49
1968	-0.55	-0.11	+0.63	+0.28	+0.63	+0.96
1972	-0.51	-0.22	-0.62	+0.08	-0.19	+0.24

Year	Less Than High School Education		High School Education But No More		More Than High School Education	
	Working Class	Middle Class	Working Class	Middle Class	Working Class	Middle Class
1952	-1.03	+0.75	-0.55	+1.64	-0.55	+1.72
1956	-0.86	-0.07	-0.94	+0.55	-0.25	+0.49
1960	-0.63	+0.05	-1.05	+0.40	-0.30	+0.79
1964	-1.23	-0.40	-1.22	+0.04	-1.25	+0.49
1968	-0.55	+0.28	-0.11	+0.63	+0.63	+0.96
1972	-0.51	+0.08	-0.22	-0.19	-0.62	+0.24

middle class is more sensitive to the status differences derived from educational attainment than is the working class.

Working class individuals with more than a high school education have been almost quixotic in their party images over the past three elections. These individuals may suffer from status incongruency; their educational level is inconsistent with their subjective social status, and this inconsistency may cause psychological discomfort and volatile political behavior. Similarly, middle class individuals with less than a high school education have been most unstable within the middle class, possibly because they too sense the inconsistency of their situation.

These data can also be juxtaposed to compare class differences within educational categories, as presented in the bottom half of Table 5.7. Among individuals with less than a high school education, the 1952 election was particularly polarizing. In 1964, on the other hand, working class and middle class individuals both moved in a pro-Democratic direction. Among individuals with a high school education but no more, working class images became more extreme from 1952 through 1964 while middle class images became less and less extreme. In 1968, working class individuals were almost neutral (-0.11) but middle class individuals moved to a strong pro-Republican position ($+0.63$). Finally, in 1972 middle class individuals became pro-Democratic in their images, almost as strongly as were working class individuals.

Among individuals with more than a high school education, middle class individuals were strongly pro-Republican in 1952 ($+1.72$) and almost neutral ($+0.24$) in 1972, but without a consistent decline in between. Working class individuals were strongly pro-Democratic in 1964, only to be strongly pro-Republican ($+0.63$) in 1968.

Scores on the Index of Class Polarization have declined within the two lower educational categories, but not in response to simple patterns of decline for each of the classes. For the highest level of educational attainment, the Index scores have not declined.

CLASS DIFFERENCES IN PARTY IMAGES AMONG AGE AND EDUCATIONAL GROUPS

By combining age and educational controls we can determine whether class differences have been altered in spite of or because of changing patterns in educational and age distributions. If class differences in 1972 differ from those in 1952 only because of the changes in education and age (the younger, better-educated American electorate), then simultaneous controls for age and education should eliminate any difference between the 1972 and 1952 data. If class differences in 1972 are smaller than they were in 1952, despite the age and education controls, then we can conclude that class is no longer so significant for American politics.

Table 5.8 presents the comprehensive cross-sectional data on class differences in the party images of Americans within each of the 15 age-education groups for each of the years of the study. The impact of class on mean party images is evident throughout the table. The middle class is consistently more pro-Republican than the working class, which can be seen in the strong nonzero values for the Index of Class Polarization. There are exceptions to this consistency. First, in 1972, especially for individuals with a high school education but no more, the middle class is more pro-Democratic than the working class. Thus, class differences persist but are reversed. Second, among individuals with more than a high school education, those who were 61 to 70 years old had a negative distance between the middle class and the working class four times in the six years. That is, for these elderly, better-educated individuals, the Index of Class Polarization reveals instability and a frequency, if not willingness, for the middle class members to be relatively more pro-Democratic than the working class members. Third, 21 to 30 year olds betray a class reversal in 1960 (the less than high school group) and in 1968 (the more than high school group). The latter reflects pro-Republican images among the young, better-educated working class in 1968.

On closer inspection we can find tentative evidence of the effects on class partisanship of the process of generational replacement, of increasing levels of education, and of individual election campaigns, as well as the unmistakable decline of the salience of class among certain birth cohorts. Table 5.8 is divided into three sections, and it is helpful to explain the arrangement of data so that each of the above phenomena can be found more easily in the table. For each class there are separate matrices for each educational category, producing the first six matrices in the table. The last three matrices present Index of Class Polarization scores for each age group for each year within the appropriate educational category. The effects of generational replacement can be found by comparing the cells in the lower left-hand corner of any one of these matrices with the cells in the upper right-hand corner of the same

TABLE 5.8 Mean Party Image Scores by Class, Educational Grouping, and Age, by Year

	Age				
	21 to 30	31 to 40	41 to 50	51 to 60	61 to 70
Working Class Individuals with Less Than High School Education					
1952	-0.93	-1.58	-1.31	-0.45	-0.80
1956	-0.61	-1.11	-0.96	-1.06	-0.40
1960	-0.12	-1.11	-0.49	-0.98	-0.38
1964	-1.02	-1.19	-1.18	-1.43	-1.50
1968	-0.03	-0.90	-0.96	-0.53	-0.64
1972	-0.23	-0.35	-0.72	-0.51	-0.46
Working Class Individuals with High School Education But No More					
1952	-0.87	-0.94	-0.32	+1.60	+0.50[a]
1956	-1.39	-0.74	-1.40	-1.00	+3.50[a]
1960	-1.41	-1.09	-0.88	-1.33	-1.39
1964	-1.41	-1.29	-1.19	-0.47	-1.67
1968	-0.46	+0.23	+0.39	-0.77	+0.27
1972	-0.47	-0.31	+0.17	-0.79	+0.28
Working Class Individuals with More Than High School Education					
1952	+0.44	+1.06	-0.92	+1.00[a]	+2.75[a]
1956	-0.33	-1.29	+0.57	+0.62	-4.00[a]
1960	-0.23	-0.05	-1.37	-0.57	+0.44
1964	-2.17	-0.42	-1.35	-1.30	-0.05
1968	+0.94	-0.51	+0.45	+0.52	+1.15
1972	-0.42	-0.68	-1.42	-0.69	+1.33[a]

TABLE 5.8 Cont.

			Age		
	21 to 30	31 to 40	41 to 50	51 to 60	61 to 70

Middle Class Individuals with Less Than High School Education

Year	21 to 30	31 to 40	41 to 50	51 to 60	61 to 70
1952	-0.75	-1.12	+0.77	+1.13	+1.70
1956	-0.09	+0.21	-0.94	-0.07	+0.46
1960	-3.00[a]	-0.42	-0.37	-0.10	+2.11
1964	+0.69	-0.53	-0.90	-1.23	-0.56
1968	+0.36	+0.28	-0.32	-0.24	+0.92
1972	+0.16	-0.29	+0.46	+0.21	-0.47

Middle Class Individuals with High School Education But No More

Year	21 to 30	31 to 40	41 to 50	51 to 60	61 to 70
1952	+1.76	+1.13	+1.84	+2.92	+1.47
1956	-0.37	+0.44	+0.27	+1.33	+2.00[a]
1960	+0.83	-0.81	+0.31	+0.94	+4.10
1964	-0.33	-0.07	-0.24	+1.11	+0.44
1968	+0.42	-0.16	+1.00	+0.68	+1.21
1972	-0.56	-0.75	+0.03	+0.28	-0.13

Middle Class Individuals with More Than High School Education

Year	21 to 30	31 to 40	41 to 50	51 to 60	61 to 70
1952	+0.62	+1.30	+3.26	+3.93	
1956	+0.51	-0.21	+1.09	+0.96	+0.40
1960	+1.18	+0.36	+1.75	+0.75	-0.23
1964	+0.51	+0.30	+0.95	-0.25	+0.97
1968	+0.67	+1.13	+0.84	+1.57	+1.13
1972	-0.12	+0.40	+0.18	0.00	+1.00

TABLE 5.8   Cont.

	Age				
	21 to 30	31 to 40	41 to 50	51 to 60	61 to 70
Index of Class Polarization -- Less Than High School Education					
1952	+0.18	+0.46	+2.08	+1.58	+2.50
1956	+0.52	+1.32	+0.02	+0.99	+0.86
1960	-2.88	+0.69	+0.12	+0.88	+2.49
1964	+1.71	+0.66	+0.28	+0.20	+0.94
1968	+0.39	+1.18	+0.64	+0.29	+1.56
1972	+0.39	+0.06	+1.18	+0.72	-0.01
Index of Class Polarization -- High School Education But No More					
1952	+2.63	+2.07	+2.16	+1.32	+0.93
1956	+1.02	+1.18	+1.67	+2.33	-1.50
1960	+2.24	+0.28	+1.19	+2.27	+5.49
1964	+1.08	+1.22	+0.95	+1.58	+2.11
1968	+0.88	+0.39	+0.61	+1.45	+1.48
1972	-0.09	-0.44	-0.14	+1.07	-0.41
Index of Class Polarization -- More Than High School Education					
1952	+0.18	+2.36	+4.18	+0.14	+1.43
1956	+0.84	+1.50	+0.52	+0.34	+4.40
1960	+1.41	+0.41	+3.12	+1.32	-0.67
1964	+2.68	+0.72	+2.30	+1.05	+1.02
1968	-0.27	+1.64	+0.39	+1.05	-0.02
1972	+0.30	+1.08	+1.60	+0.69	-0.33

[a]Based on fewer than ten cases.

matrix. The impact of education can be inferred by comparing a given age category in a given year across educational categories and by remembering that the proportions in the two higher categories of educational attainment have increased over time. The impact of particular election campaigns can be observed by reading across the appropriate row. The declining salience of class must be found by comparing the means of critical birth cohorts over time.

Beginning with the working class, the effects of generational replacement are obvious within each of the three educational categories. Among individuals with less than a high school education, strongly pro-Democratic images have been replaced with less strongly pro-Democratic images. Among individuals with at least a high school education, strongly pro-Republican images have been replaced with pro-Democratic images. The older age groups in 1952 who had had at least a high school education were apparently unaffected by the Depression (having reached political maturity before the Depression) and had pro-Republican images in 1952. The older age groups with less than a high school education did have pro-Democratic images in 1952; apparently these individuals had been mobilized by the Depression despite their age, since their relative lack of education made them more susceptible to its impact. But they felt the impact less than younger individuals who were reaching political maturity. Nevertheless, all of these older individuals have taken their images with them out of the electorate and have been replaced by younger individuals with mildly pro-Democratic leanings.

The effects of education are more difficult to assess. Certainly in 1972 young individuals with more than a high school education were more pro-Democratic than their less educated peers, but it is difficult to tell if this is a function of the 1972 campaign rather than of education itself. However, educational effects are intertwined with generational replacement effects, since young individuals today tend to be better educated than the older individuals who they are replacing in the electorate.[11]

Working class individuals were particularly responsive to the 1964 election campaign, moving in a pro-Democratic direction irrespective of age or educational attainment. This was a real class phenomenon, and not the result of the general pro-Democratic shift in that year, since middle class individuals were not particularly affected by the campaign. Working class individuals with more than a high school education were also responsive to the campaign in 1968, moving this time in a pro-Republican direction, especially the youngest and the oldest in their midst.[12]

Finally, for the youngest birth cohorts in the 1952 data, there is distinctive movement in their mean party images between 1952 and 1972, but the patterns differ by educational category. For individuals with less than a high school education, pro-Democratic images move toward the neutral point in proportion to the degree of partisanship in 1952. Thirty-one to forty year olds, with the most pro-Democratic image in 1952, moved the furthest by 1972. All three cohorts were less partisan in 1972 than they had been in 1952, even though they were still fairly strongly pro-Democratic.

Among working class individuals with a high school education but no more, 21 to 30 and 41 to 50 year olds in 1952 moved away from their pro-Democratic images of that year and became pro-Republican in their images by 1972. The 31 to 40 year olds also moved away, but only slightly, from their strong pro-Democratic images of 1952.

Among working class individuals with more than a high school education, the 21 to 40 year olds in 1952 moved in a Democratic direction between 1952 and 1972, as did the population of working class individuals with more than a high school education. Individuals under 41 in 1952 constitute the post-Depression generation. Among them, those with more than a high school education were pro-Republican in their images in 1952, unlike their age mates with lesser amounts of education, but became strongly pro-Democratic by 1972, demonstrating the increasing Democratic appeal to the better educated. But individuals 41 to 50 in 1952 had been affected most strongly by the Depression (being 21 to 30 at the time), and the 20 years of our study reveal that they gave up the Democratic imprint of the Depression in favor of strong pro-Republican images. For these individuals class did not lose its salience so much as it reversed its impact.

Among middle class individuals the effects of generational replacement are also evident. Older individuals in 1952 and 1956, who possessed strong pro-Republican party images, have moved out of the electorate and have been replaced by young individuals in 1968 and 1972 who possess weak pro-Republican or even pro-Democratic images. Especially among individuals with a high school education but no more, generational replacement has not simply reduced class cleavage as it has reversed it. If this process continues, then class differences may increase in the future as the middle class becomes more and more pro-Democratic than it ever was and than the working class presently is. In general, however, the impact of generational replacement is to reduce class differences by removing relatively partisan individuals from the electorate and replacing them with individuals whose mean party images have absolute values nearer to zero.

The impact of educational attainment is again more difficult to evaluate. In general the impact of education is to shift more and more individuals from the first into the second and third matrices, for both the middle and working class. For the middle class, as people are shifted from the first matrix to the second, the effects of generational replacement will be accentuated, since differences between the departing segment and the incoming segment of the electorate are great. As individuals are shifted from the second into the third matrix the effects of generational replacement will be dampened somewhat, since differences between the departing and incoming segments are not so great as for the second educational category. For the working class, however, educational advancement will hasten generational effects, since the most pro-Republican elements are elderly individuals with more than a high school education.

There is no evidence within the data for the middle class that the 1964 election heightened or otherwise affected class consciousness. On the other hand, the 1968 election did bring with it a pro-Republican movement on the part of middle class individuals with more than a high school education. In 1972 young age groups of all educational levels tended to be pro-Democratic in their images.

Cohort movements also reveal mixed effects. Among middle class individuals with less than a high school education, 41 to 50 year olds clearly were affected by the Depression. They were less pro-Republican than older individuals in the same year and less pro-Republican than their age mates with more education. Their relative lack of education no doubt made them vulnerable to the perils of the Depression, and minimized their middle class tendencies to be pro-Republican. Actually, those among them who had been middle class in 1932 might have been strongly pro-Republican in 1952, while the others, who had risen from the working class only after the Depression, might have brought pro-Democratic images with them, which would combine with the pro-Republican images of the long-time middle class individuals in their midst to produce the relatively depressed value of +0.77. At any rate, these middle class individuals with less than a high school education developed pro-Democratic images by 1972. The individuals under 41 in 1952 moved from strongly pro-Democratic images in 1952 to pro-Republican images in 1972.

For the three birth cohorts of interest, for individuals with a high school education but no more, there is a striking drop in their mean party images from strongly pro-Republican in 1952 to mildly so in 1972. The drop was substantial, even if it was not as great as for the population of middle class individuals with a high school education but no more, and it points out that these individuals no longer manifested strong class partisanship.

For all three of the relevant cohorts, for those with more than a high school education, the 20 years brought with it a decaying salience of class. In their case, the process of decay has led to a neutralization, not to a reversal in the traditional class patterns. These cohorts still have pro-Republican images, but images that are much less partisan than they had been in 1952 and that have changed considerably more than those of the population of middle class individuals with more than a high school education.

In summary, we have found evidence in the cross-sectional data of the effects of generational replacement, of educational attainment, of period effects, and of the decaying salience of class above and beyond these other effects. Class differences have dissipated because of generational replacement, because of increasing levels of education, and also because the imprint of the Depression is no longer as visible to many of the individuals once incited by it. In other words, generational replacement and educational change do not account for all the declining salience of class, but they are the most important factors for two reasons. First, they account for the bulk of the change that has already occurred. Second, and more significant for the future of American politics, they are ongoing processes whose effects will continue to be felt.

When we turn to the more complete cohort data of Table 5.9, the cross-sectional data of Table 5.8 are put into perspective. Immediately obvious is the absence of strong generational factors. Over the 20 years of this study, no cohort in Table 5.9 possesses and maintains a distinctive pattern of mean party images. More notable is the presence of period effects, some of which erroneously inflated cohort change in the cross-sectional data of Table 5.8. Specifically, the cohort change analyzed in Table 5.8 involved only 1952 and 1972 data. Table 5.9 reveals that no

TABLE 5.9 Mean Party Image Scores for Birth Cohorts by Class and Educational Grouping, by Year

Year	Birth Years Of Cohort						
	1942-1951	1932-1941	1922-1931	1912-1921	1902-1911	1892-1901	1882-1891
Working Class Individuals with Less Than High School Education							
1952			-0.93	-1.58	-1.31	-0.45	-0.80
1956			-0.70	-1.09	-0.99	-0.97	
1960			-0.92	-0.65	-0.58	-0.88	
1964		-0.90	-1.26	-1.03	-1.60		
1968		-0.79	-0.84	-0.68	-0.71		
1972	-0.23	-0.35	-0.72	-0.61	-0.46		
Working Class Individuals with High School Education But No More							
1952			-0.87	-0.94	-0.32	+1.60[a]	+0.50[a]
1956			-1.06	-0.91	-1.78[a]	+1.33[a]	
1960			-1.22	-0.90	-1.32	-0.75	
1964		-1.32	-1.26	-1.04	-0.76		
1968		+0.07	+0.16	-0.09	+0.46		
1972	-0.47	-0.31	+0.17	-0.51	+0.28		
Working Class Individuals with More Than High School Education							
1952			+0.44	+1.06	-0.92	+1.00[a]	+2.50[a]
1956			-0.35	-0.38	+0.71	-0.29[a]	
1960			+0.31	-2.40	+0.68	-0.52	
1964		-1.80	-0.39	-1.83	-0.59		
1968		-0.02	-0.14	+1.27	+0.52[a]		
1972	-0.42	-0.68	-1.42	-0.79	+1.33[a]		

TABLE 5.9 Cont.

Year	Birth Years of Cohort						
	1942–1951	1932–1941	1922–1931	1912–1921	1902–1911	1892–1901	1882–1891

Middle Class Individuals with Less Than High School Education

Year	1942–1951	1932–1941	1922–1931	1912–1921	1902–1911	1892–1901	1882–1891
1952			−0.75	−1.12	+0.77	+1.13	+1.70
1956			+0.52	−0.49	−0.59	+0.35	
1960			−1.64	+0.13	+1.11	−0.22	
1964		+0.72	+0.68	−1.27	−0.96		
1968		−0.37	+0.44	−0.35	+0.55		
1972	+0.16	−0.29	+0.46	+0.21	−0.47		

Middle Class Individuals with High School Education But No More

Year	1942–1951	1932–1941	1922–1931	1912–1921	1902–1911	1892–1901	1882–1891
1952			+1.76	+1.13	+1.84	+2.92	+1.47
1956			−0.20	+0.68	+0.26	+1.89[a]	
1960			−0.70	+0.62	+0.07	+3.33	
1964		−0.28	−0.05	+0.13	+0.88		
1968		+0.09	+0.44	+1.11	+0.73		
1972	−0.56	−0.75	+0.03	+0.28	−0.13		

Middle Class Individuals with More Than High School Education

Year	1942–1951	1932–1941	1922–1931	1912–1921	1902–1911	1892–1901	1882–1891
1952			+0.62	+1.30	+3.26	+1.14	+3.93
1956			−0.33	+0.68	+1.49	+0.21	
1960			+0.55	+1.33	+1.09	−0.35	
1964		+0.57	+0.50	+0.38	−0.39		
1968		+1.27	+0.79	+1.05	+1.22		
1972	−0.12	+0.40	+0.18	0.00	+1.00		

TABLE 5.9 Cont.

Year	Birth Years of Cohort						
	1942-1951	1932-1941	1922-1931	1912-1921	1902-1911	1892-1901	1882-1891

Index of Class Polarization -- Less Than High School Education

Year	1942-1951	1932-1941	1922-1931	1912-1921	1902-1911	1892-1901	1882-1891
1952			+0.18	+0.46	+2.08	+1.58	+2.50
1956			+1.22	+0.60	+0.40	+1.32	
1960			+1.44	+0.78	+1.69	+0.66	
1964		+1.62	-0.38	-0.24	+0.64		
1968		+0.42	+1.52	+0.33	+1.26		
1972	+0.39	+0.06	+1.18	+0.82	-0.01		

Index of Class Polarization -- High School Education But No More

Year	1942-1951	1932-1941	1922-1931	1912-1921	1902-1911	1892-1901	1882-1891
1952			+2.63	+2.07	+2.16	+1.32	+0.97
1956			+0.86	+1.59	+2.04	+0.56	
1960			+0.52	+1.52	+1.39	+4.08	
1964		+1.04	+1.21	+1.17	+1.64		
1968		+0.02	+0.28	+1.20	+0.27		
1972	-0.09	-0.44	-0.14	+0.79	-0.41		

Index of Class Polarization -- More Than High School Education

Year	1942-1951	1932-1941	1922-1931	1912-1921	1902-1911	1892-1901	1882-1891
1952			+0.18	+0.24	+4.18	+0.14	+1.43
1956			+0.02	+1.08	+0.78	+0.50	
1960			+0.24	+3.73	+0.41	+0.17	
1964		+2.37	+0.89	+2.11	+0.20		
1968		+1.29	+0.93	-0.22	+0.70		
1972	+0.30	+1.08	+1.60	+0.79	-0.33		

aBased on fewer than ten cases.

trend operated throughout this 20-year period; instead, mean party images were distinctively and temporarily pro-Republican in 1952 and distinctively and temporarily neutral or pro-Democratic in 1972. Other period effects can be found in the pro-Democratic movements in 1964 of individuals with less than a high school education and in 1972 of individuals with a high school education but no more.

In severely limiting the distinctiveness of birth cohorts the data of Table 5.9 thus reaffirm the changing age and educational composition of the American electorate as primarily responsible for the declining salience of class in the party images of Americans. As younger, better-educated individuals replace older, less-educated individuals, mean party images become less extreme and class differences subside. The cohort data of Table 5.9 thus strengthen the inference about generational replacement that was prompted by the cross-sectional data of Table 5.8. Though numbers of cases for the earlier birth cohorts in our study are frequently low, the mean party images in 1952 and 1956 for cohorts born before 1902 nevertheless seem more extreme than the mean party images in 1968 and 1972 for cohorts born after 1931.

Despite the general absence of cohort distinctiveness in Table 5.9, the Index of Class Polarization for individuals born between 1922 and 1931 who later received more than a high school education has actually increased since 1952. Class differences have been exacerbated for this cohort. Through 1960 working class and middle class individuals within this cohort closely resembled each other in their mean party images. The working class became sharply more pro-Democratic in 1964 and in 1972, thus separating itself from the middle class. Better-educated working class individuals would not likely be the first working class individuals to experience economic hardship; instead, the sensitivity of their party images would seemingly derive from the relative perceptiveness their education provides of the issues debated in the campaign. What is more difficult to explain is why such behavior characterizes only one cohort rather than all cohorts born prior to the Depression and only this cohort rather than all cohorts reaching political maturity at the time of the Depression. Even though these questions remain unanswered, it seems clear that this cohort is not manifesting the effects of a general aging process, since no other cohort displays a similar pattern.

CONCLUSION

Class differences have dissipated not in any simple manner but in response to a set of societal forces whose impact no doubt has been felt throughout the political arena. Generational replacement has brought into the electorate younger individuals whose party images are less extreme than the older individuals removed by death from the electorate. More specifically, younger working class individuals are somewhat less pro-Democratic and younger middle class individuals are somewhat less pro-Republican, if not actually pro-Democratic. The political relevance of generational replacement is intensified by the changing patterns of education among the young, since differences in educational achievement have generally created differences in mean party images. Yet the process of generational replacement is not identical to the changing levels of educational attainment among the electorate, since controlling for education reveals a recent tendency for young middle class individuals to be more pro-Democratic than are young working class individuals.

The declining salience of class also results from the shrinking size of the working class. Consequently there are fewer individuals in the electorate as likely as there were previously to be concerned with material needs. Instead the present middle class not only includes a growing professional elite but also an ever-increasing number of individuals committed not to the acquisition and possession of material goods but to an emerging set of nonmaterial values.[13] The recent pro-Democratic nature of the young middle class is a likely sign of this shift in values, but the data through 1972 provide clearly insufficient evidence of this possibly emerging trend. In fact so far the 1972 data appear as idiosyncratic, in comparison at least to earlier years, and only time will reveal whether the 1972 data mark the beginning of a trend. Nevertheless some sense for the growing aggregate rejection of materialism can be attained by examining in more detail the Depression-related themes introduced in Chapter 4, and we turn next, in Chapter 6, to declining class differences in these themes.

NOTES

1. Actually, the occasional respondent who did classify himself or herself as "upper class" was included in the middle class. Variables used for the assignment of class were as follows:

1952: v 126
1956: v 224
1960: v 155
1964: v 231
1968: v 209
1972: v 400

The use of a subjective measure of class membership corresponds with the strategy of the authors of *The American Voter*, who refer to the political differences that follow from subjective class differences as "status polarization." A critical difference between their work and the present one is that they also distinguished between voluntary self-assignment of the individual to a subjective class and forced assignment accomplished through the follow-up question. They interpreted individual self-assignment, quite reasonably, as evidence of stronger identification with the class. See Angus Campbell, Philip E. Converse, Warren E. Miller, and Donald E. Stokes, *The American Voter* (New York: Wiley, 1960), pp. 333–380. Also see Robert R. Alford, *Party and Society* (Chicago: Rand McNally, 1963). On page 80 Alford measures class polarization behaviorally by computing the difference between the percent of individuals in manual occupations voting for leftist parties and the percent of individuals in nonmanual occupations so voting, and refers to this difference as the "index of class voting."

2. Paul R. Abramson, "Generational Change in American Electoral Behavior," *American Political Science Review*, **68** (1975), 93–105.

3. Louis Harris, *The Anguish of Change* (New York: Norton, 1973), Ch. 12; Everett Carll Ladd, Jr. and Charles D. Hadley, *Political Parties and Political Issues: Patterns in Differentiation Since the New Deal*, Sage Professional Papers in American Politics, Series/Number 04-010 (BeverlyHills: Sage Publications, 1973), pp. 40–60. Ladd and Hadley point out that college-educated cohorts are more polarized, containing conservatives and liberals, but generally more liberal on matters of civil liberties, than in previous years.

4. Harris, *op. cit.*; Ladd and Hadley, *op. cit.*, pp. 40–60.

5. Everett Carll Ladd, Jr., *American Political Parties; Social Change and Political Response* (New York: Norton, 1970), pp. 243–312; Ladd and Hadley, *op. cit.*, pp. 40–60; Norval D. Glenn, "Class and Party Support in the United States: Recent and Emerging Trends," *Public Opinion Quarterly*, **37** (1973), 1–20; and Glenn, "Class and Party Support in 1972," *Public Opinion Quarterly*, **39** (1975), 117–122.

6. For equivalence, individuals under 21 have been excluded from the analysis, since only in 1972 did the sampling frame include individuals eligible to vote but under 21 years of age. Individuals over 70 have been excluded when controlling for age since there are too few in the samples for analysis. Finally, the cohort analysis will include seven cohorts grouped by birth years: 1882–1891, 1892–1901, 1902–1911, 1912–1921, 1922–1931, 1932–1941, and 1942–1951. No cohort will be included in the analysis unless *all* members of the cohort are at least 21 but no more than 70 years

of age at the time of the survey, in order to guard against low numbers of cases.

7. On political participation over the life cycle, see Norval D. Glenn and Michael Grimes, "Aging, Voting, and Political Interest," *American Sociological Review*, **33** (1968), 563–575; John Crittenden, "Aging and Political Participation," *Western Political Quarterly*, **16** (1963), 323–331; and Neal Cutler, "Aging and Generations in Politics: The Conflicts of Explanations and Inference," pp. 440–448 in Allen R. Wilcox, ed., *Public Opinion and Political Attitudes* (New York: Wiley, 1974); and Campbell, et al. *The American Voter, op. cit.*, pp. 156–157, 160–167. Of course period effects are not necessarily theoretically uninteresting; in the present context they reflect differences in the campaigns and climates of the Presidential election years. Period effects are not so interesting in the present context in which trends constitute the object of our attention.

8. On the declining class basis, see Abramson, *op. cit.*; Ladd, *op. cit.*; Gerald M. Pomper, *Voters' Choice* (New York: Dodd, Mead, 1975), Ch. 3; and Ladd and Hadley, *op. cit.*

9. Richard F. Hamilton, *Class and Politics in the United States* (New York: Wiley, 1972).

10. Period effects are "corrected for" by subtracting class means from population means. Period effects peculiar to a class are corrected for by subtracting age means within each class from class means. Both effects can be corrected for by undertaking, in order, both series of subtractions.

11. Note, however, that in 1972 18 to 20 year olds were pro-Democratic in their mean party images and those among them who were middle class individuals with more than a high school education were the most pro-Democratic of all (−0.73, based on 11 cases). This is not simply an inversion of traditional class differences, since working class individuals with less than a high school education were the group of 18 to 20 year olds with the next most extreme mean party image score (−0.64, also based on 11 cases).

12. The young and the old were disproportionately supportive of George Wallace. See Philip E. Converse, Warren E. Miller, Jerrold C. Rusk, and Authur C. Wolfe, "Continuity and Change in American Politics: Parties and Issues in the 1968 Election." *American Political Science Review*, **63** (1969), 1083–1105.

13. Evidence about the change in values has been collected in the Western European context. See Ronald Inglehart, "The Silent Revolution in Europe: Intergenerational Change in Post-Industrial Societies," *American Political Science Review*, **65** (1971), 991–1017.

chapter 6

Further class differences in the party images of Americans

We have two further questions to attempt to answer with regard to class differences in the party images of Americans. Have the two classes responded specifically to those issues in American politics we might expect them to respond to, and have class differences in the party images of Americans affected voting behavior in any discernible way? To answer the first question, we shall compare mean party image scores for the two classes on the DOMESTIC POLICIES, GROUPS, and Economics indexes developed in Chapter 4. To answer the second question, we have cross-tabulated collapsed versions of these three indexes with voting choice for each class.

These three indexes were chosen because they deal directly or indirectly with the substantive concerns we would expect to be relevant to the traditional class cleavage in American society. The DOMESTIC POLICIES index measures likes and dislikes for the parties with regard to all domestic policies, the GROUPS index measures likes and dislikes with regard to groups in society seen to benefit or suffer from the activities of the parties, and the Economics index measures likes and dislikes with regard to economic and welfare matters (a subset of the domestic policies). Groups in society mentioned in responses to the likes and dislikes of Americans toward their parties include such economically related groups as the "common man" and "big business," which explains why we might expect to find class differences on this index.

CLASS DIFFERENCES OVER TIME

Table 6.1 presents mean party image scores on each of the three indexes for the working and middle classes over time. The original mean values indicate that the working class has been transformed from strongly pro-Democratic to only mildly pro-Democratic. The middle class has moved from mildly pro-Democratic to levels much closer to neutrality, except on the GROUPS index, where it has remained fairly strongly pro-Democratic. In other words, over time the Democratic Party has been losing its appeal for both classes, but it is important to remember that on topics dealing with the economy even the middle class has been pro-Democratic in its party images. The corrected means and the Index of Class Polarization (the difference between the mean for the middle class and the mean for the working class) indicate that class differences have diminished over time and that the working class is not nearly so much more pro-Democratic compared to the middle class as it once was. The difference between the two classes on these three indexes was exceptionally high in 1952 and exceptionally low in 1972. On these three indexes class differences for the entire population have diminished much more clearly than on the general party image index discussed in Chapter 5.

CLASS DIFFERENCES WITHIN EDUCATION CATEGORIES

As in Chapter 5, we introduce age and education controls on these class differences to determine if the decreasing differences between the classes are due only to changes in the age and educational attainment of Americans or if they also result from the declining relevance of the class

TABLE 6.1 Mean Scores on the DOMESTIC POLICIES, GROUPS, and Economic Party Image Indexes for the Working and Middle Classes, by Year

Year	DOMESTIC POLICIES		GROUPS		Economics	
	Working Class	Middle Class	Working Class	Middle Class	Working Class	Middle Class
			Original Means			
1952	-0.62	-0.12	-0.72	-0.42	-0.52	-0.11
1956	-0.36	-0.13	-0.75	-0.60	-0.23	-0.09
1960	-0.30	+0.01	-0.58	-0.39	-0.23	+0.03
1964	-0.36	-0.04	-0.57	-0.40	-0.34	-0.10
1968	-0.18	+0.02	-0.50	-0.38	-0.21	-0.07
1972	-0.15	-0.01	-0.51	-0.51	-0.16	-0.01
			Corrected Means			
1952	-0.19	+0.31	-0.11	+0.19	-0.15	+0.26
1956	-0.09	+0.14	-0.06	+0.09	-0.05	+0.09
1960	-0.10	+0.21	-0.06	+0.13	-0.09	+0.17
1964	-0.13	+0.19	-0.07	+0.10	-0.10	+0.14
1968	-0.19	+0.11	-0.06	+0.06	-0.06	+0.18
1972	-0.06	+0.08	0.00	0.00	-0.06	+0.09
		Population Mean (P) and Index of Class Polarization (ICP) Scores				
	P	ICP	P	ICP	P	ICP
1952	-0.43	+0.50	-0.61	+0.30	-0.37	+0.41
1956	-0.27	+0.25	-0.69	+0.15	-0.18	+0.14
1960	-0.20	+0.31	-0.52	+0.19	-0.14	+0.26
1964	-0.23	+0.32	-0.50	+0.17	-0.24	+0.24
1968	-0.09	+0.20	-0.44	+0.12	-0.15	+0.14
1972	-0.09	+0.14	-0.51	0.00	-0.10	+0.15

cleavage for their party images. Tables 6.2, 6.3, and 6.4 respectively present the complete set of means on the DOMESTIC POLICIES, GROUPS, and Economics Indexes by class, age and education. We begin our discussion by considering the process of generational replacement. In general the data in these tables do not so clearly reflect the effects of generational replacement as do the data in Chapter 5. Younger members of the present electorate are somewhat less partisan than the electorates of the 1950s whom they have replaced. This is more

TABLE 6.2 Mean DOMESTIC POLICIES Party Image Index Scores by Class, Educational Grouping, and Age, by Year

Year	Age					Mean for Educational Grouping
	21 to 30	31 to 40	41 to 50	51 to 60	61 to 70	
Working Class Individuals with Less Than High School Education						
1952	-0.66	-0.84	-0.76	-0.49	-0.66	-0.68
1956	-0.25	-0.45	-0.39	-0.54	-0.30	-0.40
1960	-0.16	-0.39	-0.26	-0.49	-0.29	-0.30
1964	-0.21	-0.28	-0.43	-0.43	-0.43	-0.36
1968	0.00	-0.31	-0.15	-0.25	-0.33	-0.21
1972	-0.16	-0.25	-0.34	-0.13	-0.11	-0.19
Working Class Individuals with High School Education But No More						
1952	-0.51	-0.52	-0.47	+0.10	-0.67[a]	-0.46
1956	-0.39	-0.10	-0.47	-0.29[a]	+0.50[a]	-0.27
1960	-0.36	-0.36	-0.20	-0.44	-0.94	-0.34
1964	-0.32	-0.36	-0.33	-0.20	-0.58	-0.32
1968	-0.15	-0.10	-0.16	-0.30	+0.10	-0.15
1972	-0.14	-0.02	-0.15	-0.26	+0.17	-0.09
Working Class Individuals with More Than High School Education						
1952	-0.16	-0.44	-1.17	-0.57[a]	-0.50[a]	-0.43
1956	-0.29	-0.29	+0.29	0.00	-0.33[a]	-0.07
1960	+0.08	+0.10	-0.79	-0.13	-0.22	-0.13
1964	-0.51	-0.19	-0.25	-0.65	-0.16	-0.41
1968	+0.94	-0.43	-0.50	+0.04	-0.15	-0.13
1972	-0.13	-0.40	-0.10	-0.25	+0.33[a]	-0.17

TABLE 6.2 Cont.

Year	21 to 30	31 to 40	41 to 50	51 to 60	61 to 70	Mean for Educational Grouping
			Age			
Middle Class Individuals with Less Than High School Education						
1952	-0.95	-0.85	-0.10	-0.22	-0.11	-0.29
1956	-0.37	-0.13	-0.50	-0.09	+0.02	-0.25
1960	-0.33a	+0.12	-0.49	-0.17	+0.11	-0.18
1964	+0.12	-0.11	-0.21	-0.34	-0.11	-0.13
1968	-0.03	+0.08	-0.19	-0.13	-0.18	-0.06
1972	+0.05	+0.14	+0.18	-0.04	-0.12	+0.03
Middle Class Individuals with High School Education But No More						
1952	+0.04	-0.02	+0.19	+0.36	-0.40a	+0.07
1956	-0.32	+0.07	-0.23	-0.13	+0.17a	-0.09
1960	-0.17	-0.38	+0.44	+0.17	+0.80	+0.09
1964	-0.04	-0.16	-0.11	+0.15	+0.06	-0.05
1968	+0.10	-0.04	+0.08	+0.10	+0.05	+0.08
1972	-0.33	-0.37	+0.03	+0.19	+0.20	+0.09
Middle Class Individuals with More Than High School Education						
1952	-0.36	-0.21	+0.23	-0.07	+0.47	-0.07
1956	-0.07	-0.13	+0.07	-0.15	+0.25	-0.01
1960	+0.28	-0.09	+0.29	-0.07	0.00	+0.07
1964	+0.07	-0.04	+0.15	-0.21	-0.13	+0.01
1968	0.00	-0.06	+0.16	+0.13	-0.10	+0.03
1972	+0.04	+0.15	-0.03	+0.22	+0.35	-0.16

[a]Based on fewer than ten cases.

TABLE 6.3 Mean GROUPS Party Image Index Scores by Class, Educational Grouping, and Age, by Year

Year	Age					Mean for Educational Grouping
	21 to 30	31 to 40	41 to 50	51 to 60	61 to 70	
Working Class Individuals with Less Than High School Education						
1952	-0.57	-0.83	-0.75	-0.65	-0.63	-0.68
1956	-0.65	-0.74	-0.68	-0.82	-0.77	-0.72
1960	-0.40	-0.72	-0.47	-0.79	-0.39	-0.55
1964	-0.40	-0.56	-0.43	-0.63	-0.69	-0.52
1968	-0.24	-0.42	+0.08	-0.53	-0.51	-0.53
1972	-0.29	-0.45	-0.46	-0.57	-0.56	-0.48
Working Class Individuals with High School Education But No More						
1952	-0.99	-0.70	-1.05	-0.45	-0.50[a]	-0.85
1956	-1.07	-0.79	-0.60	-1.43[a]	+0.50[a]	-0.86
1960	-0.41	-0.83	-0.79	-1.18	-1.00	-0.74
1964	-0.48	-0.68	-0.73	-0.46	-0.42	-0.59
1968	-0.63	-0.37	-0.37	-0.63	-0.63	-0.50
1972	-0.49	-0.41	-0.56	-0.56	-0.56	-0.46
Working Class Individuals with More Than High School Education						
1952	-1.12	-0.12	-0.75	-0.71[a]	0.00[a]	-0.72
1956	-0.54	-1.42	-0.90	-0.38	-1.67[a]	-0.84
1960	-0.15	-0.15	-0.21	-1.22	-0.78	-0.27
1964	-0.71	-0.87	-0.55	-1.05	-0.63	-0.79
1968	-0.24	-0.34	-0.60	-0.63	-0.08[a]	-0.36
1972	-0.47	-0.76	-1.10	-1.00	+0.33[a]	-0.69

TABLE 6.3 Cont.

Year	Age					Mean for Educational Grouping
	21 to 30	31 to 40	41 to 50	51 to 60	61 to 70	
Middle Class Individuals with Less Than High School Education						
1952	-0.45	-0.71	-0.31	-0.59	-0.41	-0.45
1956	-0.52	-0.48	-0.69	-0.74	-0.83	-0.63
1960	-1.67[a]	-0.54	-0.46	-0.70	+0.11	-0.50
1964	+0.12	-0.53	-0.68	-0.53	-0.65	-0.47
1968	-0.23	-0.42	-0.56	-0.54	-0.38	-0.39
1972	-0.26	-0.64	-0.27	-0.05	+0.07	-0.40
Middle Class Individuals with High School Education But No More						
1952	-0.35	-0.38	-0.59	-0.28	-0.60[a]	-0.41
1956	-0.68	-0.90	-0.46	-0.47	-0.50[a]	-0.60
1960	-0.07	-0.50	-0.53	-0.17	+0.60	-0.34
1964	-0.42	-0.51	-0.55	-0.48	-0.22	-0.45
1968	-0.38	-0.40	-0.43	-0.44	-0.21	-0.41
1972	-0.42	-0.47	-0.71	-0.26	-0.31	-0.56
Middle Class Individuals with More Than High School Education						
1952	-0.34	-0.47	-0.21	-0.29	-0.20	-0.40
1956	-0.51	-0.89	-0.31	-0.35	-0.85	-0.57
1960	-0.20	-0.53	-0.15	-0.60	-0.06	-0.35
1964	-0.13	-0.26	-0.54	-0.64	-0.07	-0.32
1968	-0.28	-0.42	-0.35	-0.13	-0.63	-0.36
1972	-0.52	-0.34	-0.67	+0.04	+0.11	-0.54

[a] Based on fewer than ten cases.

133

134

TABLE 6.4 Mean Economics Party Image Index Scores by Class, Educational Grouping, and Age, by Year

Year	Age					Mean for Educational Grouping
	21 to 30	31 to 40	41 to 50	51 to 60	61 to 70	
Working Class Individuals with Less Than High School Education						
1952	-0.54	-0.72	-0.59	-0.47	-0.60	-0.58
1956	-0.14	-0.29	-0.31	-0.37	-0.19	-0.17
1960	-0.17	-0.35	-0.17	-0.40	-0.30	-0.27
1964	-0.19	-0.30	-0.43	-0.40	-0.44	-0.36
1968	-0.01	-0.37	-0.24	-0.31	-0.34	-0.26
1972	-0.16	-0.37	-0.35	-0.12	-0.09	-0.19
Working Class Individuals with High School Education But No More						
1952	-0.40	-0.44	-0.47	-0.05[a]	-0.50[a]	-0.40
1956	-0.36	-0.05	-0.13	0.00[a]	+0.50[a]	-0.15
1960	-0.13	-0.24	-0.05	-0.20	-0.61	-0.17
1964	-0.25	-0.28	-0.32	-0.21	-0.50	-0.28
1968	-0.14	-0.12	-0.20	-0.30	+0.12	-0.15
1972	-0.19	-0.04	-0.24	-0.18	+0.06	-0.13
Working Class Individuals with More Than High School Education						
1952	-0.04	-0.19	-1.08	-0.57[a]	-0.50[a]	-0.32
1956	-0.04	-0.12	+0.29	+0.08	0.00[a]	+0.06
1960	-0.08	-0.05	-0.58	-0.13	0.00	-0.15
1964	-0.36	-0.18	-0.14	-0.70	-0.32	-0.35
1968	+0.06	-0.34	-0.50	+0.15	-0.15[a]	-0.15
1972	-0.04	-0.56	-0.05	-0.19	+0.33[a]	-0.15

TABLE 6.4 Cont.

Year	Age					Mean for Educational Grouping
	21 to 30	31 to 40	41 to 50	51 to 60	61 to 70	
Middle Class Individuals with Less Than High School Education						
1952	-0.90	-0.82	-0.10	-0.22	-0.06	-0.28
1956	-0.17[a]	-0.09	-0.34	-0.07	+0.02	-0.16
1960	-0.33[a]	-0.04	-0.34	-0.13	+0.18	-0.12
1964	-0.11	-0.32	-0.19	-0.34	-0.16	-0.22
1968	-0.03	-0.08	-0.16	-0.18	-0.15	-0.08
1972	-0.05	+0.07	+0.18	-0.08	-0.09	-0.07
Middle Class Individuals with High School Education But No More						
1952	+0.13	0.00	+0.16	+0.12	-0.33[a]	+0.06
1956	-0.10	0.00	-0.08	-0.27	+0.33[a]	-0.05
1960	+0.07	-0.17	+0.25	+0.17	+0.80	+0.12
1964	-0.17	-0.18	-0.07	+0.07	0.00	-0.09
1968	-0.06	-0.04	+0.02	-0.22	-0.05	-0.06
1972	-0.26	-0.31	+0.07	+0.13	+0.13	-0.08
Middle Class Individuals with More Than High School Education						
1952	-0.09	-0.08	+0.23	-0.32	+0.33	-0.03
1956	0.00	-0.07	-0.02	-0.08	+0.10	-0.02
1960	+0.16	-0.03	+0.23	-0.05	+0.03	+0.07
1964	+0.06	-0.08	+0.02	-0.19	-0.12	-0.03
1968	-0.03	-0.18	+0.02	-0.05	-0.24	-0.07
1972	+0.04	+0.11	-0.03	+0.17	+0.20	+0.05

[a]Based on fewer than ten cases.

135

true for the working class and for the least-educated segment of the electorate, about which we shall shortly say more. The evidence for the effects of generational replacement is not overwhelming, however, and is particularly lacking with regard to the GROUPS index.

Of course generational replacement tends to supplant less-educated individuals with better-educated individuals, which for the data of Tables 6.2, 6.3, and 6.4 is highly relevant. The right-hand column of each of these tables presents the mean for the educational category for the respective index for each year. Data in this column show that class differences within educational categories have diminished somewhat over time, especially for the working class on the DOMESTIC POLICIES index. Working class individuals with no more than a high school education and middle class individuals with less than a high school education have become less and less extreme on this index. Other middle class individuals have been somewhat volatile but their means have not moved in any particular direction. Working class individuals with more than a high school education were particularly partisan in 1952 and 1964, but otherwise manifest no pattern.

Educational attainment thus seems particularly related to the persistence or disappearance of extreme DOMESTIC POLICIES means. Such policies include economic and noneconomic topics. There is no evidence, as measured by the Economics index, that economic topics are any more or less relevant to the two classes. Thus the less extreme nature of many of the DOMESTIC POLICIES means must be due to the declining salience of noneconomic domestic policies.

Furthermore, the overall decline in the salience of the economic theme, which we discussed in Chapter 4, is clearly due to the changing patterns of educational attainment among Americans. Reading down the right-hand column in Table 6.4, for the Economics theme, reveals no clear decline in the values of the mean, even though we found such a decline for the entire population (see Table 4.5). Education, very simply, is the cause of the decline for the population as a whole. The increasing levels of education among Americans have caused extreme partisanship on the Economics theme to dissipate. An examination of these tables reveals, in general, that better-educated individuals are less pro-Democratic than less-educated individuals. As more and more Americans have attained higher levels of education, overall concern with the Economics theme has ebbed. Better-educated individuals no doubt are concerned with issues other than material wants, such as quality of life matters, so the movement of the population into categories of higher education has the effect of transforming the set of issues of relevance to the American public. Yet this reasonable and important observation about the impact of education is also somewhat simplistic, for educational attainment is itself a function of increased affluence among Americans, of the changing nature of the economy which demands greater education for the newly created professions, and of the changing age composition of the public, since higher levels of educational attainment are more characteristic of the post-World War II generation.

If educational change seems to account for the declining salience of the Economics theme found in Chapter 4, it does not yet fully explain some of the data for the DOMESTIC POLICIES index (Table 6.2). For less-educated individuals, there is clearly a trend for domestic policies to be less and less relevant over the years, but these policies cannot be of an economic nature since there is no declining trend in the Economics table. The decline is significant for the less educated but not for the better educated. An index similar to the Economics index was devised for domestic policy matters *other than* economic ones, but no clear pattern emerged. That is, class-education category means on such an index do not decline in any consistent way, are not related to the amount of education of the group, and seem only weakly related to class. The means for both classes are always close to 0.0, but through 1968 at least they are more pro-Democratic for the working class than for the middle class.

It is not clear immediately which noneconomic policies have their relevance affected by education. These noneconomic topics include civil rights and integration; domestic communism; farm policy; general labor policy; conservation, public power, and the environment; veterans policy; law and order; busing; gun control; and public morality, including drugs and abortion.[1] The issues from this list that did not appear as campaign issues until 1968 or 1972 have already been dismissed (in Chapter 4), since so few individuals had other than neutral party images on these topics. Clearly the issue on the list that dominates the others in terms of its impact on the politics of the United States since 1952 is civil rights and integration.

A plausible explanation for the decline in partisanship among less-educated working class individuals has to do with status. As class matters have become less important for American society, because of rising affluence or whatever, questions of status have come to the fore.[2]

Perhaps less-educated working class individuals have been very sensitive to such status questions, and for them the declining salience of class may reflect the increasing salience of status in American politics. Certainly the problem of integration and civil rights deals with questions of status, and the white working class person's reluctance to accept integration has often been explained on the basis of his desire to maintain relative status vis-à-vis blacks.[3] Also, "white backlash" support for George Wallace has been attributed to similar motivations among whites.[4] It is true that partisanship on the DOMESTIC POLICIES index has declined, *among whites*, only for those with less than a high school education, presumably those most concerned with such questions of status, but this finding holds for middle class whites with little education as well as working class whites with little education. Furthermore, partisanship has not declined on this index for blacks of any class/educational grouping.[5] The issue of civil rights and integration will be examined in considerable detail in Chapter 7.

POLITICAL COHORTS AND PARTY IMAGES

Within these data we can examine the behavior over time of three birth cohorts in order to determine whether factors other than age, generational replacement, and education have contributed to the declining salience of class. The Depression generation is well represented in our samples by people who were 41 to 50 years old in 1952, who had been 21 to 30 years old in 1932 and would be 61 to 70 years old in 1972. In addition, the two post-Depression-generation cohorts, those who were 21 to 30 or 31 to 40 years old in 1952, offer relevant comparisons to the Depression generation. To control for the effects of education, comparisons are made again within the three categories of educational attainment.[6]

Within the working class the Depression generation became much less pro-Democratic between 1952 and 1972. This was true regardless of the issue and regardless of the educational level. In each of the nine comparisons, the working class individuals who were 41 to 50 years old in 1952 changed more in 20 years than their respective educational peer group. In short, these individuals moved from strongly pro-Democratic images in 1952 to weak images in 1972, images that occasionally were pro-Republican, and so experienced a declining salience of class consciousness not explained by education or generational replacement. Individuals under 41 in 1952 also moved away from their pro-Democratic positions but frequently changed less than their respective educational peer groups. Thus among these three cohorts it was the very individuals polarized by the Depression who contributed most to its lessened impact in 1972.

Within the middle class we also encounter depolarization among the Depression generation, who moved from mildly pro-Democratic or mildly pro-Republican positions in 1952 to more *Democratic* positions in 1972. Thus working class movement in a Republican direction and middle class movement in a Democratic direction have produced convergence among the Depression generation. Middle class individuals under 41 in 1952 have moved in a Republican direction, though not decidedly, so that the depolarization of the Depression is all the more notable.

Consequently, the salience of the substantive issues of concern to the classes has decreased not just because of education and generational replacement, but also as a result of lessened impact of the Depression among those who experienced it most intensely. No doubt the Depression means less today because affluence has pervaded most of American society. But as memories of the Depression wane, other issues have not yet come to define parties as did the economic crisis of the Depression.

STRUCTURING THE VOTE

At this point we try to determine how effective these indexes have been in structuring the vote of Americans. As we did in Chapter 4, we argue that if party image can structure the vote, then individuals with pro-Democratic images will vote Democratic and individuals with pro-Republican images will vote non-Democratic. Each of these three indexes dealing with class-related themes was collapsed into pro-Democratic, neutral, and pro-Republican categories, and these collapsed versions of the indexes were cross-tabulated with the vote. From these cross-tabulations, the structuring abilities of the indexes were determined by dividing the number of pro-Democratic image-holders voting Democratic by the total number of pro-Democratic image-holders; by dividing the number of pro-Republican image-holders voting non-Democratic by the total number of pro-Republican image-holders; and by dividing the number of nonneutral (pro-Democratic plus pro-Republican) image-holders voting for their respective parties by the total number of non-neutral image-holders. These procedures were followed within each of the two classes, and the results are presented in Table 6.5.

In Table 6.5 column 9 reveals evidence over time of the declining ability of these three indexes to structure the vote of Americans, replicating the decline we observed in Chapter 4. For the GROUPS and Economics indexes, the decline has occurred only since 1964. For the

TABLE 6.5 Vote Structuring Abilities of the DOMESTIC POLICIES, GROUPS, and Economics Party Image Indexes, by Class and Party, by Year[a]

Year	Working Class			Middle Class			Totals		
	D	R	Total	D	R	Total	D	R	Total
DOMESTIC POLICIES Party Image Index								
1952	85.0	83.8	84.7	62.5	94.6	78.5	77.3	90.1	82.0
1956	76.4	92.6	81.1	61.5	90.9	75.0	71.4	91.8	78.7
1960	72.0	82.7	74.8	62.7	94.1	78.9	69.4	88.9	76.4
1964	94.4	52.8	86.4	88.5	57.7	74.6	92.6	55.7	81.8
1968	71.9	90.5	73.8	52.0	88.9	71.6	63.9	89.6	75.3
1972	66.7	91.2	75.8	48.4	89.3	70.8	60.0	90.2	73.7
GROUPS Party Image Index								
1952	80.4	84.2	80.6	58.9	97.9	68.0	73.4	94.0	82.4
1956	79.2	93.3	80.4	63.4	97.7	69.7	73.2	95.9	76.1
1960	78.1	90.2	79.5	75.9	95.2	81.8	77.5	93.2	80.3
1964	93.9	58.3	61.9	86.9	68.8	83.8	91.3	64.6	88.2
1968	74.7	93.8	77.5	62.4	93.7	69.9	69.8	93.8	74.1
1972	60.2	92.6	64.6	52.7	100.0	60.1	56.7	96.4	62.5
Economics Party Image Index								
1952	84.7	82.7	84.2	63.9	93.4	78.2	77.8	88.9	81.7
1956	80.1	94.3	84.2	62.9	98.4	79.7	75.1	96.2	82.6
1960	78.9	82.1	79.7	66.7	95.2	82.1	75.2	89.6	80.7
1964	92.4	43.9	89.3	87.7	62.2	79.7	91.0	57.2	85.8
1968	71.5	88.2	76.1	48.3	89.9	67.8	62.7	89.2	72.3
1972	65.6	89.1	73.5	47.3	92.4	71.9	58.6	91.1	72.8

[a]Entries for columns labelled "D" are the percent of all individuals with pro-Democratic images who voted Democratic. Entries for columns labelled "R" are the percent of all individuals with pro-Republican images who voted non-Democratic. Entries for columns labelled "Total" are the percent of all non-neutral image-holders who voted for their respective parties.

DOMESTIC POLICIES index, the decline has been slow but persistent since 1952, offset somewhat in 1964.

The columns on class and party permit us to specify this decline. We see immediately that the decline has characterized the Democratic Party only (compare columns 7 and 8). For the Democrats the decline has been steady since 1952 on the DOMESTIC POLICIES index but has occurred only since 1964 on the other two indexes. Throughout these 20 years, individuals with pro-Republican images have been consistently likely to vote Republican, with the single exception of 1964.

With regard to class (columns 3 and 6), the DOMESTIC POLICIES index has slowly but increasingly failed to structure the vote of middle class individuals throughout these 20 years (except again in 1964). For working class individuals, there is a marked decline from 1952 through 1960, a rise in 1964, and then another decline between 1964 and 1972. For the GROUPS index, a decline is not evident; instead, the structuring ability is low for both classes in 1972 and low for the working class in 1964 but high for the middle class in 1960 and 1964. For the Economics index, the middle class is distinctively low in 1968 and 1972. In sum, class data by themselves reveal a rather mixed picture — some evidence of steady decline, other evidence of unique elections.

When class and party factors are combined (in columns 1, 2, 4, and 5), we see that Republican images steadily and strongly structured the vote, for working class as well as middle class individuals (except in 1964). For pro-Democratic images, there is a different story. For working class individuals, images increasingly failed to structure the vote, dropping in their ability to do so from high levels of 1952 (from 80 to 85%) to moderate values (near 65%) in 1972. For middle class individuals, a decline is also noticeable, from lower values in 1952 (around 60%) to still lower values in 1972 (around 50%).

In summary we have stallwart Republicans and less loyal Democrats. The steady structuring ability for the Republicans in these data is less a tribute to the ability of the Republican Party to hold the allegiance of its supporters with domestic policy themes than it is evidence that such themes never constituted a significant element in that allegiance. That is, the steady structuring ability stems instead from the persistent loyalty of Republican supporters, a persistence based on other themes and other concerns. In fact, as we have suggested in Chapter 2, these loyalties were forged during the Depression; having survived the challenges of the 1930s, when domestic matters were not able to shake them, it is less surprising that these loyalties should resist the erosive influence of more contemporary issues and events.

For the Democrats, on the other hand, we have found strong evidence that the party has not been able to hold its own among its supporters with the very theme that has contributed so much to the party's meaning and success in contemporary American politics. Both classes have been less and less motivated in their voting by the economics theme. The working class was more likely in 1952 to follow its images and vote for the Democratic Party than was the middle class, but the support of both has deteriorated, especially that of the working class. It is not so surprising that the middle class should not support the Democratic Party on economic matters; other kinds of issues occupy the attention of the contemporary middle class. But even as the working class seems willingly responsive to economic themes (witness 1964), over time there has been a general attrition of support on these grounds.

To what extent, however, do data about the declining salience of the Depression theme for the voting behavior of Americans inform us about the process of party decomposition? The data seem first to testify to the declining salience of the issue itself, as we have seen the issue divide the two classes less and less over time (because of generational replacement, educational change, and decreasing salience among the Depression generation). Only when all issues fail to structure the vote as they once did, and no new issues appear that begin to structure the vote, and a generalized measure of affect (such as party identification, or the general party image index developed in Chapter 2) also fails to motivate behavior as it once did, does it seem reasonable to conclude that party decomposition has occurred. Several forms of the required evidence are already in hand, however, for such a conclusion. The generalized measure of affect does not structure voting the way it once did. Many of the issues that once did so in a highly constrained fashion do so no longer, including the defining theme of the Depression, and other issues do not appear ready to provide the consistent and directed focus once provided (see Chapter 7). Thus political parties seem less and less meaningful to Americans.

Since this conclusion is based only on party image data, it obviously is not a complete search of possible influences on the electoral behavior of individuals. But we must point out again that one of our tasks is to discover what *parties* mean to voters; thus, even if other factors, such as opinions on the issues or feelings about the candidates, effectively determine electoral behavior, it is nevertheless meaningful to conclude that political parties no longer perform the function of linking voters to government.

POLITICAL COHORTS AND VOTING BEHAVIOR

It is not possible to probe comprehensively the several possible causes of the declining structuring abilities of these indexes because multiple controls quickly reduce the number of cases available for study. Education, consequently, will not be employed in our investigation of whether significant cohorts have experienced the same decline that we have just identified for the population as a whole. Table 6.6 presents the percentage of the respective categories for each of the three cohorts that has had its vote structured by these indexes.[6]

In absolute terms we see at once that each of these cohorts has experienced the same decline we found in Table 6.5 on all three indexes, but that the decline is restricted to working class individuals with pro-Democratic images, again. In fact, for working class individuals with pro-Republican images, the structuring abilities of the indexes have actually increased. Thus it is premature to speak about uniform party decomposition. The consequence of this phenomenon, moreover, is to reduce even further the electoral advantage that has accrued to the Democrats from the DOMESTIC POLICIES theme.

Relative to the overall change in the population, these cohorts are still likely to show a decline in the ability of the indexes to structure the vote of working class individuals with pro-Democratic images, though not consistently for the Depression generation. The inclination for the votes of working class individuals with pro-Republican images to be non-Democratic has increased especially strongly relative to the population as a whole.

CONCLUSION

Consequently, in probing the phenomenon of party decomposition, one is forced to attend to the concerns and political inclinations of working class individuals with pro-Democratic images. The backbone of the Democratic Party, so to speak, the working class element of support is

TABLE 6.6   Vote Structuring Abilities of DOMESTIC POLICIES, GROUPS, and Economics Party Image Indexes for Selected Political Cohorts (in percentages)

Year	Working Class			Middle Class			Totals		
	D	R	Total	D	R	Total	D	R	Total

DOMESTIC POLICIES Party Image Index

Population as a Whole

1952	85.0	83.8	84.7	62.5	94.6	78.5	77.3	90.1	52.0
1972	66.7	91.2	75.8	48.4	89.3	70.8	59.5	90.2	73.7
Change	-18.3	+7.4	-8.9	-14.1	-5.3	-7.7	-17.8	+0.1	-8.3

Cohort Born Between 1902 and 1911 (Age 21 to 30 in 1932)

1952	90.9	73.3	87.7	53.6	97.6	80.0	79.8	91.2	84.1
1972	55.6	90.0	73.7	60.0	76.9	72.2	57.1	82.6	73.0
Change	-35.3	+16.7	-14.0	+6.4	-20.7	-7.8	-22.7	-8.6	-11.1

Cohort Born Between 1912 and 1921 (Age 11 to 20 in 1932)

1952	85.9	80.0	84.6	61.5	87.5	73.2	78.6	84.2	80.3
1972	60.0	71.4	70.6	50.0	62.5	45.8	75.9	61.0	67.1
Change	-25.9	-8.6	-14.0	-11.5	-25.0	-27.4	-2.7	-23.2	-13.2

Cohort Born Between 1922 and 1931 (Age 1 to 10 in 1932)

1952	80.6	80.6	80.6	75.0	91.3	82.4	78.9	85.7	81.3
1972	60.0	100.0	75.0	61.1	93.3	75.8	60.5	96.3	75.4
Change	-20.6	+19.4	-5.6	-13.9	+2.0	-6.6	-18.4	+10.6	-5.9

GROUPS Party Image Index

Population as a Whole

1952	80.4	84.2	80.6	58.9	97.9	68.0	73.4	94.0	82.4
1972	60.2	92.6	64.6	52.7	100.0	60.1	56.7	96.4	62.5
Change	-20.2	+8.4	-16.0	-6.2	+2.1	-7.9	-16.7	+2.4	-19.9

Cohort Born Between 1902 and 1911 (Age 21 to 30 in 1932)

1952	81.3	100.0	82.3	51.4	100.0	63.0	70.5	100.0	74.0
1972	65.2	100.0	69.2	50.0	87.5	61.5	58.5	90.9	65.4
Change	-16.1	0.0	-13.1	-1.4	-12.5	-1.5	-12.0	-9.1	-8.6

TABLE 6.6   Cont.

Year	Working Class			Middle Class			Totals		
	D	R	Total	D	R	Total	D	R	Total

Cohort Born Between 1912 and 1921 (Age 11 to 20 in 1932)

1952	86.2	100.0	86.5	53.3	100.0	62.2	85.1	100.0	86.2
1972	45.2	100.0	48.5	59.1	100.0	67.9	50.9	100.0	57.4
Change	-41.0	0.0	-38.0	+5.8	0.0	+5.7	-34.2	0.0	-28.8

Cohort Born Between 1922 and 1921 (Age 1 to 10 in 1932)

1952	74.0	80.0	74.4	62.5	61.1	64.6	70.5	65.2	69.5
1972	66.7	76.9	71.4	50.0	100.0	56.8	58.1	83.3	63.8
Change	-7.3	-3.1	-3.0	-12.5	+38.9	-7.8	-12.4	+18.1	-5.7

Economics Party Image Index

Population as a Whole

1952	84.7	82.7	84.2	63.9	93.4	78.2	77.8	88.9	81.7
1972	65.6	89.1	73.5	47.3	92.4	71.9	58.6	91.1	72.8
Change	-19.1	+6.4	-10.7	-16.6	-1.0	-6.3	-19.2	+2.2	-8.9

Cohort Born Between 1902 and 1911 (Age 21 to 30 in 1932)

1952	90.7	76.9	88.1	54.2	94.6	78.7	79.5	90.0	83.6
1972	62.5	87.5	68.8	60.0	80.0	73.3	61.5	83.3	74.2
Change	-28.2	+10.6	-19.3	+5.8	-14.6	-5.4	-18.0	-6.7	-9.4

Cohort Born Between 1912 and 1921 (Age 11 to 20 in 1932)

1952	84.1	78.3	82.9	64.7	96.3	78.7	78.4	88.0	81.3
1972	55.6	85.7	65.6	50.0	93.3	78.3	50.0	90.0	70.9
Change	-28.5	+7.4	-17.3	-14.7	-3.0	-0.4	-28.4	+2.0	-10.4

Cohort Born Between 1922 and 1931 (Age 1 to 10 in 1932)

1952	80.3	75.0	79.0	78.3	81.0	79.5	91.7	78.0	72.0
1972	66.7	100.0	76.9	85.7	100.0	94.7	72.0	100.0	84.1
Change	-13.6	+25.0	-2.1	+7.4	+19.0	+15.2	-19.7	+22.0	+8.1

wavering from its concern with the traditional meaning of the Democratic Party. Such wavering is to be expected, perhaps, in a society of growing affluence. Its political implications are not that working class individuals will no longer support the Democratic Party, but rather that their support cannot be assumed for the traditional reasons. Whether they do support the Democratic Party or not depends on other matters.

Yet what is perplexing is that individuals still seem willing and able to identify themselves as "working class." Even as late as 1972, 55.6% of all Americans regarded themselves as working class (see Table 5.1). Consequently one is tempted to conclude that working class means something quite different in contemporary American politics than it did as recently as 1952. If middle class Americans have developed a concern for quality of life issues, could the concept of class have been transformed from a measure of material wealth to an indicator of lifestyle and culture? Is the working class still different from the middle class — even while relative affluence among the working class makes less significant material differences with the middle class — primarily because the working class has not participated in the "silent revolution" in values that is sweeping postindustrial societies?[7]

As we have pointed out, the slow disappearance of class differences, stemming from the declining salience of the Depression theme among working class individuals, is likely to introduce new forms of conflict over status. In the next chapter, then, we turn to the political significance of the racial issue, the most contentious of all status issues in contemporary American politics. Eventually we shall return to the process of party decomposition, for we shall have to conclude that such a process has occurred if we find no evidence that issues such as race have replaced class and economics in defining American political parties. Anticipating the analysis in the next chapter, we shall find strong evidence that race had the potential to redefine the coalitional base of American parties but failed to do so. In the Conclusion, then, we shall speculate about how the dynamics of the party system revolve around the emergence, and disappearance, of issues such as class and race.

NOTES

1. This is virtually a complete list of the noneconomic topics included in the SRC/CPS Master Codes under the label, "Domestic Policies." See the

codebooks provided by the ICPR (Inter-University Consortium for Political Research).

2. See Everett Carll Ladd, Jr., *American Political Parties: Social Change and Political Response* (New York: Norton, 1970), pp. 267–275.

3. *Ibid.* See also the related discussion on working class authoritarianism in Seymour Martin Lipset, *Political Man* (Garden City, N.Y.: Doubleday-Anchor Books), Ch. 4. For criticism of the "working class authoritarianism" theme, see Richard F. Hamilton, *Class and Politics in the United States* (New York: Wiley, 1972), Ch. 11.

4. Theodore H. White, for instance, claims that Wallace's 1964 primary successes stemmed in part from antiblack sentiments among whites. See his *The Making of the President 1964* (New York: Atheneum, 1965), p. 234. For evidence disputing the claim of a white, working class, authoritarian, antiblack backlash, see Michael Rogin, "Wallace and the Middle Class: The White Backlash in Wisconsin," *Public Opinion Quarterly*, **30** (1966), 98–108. For survey data on the Wallace voter, see Philip E. Converse, Warren E. Miller, Jerrold G. Rusk, and Arthur C. Wolfe, "Continuity and Change in American Politics: Parties and Issues in the 1968 Election," *American Political Science Review*, **63** (1969), 1083–1105; and Seymour Martin Lipset and Earl Raab, *The Politics of Unreason* (New York: Harper and Row, 1970), Ch. 10. Also see Hamilton, *op. cit.*, pp. 460–467, who claims (p. 467), "the working class Wallace supporters proved to be more tolerant than the middle class Wallaceites."

5. The DOMESTIC POLICIES means are given below:

	< HS		HS		> HS	
	WC	MC	WC	MC	WC	MC
YEAR			WHITES			
1952	−0.63	−0.25	−0.40	+0.10	−0.31	−0.05
1956	−0.36	−0.23	−0.26	−0.09	−0.08	0.00
1960	−0.21	−0.17	−0.36	−0.08	−0.13	+0.07
1964	−0.29	−0.11	−0.29	−0.03	−0.37	+0.03
1968	−0.10	−0.01	−0.05	+0.09	−0.06	+0.04
1972	−0.12	−0.01	+0.01	−0.07	−0.06	+0.09
			BLACKS			
1952	−0.94	−0.85	−1.19	−1.25[a]	−1.50[a]	−1.00[a]
1956	−0.60	−1.50[a]	−0.37[a]	0.00[a]	+0.17	−1.00[a]
1960	−0.87	−0.57[a]	−0.21	−1.00[a]	−0.14	−1.00[a]
1964	−0.72	−0.48	−0.66	−0.85	−0.77	−0.83
1968	−0.78	−0.62	−0.84	−0.43[a]	−0.78	−0.47
1972	−0.65	−0.40	−0.83	−0.83[a]	−0.82	−0.37

[a] Based on fewer than 10 cases.

6. Comparisons between 1952 and 1972 can be made for both the Depression generation and the post-Depression cohorts with the data in Tables 6.2, 6.3, and 6.4. In 1972, 21 to 30 year olds in 1952 were 41 to 50, 31 to 40 year olds in 1952 were 51 to 60, and 41 to 50 year olds in 1952 were 61 to 70. Change between 1952 and 1972 for each of these cohorts can then be compared to change between 1952 and 1972 for the relevant educational grouping by noting the 1952 and 1972 entries in the right-hand column of the tables. The Depression generation refers of course to those individuals coming to political maturity at the time of the Depression (21 to 30 years old in 1932). The post-Depression cohorts are those individuals coming to political maturity after the Depression (reaching age 21 after 1932).

7. On the "silent revolution," see Ronald Inglehart, "The Silent Revolution in Europe: Intergenerational Change in Post-Industrial Societies," *American Political Science Review,* **65** (1971), 991–1017.

chapter 7

Party images among racial and regional groups

The significance of the racial issue for the party images of Americans has been suggested in Chapter 4, particularly for the 1960–1964 period. Consequently, it is appropriate to examine in more detail the attitudes and behavior of those groups in American society that have been most attuned to this political issue. In this chapter, then, we discuss the political behavior of blacks and whites, whose reactions to the civil rights movement and to government involvement in that movement are clearly detectable in their party images. We begin by tracing the mean party image scores of racial and regional groups over time. Then we examine the distributions of racial and regional groups along the collapsed party image index. Next we turn to the particular response of party images of Southern whites to events of the 1960s and we examine the process of electoral realignment among Southern whites in the period 1960–1968.

MEAN PARTY IMAGE SCORES AMONG
RACIAL AND REGIONAL GROUPS

Although in Chapter 2 we noted the great stability in the aggregate of the distribution of party image-holders, this stability masks important change among racial and regional groups. Table 7.1 presents mean party image scores for several different groups in society over time: for the population as a whole, for each region,[1] for each race, and for each of the four regional and racial combinations.

These data reveal that regional differences declined fairly steadily throughout the 20-year period but that racial differences, while declining initially from 1952 through 1960, were accentuated in 1964 and 1968 and remained at a high, though somewhat subdued, level in 1972. Among whites only, regional differences began to narrow in 1960, were eliminated if not slightly reversed in 1968 as Southern whites became even more pro-Republican in their party images than non-Southern whites, and remained small in 1972. Among blacks only, regional differences were great only in 1960, and as a group, Southern and non-Southern blacks moved away from whites in 1964 and have remained strongly pro-Democratic while whites have been mildly pro-Republican in recent years.

TABLE 7.1   Mean Party Image Scores for Racial and Regional Groups, by Year

	1952	1956	1960	1964	1968	1972
Population	−0.01	−0.36	−0.37	−0.61	−0.16	−0.21
Racial Groups						
Whites	+0.19	−0.32	−0.29	−0.42	+0.47	−0.01
Blacks	−1.85	−1.48	−1.19	−2.51	−2.59	−1.95
Difference	+2.04	+1.16	+0.90	+2.09	+3.06	+1.94
Regional Groups						
Non-Southerners	+0.27	−0.11	−0.24	−0.42	+0.32	−0.13
Southerners	−0.84	−1.29	−0.66	−1.16	−0.28	−0.41
Difference	+1.11	+1.18	+0.42	+0.74	+0.60	+0.28
Racial and Regional Groups						
Non-Southern Whites	+0.37	−0.06	−0.17	−0.35	+0.45	−0.04
Southern Whites	−0.47	−1.25	−0.60	−0.66	+0.49	+0.13
Non-Southern Blacks	−2.03	−1.72	−1.84	−2.58	−2.03	−1.82
Southern Blacks	−1.80	−1.41	−0.88	−2.52	−2.87	−2.00

The 1952 election was marked by a politics of both race and region: mild regional differences existed among whites and among blacks, strong racial differences existed among Southerners and especially among non-Southerners. Throughout the 20-year period there was a decline in regional differences and an increase in racial differences, especially at the time of Wallace's third party campaign for President (1968).[2] But the most impressive feature of the data is the strong increase in differences between the races that occurred between 1960 and 1964 and again between 1964 and 1968. This eight-year period created sharp, wide cleavages within the Southern electorate, and did so in two steps.

The differences by race in images of the parties resulted first from the pro-Democratic movement of blacks, very much a mobilization at least in terms of the forging of political attitudes.[3] Southern blacks had a pro-Democratic mean party image score in 1960 of −0.88, which, however, became three times more pro-Democratic by 1964 (−2.52). During this period (1960–1964), on the other hand, Southern white party images remained virtually identical (−0.60 and −0.66, respectively).[4] The second step in the creation of sharp racial cleavages was taken by Southern whites, whose mean party image score between 1964 and 1968 moved from −0.66 (fairly strongly favoring the Democrats) to +0.49 (mildly favoring the Republicans), while the mean party image score of blacks moved only from −2.52 to −2.87. Thus the creation of racial cleavage resembles a process of mobilization and countermobilization, in which blacks presumably reacted favorably to the Civil Rights Movement of the early 1960s and whites reacted unfavorably, presumably to the gains achieved by blacks.[5] This is not to minimize the increased pro-Democratic nature of Southern black party images between 1964 and 1968. (Corrected means reveal that Southern black party images moved from −0.22 in 1960 to −1.36 in 1964 to −2.59 in 1968.) Relatively, then, the mobilization of blacks into the Democratic camp continued between 1964 and 1968, but the path of the uncorrected means reveals that absolute change in favorability occurred between 1960 and 1964 primarily for blacks and between 1964 and 1968 primarily for whites. In the first instance, the movement was pro-Democratic; in the second, pro-Republican. Together, the processes of mobilization and countermobilization have produced striking racial differences among Southerners.

In 1972 we note a slight tempering of racial differences. This may have resulted from a normal "regression toward the mean"[6] or from the dissipation of the salience of the racial issue, as was argued in Chapter 4, or from a combination of both phenomena.[7] The interpretation depends, of course, on how party images among regional and racial groups behave in the future, but whatever the eventual interpretation of post-1968 politics, we must not underestimate the magnitude of change between 1960 and 1968. The aggregate stability in the party image index that we observed in Chapter 2 traces the attitudinal foundation of American electoral behavior. But Table 7.1 reveals that party images can also trace quite sensitively the preferences of blacks and whites, and this ability demonstrates considerable power for the concept of party image.

PARTY IMAGE DISTRIBUTIONS OF RACIAL AND REGIONAL GROUPS

When we examine distributions of racial and regional groups along the collapsed party image index we find further evidence of massive change in the 1960s, among Southerners especially. Table 7.2 presents these distributions. Party image data quite clearly document the processes of regional convergence and racial divergence that we have just discussed.[8]

If racial divergence ebbed somewhat in 1972, regional convergence continued. More significantly, in 1972 both parties were relatively ineffective in projecting any image at all. In 1972 the proportion of neutral image-holders among Southern whites reached the highest level (42.8%) for any of these four groups for this entire 20-year period, a result of declining proportions of pro-Republican as well as pro-Democratic image-holders. In 1972 more blacks than whites held a nonneutral party image, although non-Southern blacks were not unaffected by the relative inability of the parties to project images in 1972. Only for Southern blacks did the proportion of neutral image-holders in 1972 not constitute a respective high for this 20-year period, and in 1972 the greatest difference in distributions of party images could be found between the proportion of Southern whites and the proportion of Southern blacks holding neutral images.

In fact, the trends of these past 20 years have produced a profound political irony. In 1956 Southern blacks had been the least articulate with regard to party image (40% in the neutral category), but by 1972 they had become the strongest supporters of the Democratic Party. In 1956 Southern whites had been the strongest supporters of the Democratic Party, as they had been since Reconstruction, but by 1972 they had become the weakest supporters of the Democratic Party and the least articulate with regard to party image. In fact, they had become perhaps the strongest supporters of the Republican Party.

Among Southern blacks, the politicizing impact of the 1964 election is again clear: 78.5% of Southern blacks held pro-Democratic images in 1964, compared to 47.0% in 1960. Also, for Southern blacks the group of neutral image-holders dwindled steadily from 1956 through 1968, suggesting perhaps an increasing activism among this group, which fell off however in 1972. From 1964 on, blacks have been overwhelmingly pro-Democratic in their images, whites have wavered near the neutral point, and regional differences within racial groups have been dwarfed by racial differences within regional groups.

Among Southern whites, there has been a general attrition of support for the Democratic Party. The proportion of pro-Democratic image-holders has generally declined, and in 1968 this was accompanied by large increases in the proportions of mildly and strongly pro-Republican image-holders. In fact, in 1968 the proportion of strongly pro-Republican image-holders reached one-seventh of the entire group.[9] Increasing Republicanism among Southern whites was concentrated in the 1964–1968 period, although the proportion of strongly pro-Democratic image-holders fell fairly steadily throughout the 20 years, approaching zero in 1972.[10]

Such movement has certain obvious implications for political behavior. We saw in Chapter 2 that strongly pro-Republican image-holders can be expected to vote heavily non-Democratic, *irrespective of party identification*. Mildly pro-Republican image-holders can also be expected to vote non-Democratic, though less uniformly and less consistently. (See Table 2.7.) Consequently, aggregate changes in party images seem to explain a good deal of the recent increased Republican voting in the South. The role of party image in affecting electoral change may be fruitfully discussed, then, by examining the relationship of party image to increasing Republican voting among Southern whites.

PARTY IMAGES AND THE VOTES OF SOUTHERN WHITES

Among Southern whites, strongly pro-Republican image-holders have consistently voted strongly non-Democratic, as Table 7.3 shows. There-

TABLE 7.2 Distributions of Party Images Among Racial and Regional Groups,[a] by Year

Party Image[b]	1952				1956				1960			
	SW	NSW	SB	NSB	SW	NSW	SB	NSB	SW	NSW	SB	NSB
DD	15.9%	15.7%	26.5%	30.8%	17.6%	14.2%	22.0%	25.0%	10.4%	15.0%	12.0%	21.8%
D	34.4	24.6	33.3	41.0	34.6	26.7	26.3	39.3	36.8	27.1	35.0	43.6
N	18.6	14.6	28.0	12.8	25.9	19.2	40.7	25.0	26.7	20.2	38.5	20.0
R	16.5	23.8	9.8	15.4	18.4	25.7	10.2	10.7	19.2	25.0	12.8	10.9
RR	14.7	21.3	2.3	0.0	3.5	14.2	0.8	0.0	7.0	12.7	1.7	3.6
Total	100.1%[c]	100.0%	99.9%[c]	100.0%	100.0%	100.0%	100.0%	100.0%	100.1%[c]	100.0%	100.0%	99.9%[c]
(N)	(334)	(1284)	(132)	(39)	(347)	(1263)	(118)	(28)	(386)	(1378)	(117)	(55)

[a]Key: SW = Southern Whites; NSW = Non-Southern Whites; SB = Southern Blacks; NSB = Non-Southern Blacks. For states coded as Southern, see note 1.

[b]Key: DD = Strongly pro-Democratic; D = Mildly pro-Democratic; N = Neutral; R = Mildly pro-Republican; RR = Strongly pro-Republican.

[c]Column does not total 100.0% due to rounding errors.

TABLE 7.2 Cont.

Party Image [b]	1964				1968				1972			
	SW	NSW	SB	NSB	SW	NSW	SB	NSB	SW	NSW	SB	NSB
DD	12.1%	13.1%	29.9%	30.6%	6.2%	8.3%	33.9%	29.0%	2.2%	7.5%	26.6%	30.0%
D	33.9	31.2	48.6	53.2	25.2	24.0	48.6	42.1	22.9	25.9	42.6	35.0
N	27.9	25.9	19.3	10.8	26.8	24.2	11.9	22.4	42.8	35.4	22.3	30.0
R	21.4	20.3	2.3	4.5	27.1	27.9	5.6	6.5	26.2	24.7	8.5	2.5
RR	4.6	9.5	0.0	0.9	14.7	15.5	0.0	0.0	5.9	6.5	0.0	2.5
Total	99.9%c	100.0%c	100.1%c	100.0%	100.0%	99.9%c	100.0%	100.0%	100.0%	100.0%	100.0%	100.0%
(N)	(840)	(3357)	(311)	(111)	(612)	(2164)	(177)	(107)	(271)	(950)	(94)	(40)

[a]Key: SW = Southern Whites; NSW = Non-Southern Whites; SB = Southern Blacks; NSB = Non-Southern Blacks. For states coded as Southern, see note 1.

[b]Key: DD = Strongly pro-Democratic; D = Mildly pro-Democratic; N = Neutral; R = Mildly pro-Republican; RR = Strongly pro-Republican.

[c]Column does not total 100.0% due to rounding errors.

155

**TABLE 7.3   Non-Democratic Percentage of the Vote by Party Image, for
Southern Whites, by Year**[a]

Year	Party Image[b]				
	DD	D	N	R	RR
1952	6.7%	15.8%	52.6%	87.5%	94.4%
	(30)	(57)	(19)	(32)	(36)
1956	8.2%	28.8%	57.5%	89.2%	100.0%
	(49)	(73)	(40)	(37)	(10)
1960	13.9%	26.8%	50.0%	81.0%	89.5%
	(36)	(97)	(56)	(42)	(19)
1964	4.0%	12.7%	37.5%	77.1%	91.7%
	(75)	(213)	(96)	(105)	(36)
1968	30.8%	47.0%	81.3%	89.2%	97.0%
	(26)	(102)	(64)	(92)	(68)
1972	20.0%	53.7%	88.1%	98.4%	100.0%
	(5)	(41)	(67)	(61)	(13)

[a]Entries are the percentage of cases in the respective party
image category, given in parentheses, which voted non-Democratic.

[b]Key: DD = Strongly pro-Democratic; D = Mildly pro-Democratic;
N = Neutral; R = Mildly pro-Republican; RR = Strongly pro-
Republican.

fore, the increased Republican voting among Southern whites is not due
to a greater propensity of strongly pro-Republican image-holders to vote
non-Democratic. Instead, we have to look for the source of increased
Republican voting among Southern whites in the *numbers* of individuals
who had come to possess a strong pro-Republican image. The *number* of
strongly pro-Republican image-holders voting non-Democratic can be
expressed as the product of the percent of this group voting non-
Democratic and the size of the group. The size of the group of strongly
pro-Republican image-holders increased notably between 1964 and
1968 (from 4.6 to 14.7%; see Table 7.2); virtually all were translated into
non-Democratic votes (see Table 7.3). Thus this change in the party
images of Southern whites by itself increased the non-Democratic percentage of the vote by about 10 percentage points between 1964 and
1968.

Perhaps more significant for voting results has been the steady increase over this 20-year period in the proportion of mildly pro-Republican image-holders (see Table 7.2 again), almost 90% of whom in any year vote non-Democratic (Table 7.3). The propensity of this group to vote non-Democratic has not increased, but the increasing size of the group has nevertheless produced an increasing number of non-Democratic voters.

On the other hand, the propensity to vote non-Democratic has been more volatile among neutral image-holders, remaining near 50% from 1952 through 1960, falling markedly to 37.5% in 1964, but rising sharply to 81.3 and 81.1% in 1968 and 1972, respectively. Neutral image-holders increased in number among Southern whites, especially between 1968 and 1972. Mildly pro-Democratic image-holders have shown a substantial increase since 1964 in the propensity to vote non-Democratic at the same time that they have become fewer in number. Thus, surprisingly, it is among neutral and mildly pro-Democratic image-holders that the number of Republican voters has increased most notably, despite increasing numbers of non-Democratic voters among pro-Republican image-holders.

Table 7.4 presents data that show the changing contributions of each image category to the total non-Democratic percentage of Southern white votes. Only in 1968 did strongly pro-Republican image-holders contribute an unusually high proportion of the total non-Democratic votes cast. By 1972, of course, the Republican vote was so high that strongly pro-Republican image-holders necessarily contributed a small proportion of the Republican vote, since their size shrunk between 1968 and 1972 while the proportion of non-Democratic votes increased from 69.0 to 82.1% among Southern whites.

Among mildly pro-Republican image-holders the contributions to the non-Democratic vote increased after 1964, expecially between 1968 and 1972. Among neutral image-holders the contribution increased much more substantially, from 10.5% in 1964 to 21.8% in 1968 and to 37.7% in 1972. By 1968 about one-third of all Southern whites were mildly pro-Democratic or neutral image-holders who voted Republican. By 1972 the proportion had risen to one-half. By 1972 among all image categories except strongly pro-Democratic either large proportions or large numbers of individuals were voting Republican.

What all these data suggest is that the two-step process of electoral change was in fact a three-step process. The second stage, counter-mobilization of Southern whites, seems itself to have involved, first,

TABLE 7.4 Categories of Party Image as Sources of the Southern White Non-Democratic Vote, by Year[a]

Party Image[b]	Year					
	1952	1956	1960	1964	1968	1972
DD	1.1%	1.4%	1.4%	0.5%	2.5%	0.4%
D	5.4%	10.0%	9.9%	4.4%	11.8%	12.3%
N	9.8%	14.9%	13.4%	10.5%	21.8%	37.7%
R	14.4%	16.1%	15.6%	16.5%	18.6%	25.8%
RR	13.9%	3.5%	6.3%	4.3%	14.3%	5.9%
Total[c]	44.6%	45.9%	46.6%	36.2%	69.0%	82.1%

[a]Entries constitute the percent voting non-Democratic among Southern Whites holding the respective party image. Figures are derived by multiplying the percentage of Southern Whites within the party image category by the percentage of that category voting non-Democratic. Since these percentages are not based on the same number of cases, the results are only close approximations.

[b]Key: DD = Strongly pro-Democratic; D = Mildly pro-Democratic; N = Neutral; R = Mildly pro-Republican; RR = Strongly pro-Republican.

[c]Totals constitute the proportion of the Southern White electorate voting non-Democratic in the respective years. N's are not reported because of the manner of computation. (See note a.)

attitude and behavioral change among a "vanguard," and second, large-scale behavioral change among the masses. Between 1964 and 1968 the proportion of strongly pro-Republican image-holders increased sharply, accounting in part for the more pro-Republican mean party image score we observed earlier for 1968. This vanguard of individuals, who only recently had become strongly committed to the Republican Party, contributed significantly to the non-Democratic vote of this year — over one-fifth of the non-Democratic votes came from strongly pro-Republican image-holders (14.3/69.0%).

Between 1968 and 1972 the masses seemed to respond behaviorally to the vanguard's 1968 cues. Mildly pro-Republican and neutral image-holders raised their contribution to the total non-Democratic vote, but they did so without first having acquired the attitudinal predisposition we might have expected. That is, their behavior (non-Democratic voting) more and more resembled that of the strongly pro-Republican vanguard, but these masses still maintained neutral or perhaps mildly pro-Republican images.

Consequently, the concept of party image cannot explain all of the increased Republican voting of Southern whites. But the idea of a two- or three-step process of electoral change is an intriguing one, and the role of party image in the early stages of the process receives considerable support in the data we have examined.

PARTY IMAGE AND PARTY IDENTIFICATION AMONG SOUTHERN WHITES

Having documented a role for party image in the transformation of electoral behavior, we now examine the tangential issue of whether party images also affect party identification. This issue is crucial to the debate over a possible electoral realignment in the South. The transformation of the formerly Democratic "solid South" into a region that is electorally competitive has led scholars who define realignment in terms of aggregate political *behavior* to pronounce its accomplishment[11] and has prompted scholars who define realignment in terms of individual conversions in *party identification* to examine appropriate survey data.[12] In this section we explore the ability of party images to cause Southern white Democratic identifiers to switch identifications.

Matthews and Prothro found that Republican to Democratic and Democratic to Republican identification switchers had mean party image scores strongly favorable to the party to which they had switched identification.[13] Such evidence, however, does not conclusively demonstrate that party images cause one to switch identifications, since the time order of the aquisition of image and identification is not known. Possibly individuals are rationalizing new identifications by adopting favorable images *after* their switch in party identifications. We shall deal more fully with the time order of attitude acquisition in the next chapter, in order to test as rigorously as possible the proposition that images cause changes in identification. For now, we simply continue the investigation of the aggregate behavior of Southern whites.

Among Southern whites there has been a rapid deterioration of Democratic identification. Table 7.5 presents distributions of party identification among Whites by region. Regional covergence in identifications has occurred, similar to regional convergence in party images, evident in the declining values of gamma in the Table, but has slowed considerably. By examining successively the percentage of Democratic identifiers among Southern whites in each election, a general decline can be detected,

TABLE 7.5 Distributions of Party Identification Among Whites, by Region[a] and Year

Party Identification[b]	1952		1956		1960	
	SW	NSW	SW	NSW	SW	NSW
Democratic	83.8%	50.4%	74.8%	44.1%	67.8%	47.7%
Independent	2.8	7.0	5.5	10.3	10.4	9.2
Republican	13.4	42.7	19.8	45.6	21.8	43.1
Total	100.0%	100.1%[c]	100.0%	100.0%	100.0%	100.0%
(N)	(321)	(1261)	(329)	(1237)	(376)	(1324)
Gamma	.650		.542		.394	

	1964		1968		1972	
	SW	NSW	SW	NSW	SW	NSW
Democratic	76.2%	54.6%	62.9%	48.5%	60.3%	46.0%
Independent	7.7	8.2	12.3	11.3	12.6	12.8
Republican	16.1	37.3	24.8	40.3	27.1	41.1
Total	100.0%	100.0%	100.0%	100.0%	100.0%	99.9%[c]
(N)	(819)	(3309)	(604)	(2130)	(262)	(934)
Gamma	.447		.247		.268	

[a]Key: SW = Southern Whites; NSW = Non-Southern Whites. For states coded as Southern, see note 1.

[b]Independent Democrats and Independent Republicans are coded as partisans, not as Independents.

[c]Column may not total 100.0% due to rounding errors.

interrupted only by the increase in 1964. But the rate of decline has virtually reached zero, so that the percentage of Democratic identifiers has seemingly stabilized near 60%. Furthermore, although regional convergence seemed to progress through 1968, change between 1968 and 1972 seems to have been due to some other process (perhaps party decomposition), since the Democratic Party sustained a net loss among white identifiers in the non-South equal to its loss in the South.

During the 1952–1972 period, the relationship between party image and party identification among Southern whites decayed noticeably. This relationship is presented in Table 7.6. By 1972 only 37.4% of the Democratic identifiers held pro-Democratic images. Although the proportion of non-Southern, white, Democratic identifiers holding pro-Democratic images has also fallen since 1956, testifying perhaps to the process of party decomposition, the drop has not been as sharp as

TABLE 7.6 Percent of Party Identification Categories Holding Pro-Democratic Party Images, Among Whites, by Region, by Year[a]

Year	South			Non-South		
	Party Identification[b]			Party Identification[b]		
	D	I	R	D	I	R
1952	59.5% (269)	11.1% (9)	7.0% (43)	69.7% (635)	26.2% (88)	8.9% (538)
1956	67.5% (246)	11.2% (18)	12.3% (65)	77.5% (546)	29.1% (127)	8.2% (564)
1960	65.1% (255)	7.7% (39)	13.4% (82)	77.2% (632)	32.8% (122)	7.6% (570)
1964	60.1% (624)	9.5% (63)	4.6% (132)	69.8% (1806)	24.4% (270)	13.6% (1233)
1968	48.4% (380)	8.1% (74)	1.3% (150)	66.4% (1032)	22.5% (240)	6.5% (2130)
1972	37.4% (158)	21.2% (33)	2.8% (71)	62.8% (430)	17.5% (120)	6.8% (384)

[a]Entries are the percentage of cases, given in parentheses, holding pro-Democratic party images.

[b]Key: D = Democrat, including Independent Democrats; I = Independents; R = Republican, including Independent Republican.

for Southern whites (from 77.5 to 62.8%, compared to from 67.5 to 37.4%). This decaying relationship may be evidence of new party images inducing change in party identification, but the data of Table 7.6 are not sufficient for making such an inference. Clearly, however, images and identification are less strongly related among white Southerners than among white non-Southerners.

Table 7.7, however, presents stronger evidence for inferring that party images have weakened the Democratic identifications of Southern whites throughout the 20-year period of this study. Among Southern white Democratic identifiers, the proportion voting non-Democratic increases steadily and consistently from the strongly pro-Democratic image-holders to the strongly pro-Republican image-holders. If a strong Democratic identifier acquires a strongly pro-Republican image, we would indeed expect him to vote non-Democratic,[14] and it is not unreasonable to argue that his pro-Republican image is evidence of a weakened psychological commitment to the Democratic Party.

TABLE 7.7 Non-Democratic Percentage of the Vote by Party Image, for Southern White Democratic Identifiers, by Year[a]

Year	Party Image[b]				
	DD	D	N	R	RR
1952	6.7% (30)	13.5% (52)	46.2% (13)	80.0% (20)	88.9% (18)
1956	8.5% (47)	23.1% (65)	51.9% (27)	76.9% (13)	100.0% (1)
1960	12.1% (33)	27.8% (90)	33.3% (30)	50.0% (14)	75.0% (8)
1964	0.0% (72)	11.8% (204)	28.6% (63)	64.3% (42)	66.7% (9)
1968	30.8% (26)	42.5% (80)	68.8% (32)	72.2% (36)	83.3% (12)
1972	25.0% (4)	51.3% (39)	78.4% (37)	100.0% (27)	100.0% (6)

[a]Entries are the percentage of cases in the respective party image category, given in parentheses, which voted non-Democratic.

[b]Key: DD = Strongly pro-Democratic; D = Mildly pro-Democratic; N = Neutral; R = Mildly pro-Republican; RR = Strongly pro-Republican.

While these data demonstrate that in the aggregate party images have weakened the traditional Democratic allegiances of Southern whites, both in terms of party identification and voting behavior, it must be pointed out that party images do not constitute the only force for political change in the South. For instance, images clearly cannot explain why 30.8% of the strongly pro-*Democratic* image-holders voted *non*-Democratic in 1968. In addition, a party image explanation of Southern political change fails to incorporate the substantial evidence that social and economic change in the South, particularly urbanization, has induced political change.[15] Finally, "dealignment" or party decomposition has occurred among young Southern whites,[16] for whom it is thus an open question whether images might have any affect at all on political attitudes and electoral behavior.

THE RACIAL ISSUE AND PARTY IMAGES AMONG RACIAL AND REGIONAL GROUPS

Matthews and Prothro, among others, presented evidence that the racial issue is one of the two issues most responsible for long-term change in Southern voting patterns.[17] Although the Matthews and Prothro analysis documents substantial electoral and attitudinal change among Southern whites from 1960 to 1964, the evidence to be considered in this section reveals that the impact of the racial issue on party images was inconsistent — it was dramatically strong in the period of 1960–1964, but dramatically weak prior to that period.

The specific party image index for the racial issue, identical to the one discussed in Chapter 4, is presented in Table 7.8 for each of the four racial and regional groups and for the population as a whole. Through 1960 there is no significantly strong impact of the racial issue on the party images of Americans, either for the population as a whole or for any of the four racial and regional groups (with the inexplicable exception of non-Southern blacks' positive orientation toward the Democratic Party in 1952). In fact, through 1960 Southern whites were more positively oriented toward the Democratic Party (and negatively oriented toward the Republican Party) by the racial issue than were non-Southern whites, and Southern whites were almost as positive as Southern blacks. No doubt these data reflect the legacies of traditional American political coalitions — post-1860 Southern opposition to Republicanism; post-

TABLE 7.8 Mean Racial Issue Party Image Index Scores and Percents with Non-Neutral Images by Party for Racial and Regional Groups, by Year

	Population	Non-Southern Whites	Southern Whites	Non-Southern Blacks	Southern Blacks
Mean Racial Issue Party Image Scores					
1952	-0.01	0.00	+0.03	-0.18	-0.11
1956	-0.01	0.00	-0.03	+0.13	-0.07
1960	-0.02	-0.02	0.00	-0.14	+0.01
1964	-0.01	+0.02	+0.15	-0.81	-0.50
1968	-0.03	0.00	+0.03	-0.46	-0.45
1972	-0.01	0.00	0.00	-0.11	-0.15

Percent with Non-Neutral Racial Issue Party Image

	Pro-D	Pro-R	Pro-D	Pro-R	Pro-D	Pro-R	Pro-D	Pro-R	Pro-D	Pro-R
1952	2.8	2.1	1.3	0.9	3.3	6.6	23.1	5.1	3.3	6.6
1956	3.2	2.7	1.6	1.7	6.8	5.0	9.4	12.5	9.6	5.3
1960	3.6	1.9	2.4	0.9	6.0	4.4	10.9	0.0	6.8	6.8
1964	6.9	6.8	3.9	5.7	1.8	13.8	54.7	2.1	37.0	1.6
1968	5.5	3.4	2.9	3.0	1.6	4.9	24.7	2.2	35.2	1.1
1972	2.0	0.9	0.8	1.1	0.7	0.4	13.6	2.3	12.4	0.0

1932 tacit cooperation on the part of Southerners with National Democrats in exchange more or less for a "hands off" policy on "states' rights" and segregation issues; and post-1954 Southern resentment toward a Republican Administration that had "appointed" the Warren Court.

At the same time none of these traditions can reasonably be invoked to explain the pro-Democratic (anti-Republican) attitudes of blacks. While many blacks perhaps had not forgotten "the Party of Lincoln," and still more blacks, in the North at least, were receptive to the Warren Court's 1954 *Brown* decision (witness the 12.5% of non-Southern blacks with pro-Republican racial issue party images in 1956), many other blacks held pro-Democratic images in 1956 and 1960 (9.4 and 10.9%, respectively).

But the 1964 data dramatically document the response to Birmingham, freedom marches, and sit-ins. The data reveal a polarization around the race issue: blacks became overwhelmingly supportive of the Democratic Party, and Southern whites reacted strikingly by adopting pro-Republican, anti-Democratic images. Yet black pro-Democratic sentiment clearly outweighed white pro-Republican, anti-Democratic sentiment, so the 1960–1964 change was primarily a mobilization of black sentiment, as provided by our hypothetical model of electoral change. But the model fails us after this point, for it would cause us to overlook or minimize the important change among Southern whites between 1960 and 1964, and it would lead us to predict a Southern white countermobilization between 1964 and 1968 which simply does not appear in these data. In fact, Southern white party images are less partisan with regard to the racial issue after 1964 than before, and by 1972 had become virtually neutral. Black images remained significantly pro-Democratic, despite the large decrease among non-Southern blacks between 1964 and 1968 and among all blacks between 1968 and 1972.

By 1972 the racial issue had clearly lost its salience for white Americans but still evoked sentiment among blacks that was as pro-Democratic as white sentiment had been pro-Republican in 1964. Based on the argument put forth in Chapter 4, it seems reasonable to suppose that whites no longer saw the racial issue as helping to define American political parties. Despite the movement toward Republicanism among Southern whites in the 1960s, the Republican Party did not come to be perceived as strongly status quo or segregationist on racial matters, despite Nixon's alleged "Southern strategy."[18]

Of course another explanation can be offered, and that is that Southern whites had learned to disguise their racial attitudes. Several factors argue against this, however. We are not dealing here with concrete aspects of the racial issue; these data reveal only the freely offered reasons for liking or disliking the parties, not the structured responses to items concerning the speed of integration or the treatment of blacks or the like. Thus, there would have been no apparent need for the respondent to disguise his or her opinion. Of course the respondent might have been conditioned to offer euphemistic responses such as law and order rather than direct race-related answers. But in 1968, just when Wallace's campaign might have prompted such action, the evidence suggests that the issues of race and law and order were in fact separable political dimensions in the voter's mind.[19] Finally, other scholars have also noted the "diminution in the salience and potency of racial issues during the period from 1968 to 1972."[20]

Thus either of two explanations seems reasonable. First, as we have argued, because voters perceived that parties had not and would not take opposite stands on segregation/integration, the issue no longer helped define the parties for the voters, and the issue disappeared from the party images of Americans. Or, second, Americans simply had lost interest totally in the racial issue (because parties had not polarized around the issue?). Of course, those voters still motivated by the racial issue are likely either to support third party candidates or to move back and forth between the major parties as a preferable candidate emerges first in one party and then in the other.[21]

THE RACIAL ISSUE AND VOTING

References to the racial issue have contributed greatly to the party images of Americans only beginning with the 1964 election. For Southern whites, the issue had high salience only in 1964. For blacks, the issue's salience was tremendous in 1964 but has declined since then. It is now appropriate to examine how the salience of the issue in turn affected voting behavior. Table 7.9 presents data on the vote-structuring ability of the collapsed specific racial issue party image index, for each of the four racial and regional groups.

It is clear immediately that this index has structured the votes of blacks more consistently and more strongly than those of whites. The low numbers of cases, particularly due to the small proportions of individuals with nonneutral party images, makes analysis difficult, yet some of the data are impressive. Whether we view small or large numbers of cases, Southern blacks and non-Southern blacks alike have almost uniformly voted for the Democratic Party, apparently in response to their pro-Democratic party images. Whites are not nearly so overwhelmingly uniform in their voting, whatever their party image.

For whites, however, the greater heterogeneity in party images and the less uniform voting behavior of individuals with nonneutral party images make the data of Table 7.9 more interesting and potentially helpful. Surprisingly, however, pro-Republican images neither rise dramatically among whites in 1964 and 1968, nor do they all of a sudden affect voting behavior in a profound way. Even in 1964, only 45.5% of the Southern whites with pro-Republican party images voted Republican (although this was considerably higher than the 20.0% of those Southern whites with pro-Democratic images or the 34.4% of all Southern whites). If blacks were mobilized in 1964, developing pro-Democratic images and voting overwhelmingly Democratic, white countermobilization did not occur, as the hypothetical model specifies it would not, until 1968, when large proportions of Southern and non-Southern whites with pro-Republican Party images did vote non-Democratic.

The table also contains information on the ability of this racial issue party image index to structure the vote in the aggregate. The total percentages of individuals whose votes are structured are those of all individuals possessing nonneutral images who voted for the party projecting their nonneutral image. Here again the figures for blacks far exceed those for whites. More interestingly, when we multiply these figures by the respective percent of the entire racial-regional group possessing nonneutral party images, we obtain a measure of the total percent of the group whose vote has been structured by this index. Once more the racial gap is immense. For whites, never more than 10% seem to be responding to the racial issue in their voting, and this in 1956. For blacks, the proportions are two to nine times greater. Between 1960 and 1964, the proportion of Southern blacks seemingly responding in their voting behavior to their party images increased by half (from 26.8 to 39.1%) and for non-Southern whites almost three-fifths (57.8%) seemed to be responding to their party images in 1964. The figures jumped so high because such large numbers of individuals developed nonneutral (pro-Democratic) images between 1960 and 1964. But the lesson of this part of the table is that the racial issue has played an immense role in contemporary American electoral politics primarily because of its mobilizing impact on blacks. The countermobilization that was predicted never materialized in the expected fashion.

Two comments are in order. First, if the appearance of the racial issue dramatically transformed American politics in the early 1960s, its apparent disappearance may have equally dramatic if unpredictible results. Between 1968 and 1972 the proportions of Southern and non-Southern blacks responding in their voting behavior to the party image index dropped to one-seventh. Second, if the claim of little countermobilization among whites is counterintuitive, then in addition to our earlier arguments on this point the reader should realize that we are discussing here the impact of the racial issue through the likes and

TABLE 7.9 Vote Structuring of the Racial Issue Party Image Index for Racial and Regional Groups, by Year

Racial and Regional Group	Vote Structuring[a]	Year					
		1952	1956	1960	1964	1968	1972
Non-Southern Whites	Democratic	69.2 (13)	25.0 (20)	24.1 (29)	92.3 (117)	45.8 (48)	28.6 (7)
	Republican	72.7 (11)	55.0 (20)	75.0 (12)	54.4 (171)	87.5 (48)	100.0 (6)
	Total	70.8 (17/24)	40.0 (16/40)	39.0 (16/41)	69.8 (201/288)	66.7 (64/96)	61.5 (8/13)
Southern Whites	Democratic	62.5 (8)	76.5 (17)	72.2 (18)	80.0 (15)	33.3 (6)	--- (b)
	Republican	52.9 (17)	53.3 (15)	81.8 (11)	45.5 (99)	100.0 (20)	--- (b)
	Total	56.0 (14/25)	65.6 (21/32)	75.9 (22/29)	50.0 (57/114)	84.6 (22/26)	--- (b)
Non-Southern Blacks	Democratic	100.0 (5)	100.0 (3)	100.0 (6)	100.0 (52)	100.0 (20)	100.0 (4)
	Republican	100.0 (1)	66.7 (2)	--- (b)	0.0 (1)	0.0 (2)	0.0 (1)
	Total	100.0 (6/6)	83.3 (5/6)	100.0 (6/6)	98.1 (52/53)	90.9 (20/22)	100.0 (5/5)
Southern Blacks	Democratic	100.0 (10)	83.3 (6)	100.0 (3)	99.1 (117)	100.0 (51)	100.0 (8)
	Republican	0.0 (1)	50.0 (2)	85.7 (7)	0.0 (5)	0.0 (1)	--- (b)
	Total	90.9 (10/11)	75.0 (6/8)	90.0 (9/10)	95.1 (116/122)	98.1 (51/52)	100.0 (8/8)

TABLE 7.9 cont.

Racial and Regional Group	Year					
	1952	1956	1960	1964	1968	1972

Percent with Non-Neutral Racial Issue Party Image

Non-Southern Whites	2.4	4.0	7.7	10.1	6.0	1.9
Southern Whites	11.9	14.3	11.4	16.0	6.9	0.0
Non-Southern Blacks	26.0	31.6	14.6	58.9	31.9	14.3
Southern Blacks	26.8	24.3	29.8	41.1	39.7	12.9

Percent of Non-Neutral Image-holders with Vote Structured by Racial Issue

Non-Southern Whites	70.8	40.0	39.0	69.8	66.7	61.5
Southern Whites	56.0	65.6	75.9	50.0	84.6	(b)
Non-Southern Blacks	100.0	83.3	100.0	98.1	90.9	100.0
Southern Blacks	90.9	75.0	90.0	95.1	98.1	100.0

Percent of Group with Vote Structured by Racial Issue (product of two respective figures above)

Non-Southern Whites	1.7	1.6	3.0	7.0	4.0	1.2
Southern Whites	6.7	9.4	8.7	8.0	5.8	(b)
Non-Southern Blacks	26.0	26.3	14.6	57.8	29.0	14.3
Southern Blacks	24.4	18.2	26.8	39.1	38.9	12.9

[a]Figures in the "Democratic" rows are the percent of pro-Democratic image-holders voting Democratic; figures in the "Republican" rows are the percent of pro-Republican image-holders voting non-Democratic; figures in the "Total" rows are the percent of Non-Neutral image-holders whose vote is structured. Figures in the "Total" rows are repeated in the middle matrix on the second page of the Table.

[b]No cases on which to base a percent.

169

dislikes Americans have for their parties. In this party-related sense the countermobilization failed to materialize, apparently because voters failed to perceive the parties in prointegration, anti-integration terms. In other more direct or less direct channels, the issue may have had and may continue to have profound impact on the political behavior of Americans, but if so, these channels do not include the channel of the political party.

CONCLUSION

It is difficult to overstate the ability of party images to capture the political realities of the 1960s, certainly for blacks at least. So far we have found evidence important not just for what it tells us about American politics, but also for what it tells us about the ability of the concept of party image to instruct us about American politics. This will be a major theme in our concluding chapter. But for the moment we must realize also how powerful is the concept of party image for sensitively documenting the process of mobilization, a process perhaps just the opposite of that of party decomposition. In the 1960s, blacks willingly moved into the political system, using the political party as a convenient and instrumental channel.

The lessons of this chapter suggest an irony we encountered in Chapter 4. The racial issue clearly motivated Americans, and continues unfortunately to separate them too often. Because of an issue about which they were so concerned, Americans in the early 1960s looked toward their political parties for assistance. For proponents of any party system, highly programmatic or diffuse and pluralistic, it has to be regarded as a healthy sign in a democracy that citizens attempt to resolve their dilemmas through the representative mechanism of the party system. The irony occurred, however, either when parties failed to articulate the concerns of the voters on this highly contentious, perhaps even abhorrent issue, or when the voters perceived that the parties were not polarizing on the issue and so gave up just that much more on their party system. We raised the question in Chapter 4 whether political parties, by failing to take clear and opposite stands on such contentious issues, contribute to their own destruction. In some sense it would seem that they obviously do. For instance, in times of electoral realignment, the party system is transformed because the traditional party system is ill-equipped to debate the newly relevant political issues. But with regard to the racial issue, no new party system is likely to form with parties polarized around this issue, so the uncomfortable and undesirable irony is that parties may promote not only their own destruction, but the destruction of the party system itself. Is such speculation unwarranted pessimism?[22] Hopefully it is, but one wonders whether few blacks in 1972 had their votes structured by their party images because others had given up on the party system and on the promise of the 1960s. It is not likely that the low figures result from satisfaction with the party system for a job well done.

NOTES

1. The South is defined as the 11 Confederate States: Alabama, Arkansas, Florida, Georgia, Louisiana, Mississippi, North Carolina, South Carolina, Tennessee, Texas, and Virginia. It should be noted that individuals in the SRC/CPS samples from these 11 states do not consitute a strictly representative sample of the citizens of these states.

2. For instance, in their study of the 1968 election, the SRC/CPS points out that 97% of all blacks voted for Humphrey but only 35% of all whites did so. "This percentage difference of 62% in candidate preference between blacks and whites is substantially larger than class differentiation or other social cleavages and partisanship within the United States in recent history or for democracies of Western Europe." See Philip E. Converse, Warren E. Miller, Jerrold C. Rusk, and Arthus C. Wolfe, "Continuity and Change in American Politics: Parties and Issues in the 1968 Election," *American Political Science Review,* **63** (1969), p. 1085 and note 4.

3. Bruce A. Campbell speaks of the mobilization of blacks in 1964 in his "Patterns of Change in the Partisan Loyalties of Native Southerners: 1952–1972," paper prepared for delivery at the Annual Meeting of the Midwest Political Science Association, Pick-Congress Hotel, Chicago, Ill., May 1–3, 1975.

4. This finding seems to contradict Matthews and Prothro's claim of great change between 1960 and 1964. See Donald R. Matthews and James W. Prothro, *Negroes and the New Southern Politics* (New York: Harcourt, Brace and World, 1966), pp. 369–404. There is really no contradiction at all; despite the relative stability in means, there is much change in the distribution on the collapsed party image index, as we shall see shortly.

5. On behavioral manifestations of black mobilization and white counter-mobilization, see Earl Black and Merle Black, "The Demographic Basis of

Wallace Support in Alabama," *American Politics Quarterly*, **1** (1973), 279–304; and Numan V. Bartley, *From Thurmond to Wallace* (Baltimore: Johns Hopkins University Press, 1970).

6. There is a well-known statistical phenomenon that cases with extreme values at one moment in time will have less extreme values at a second moment in time. Such a natural statistical process is not inherently interesting substantively.

7. Campbell, *op. cit.*, also discusses these possibilities.

8. On regional convergence see James L. Sundquist, *Dynamics of the Party System* (Washington: Brookings, 1973), pp. 332–337; Philip E. Converse, "On the possibility of a Major Political Realignment in the South?" pp. 212–242 in Angus Campbell, Philip E. Converse, Warren E. Miller, and Donald E. Stokes, *Elections and the Political Order* (New York: Wiley, 1964); and Bernard Cosman, *Five States for Goldwater* (University, Ala.: University of Alabama Press, 1966), pp. 121–123. On racial divergence see Cosman, *op. cit.*, pp. 123–124; Donald R. Matthews and James W. Prothro, "Southern Racial Attitudes: Conflict, Awareness, and Political Change," *Annals of the American Academy of Political and Social Science*, **344** (November, 1962), 108–121; Matthews and Prothro, "Southern Images of Political Parties: An Analysis of White and Negro Attitudes," pp. 82–111 in Avery Leiserson, ed., *The American South in the 1960's* (New York: Praeger, 1964); Walter Dean Burnham, *Critical Elections and the Mainsprings of American Politics* (New York: Norton, 1970), p. 157; and Everett Carll Ladd, Jr., and Charles D. Hadley, "Party Definition and Party Differentiation," *Public Opinion Quarterly*, **37** (1973), p. 31.

9. This figure had been reached earlier in 1952.

10. Note the exception produced by Goldwater's candidacy in 1964.

11. See, for instance, Louis M. Seagull, *Southern Republicanism* (New York: Schenkman, 1975), who follows in the tradition of V. O. Key, Jr., "A Theory of Critical Elections," *Journal of Politics*, **17** (1955), 3–18; and Key, "Secular Realignment and the Party System," *Journal of Politics*, **21** (1959), 198–210.

12. Several scholars have used survey data to study a possible Southern electoral realignment. See for instance Paul Allen Beck, "Partisan Stability and Change in the American South: 1952-1972," paper prepared for delivery at the annual meeting of the American Political Science Association, Palmer House Hotel, Chicago, Ill., August 29–September 2, 1974; and Campbell, "Patterns of Change in the Partisan Loyalties of Native Southerners: 1952-1972," *op. cit.* Also see the pioneering effort by Converse, "On the Possibility of a Major Political Realignment in the South," *op. cit.*

13. Matthews and Prothro, *Negroes and the New Southern Politics, op. cit.*, Table 13-6, p. 393. See also F. Glenn Abney, "Partisan Realignment in a One-Party System: The Case of Mississippi," *Journal of Politics*, **31** (1969), 1102–1106.

14. We must postpone again until the next chapter the question of whether images rationalize identifications. However, even if images do rationalize identifications, this does not invalidate the argument that if a strong Democratic identifier acquires a strongly pro-Republican image, he or she will vote Republican. This claim is an empirical fact, as presented in Table 7.7.

15. For instance, see Donald S. Strong, *Urban Republicanism in the South* (University, Ala.: Bureau of Public Administration, University of Alabama, 1960).

16. See Paul Allen Beck, "Partisan Stability and Change in the American South: 1952-1972," *op. cit.*

17. Matthews and Prothro, *Negroes and the New Southern Politics*, *op. cit.*, pp. 396–400. The second issue they mention is economic conservatism.

18. For discussion of Nixon's alleged "Southern Strategy," see Theodore H. White, *The Making of the President 1968* (New York: Atheneum, 1969); Nelson W. Polsby and Aaron B. Wildavsky, *Presidential Elections*, 3rd ed. (New York: Charles Scribner's Sons, 1971), pp. 83–97; Bernard Cosman and Robert J. Huckshorn, "The Goldwater Impact: Cyclical Variation or Secular Decline?" pp. 234–244 in Cosman and Huckshorn, eds., *Republican Politics* (New York: Praeger, 1968); and George B. Tindall, *The Disruption of the Solid South* (Athens: University of Georgia Press, 1972), pp. 61–64, 68–70.

19. Converse et al., *op. cit.*

20. Arthur H. Miller, Warren E. Miller, Alden S. Raine, and Thad A. Brown, "A Majority Party in Disarray: Policy Polarization in the 1972 Election," paper presented at the Annual Meeting of the American Political Science Association, Jung Hotel, New Orleans, La., September 4–8, 1973.

21. Sundquist, *op. cit.*, p. 366.

22. For a more systematic and thorough discussion of this possibility, see Walter Dean Burnham, "The End of American Party Politics," *Trans-action*, **7**:2 (December 1969), 12–22; and Burnham, "American Parties in the 1970s: Beyond Party?" pp. 238–279 in Louis Maisel and Paul M. Sacks, eds., *The Future of Political Parties*, Sage Electoral Studies Yearbook, Vol. 1 (Beverly Hills: Sage Publications, 1975).

part III
Theoretical considerations

chapter 8

Party image and partisan change

In Part I we examined an index of the number of likes and dislikes
Americans have for their political parties, the relative importance of
these likes and dislikes for political behavior, and the richness, variety,
and substance of these likes and dislikes over time. In Part II we investi-
gated the ability of party images to document the preferences of politi-
cally significant groups in American society. Now in Part III we address
more directly the theoretical role for party image in electoral behavior.
In this chapter we examine the proposition that party images can cause
changes in party identification and can affect the pursuant voting behavior of individuals who change their identification.[1] In Chapter 9 we
summarize the evidence we have considered concerning the theoretical
role of party images and we specify that role.

CHANGE IN PARTY IDENTIFICATION

Why do some people change party identifications while other people maintain existing party identifications? Party identifications are typically acquired at an early age and maintained by an individual over his or her lifetime.[2] Because identifications are learned through affective rather than cognitive processes, and because the longer they are held the stronger they become,[3] identifications possess great inertia in that they change relatively infrequently and only with much difficulty. Not surprisingly, then, party identifications are typically stable and enduring.[4]

Yet for several different reasons identifications occasionally do change. Change in social milieu, particularly moving from an urban to suburban environment, may predispose an individual to change identification[5] as may short-term forces in the political environment.[6] Or, "the highly involved voter, who is likely to be more constrained in his partisan attitudes than are voters of low involvement, is more likely to alter his party attachment so that it is consonant with his current vote intention than are voters of low involvement."[7]

There has been inadequate study of change in identification, in part because change is rare. In addition, even when changes in identification are more frequent, for instance in times of electoral realignment, insufficient data at the individual level have been collected to provide scholars the material upon which to build theories of electoral change. A panel study is of course ideally suited to the study of change, and the 1956–1958–1960 SRC/CPS panel study has provided the best evidence we have about identification change. Dreyer analyzed these data and found that measurable changes did occur, but that the pattern of change was random.[8] More recently, Brody found that strength of partisanship responds to short-term political stimuli,[9] while Dobson and St. Angelo revealed that identifications are less stable than previously thought and often are altered to conform with vote intention.[10]

In this chapter we consider evidence that the index of party image — the measure of the extent to which individuals like or dislike the two political parties — can help explain stability and change in the party identifications of Americans. We use two kinds of evidence. First, in each of the six cross-sectional surveys by the SRC/CPS that we already employed, present Democratic and Republican identifiers were asked whether they ever identified with another party and present Independents were asked whether they ever identified with either the Democratic or Republican parties.[11] These recall data, in conjunction with data on present party images and present party identifications, are consistent with the proposition that party images play an intervening role in the transformation of party identifications.

The second set of evidence includes more direct and more reliable (although not completely unambiguous) measures of the time sequence in the acquisition of image and identification. Using the SRC panel study, patterns of identification change will be compared to images whose temporal location is known. These data, too, support the argument that images can induce change in identification.

These findings do not contradict the lesson of political socialization that identifications normally endure. In fact, party images generally reinforce identifications and promote this endurance. However when images strongly contradict identifications, identifications are indeed more likely to change.

PARTY IMAGE AND ELECTORAL CHANGE

The motivation for the present examination is the theoretical role for party image described by Charles Sellers, whose comments bear repeating. In periods of electoral realignment, he speculates, individuals first adopt favorable images of the party they will come to identify with before they actually alter their party identification.[12] Speaking about the causes of electoral realignment, Sellers suggests,

> The crucial factor would seem to be the gross images of the parties as they are perceived (whether accurately or not) by voters in the process of forming or, to a lesser extent, changing identifications . . . the images that the parties project, the ways in which they do this, and the ways in which the voters perceive the parties seem to be the major determinants of political alignment.[13]

The process that occurs, Sellers continues, involves (1) a few voters with established identifications changing them to the party with the now more appealing image with regard to the circumstances causing realignment, (2) the desertion by a large number of voters for an election or two without abandoning their identifications, and (3) the formation by a great majority of the new voters of an identification with the newly advantaged party.[14]

While Sellers thus identifies an important theoretical role for the concept of party image in the transformation of party identifications, so far little empirical evidence has been collected with which to evaluate his theoretical claim. The scanty supporting evidence that does exist comes first from Matthews and Prothro's examination of Southern politics from 1960 to 1964. Matthews and Prothro found that the group of Democratic to Republican identification switchers between 1960 and 1964 had the most pro-Republican mean image score of any group of identification switchers,[15] that 1956–1960 Democratic behavioral "standpatters"[16] were the group with the highest mean pro-Democratic image score, and that 1956–1960 Republican standpatters were the group with the highest pro-Republican mean image score.[17] Additional supporting evidence is provided in Abney's replication of the Matthews and Prothro study. Abney found among white Mississippians in 1967 that a negative image of the Democratic Party was the major cause of individuals foreseaking their Democratic Party identifications.[18] Still, these two studies do not provide definitive evidence confirming Sellers' hypothesized role for party image in the transformation of party identifications. Neither study unambiguously measures the time at which present party identifications and present party images are acquired, so neither study can rule out the possibility that changes in identification cause individuals to change images as part of a process of rationalization of their changes in identification.[19]

To pursue more closely Sellers' claim for the theoretical role of party image, we undertake two different approaches. Our first examination — the successive cross-sectional comparisons of recall data and party image data — adds longitudinal scope to the suggestive analyses provided by Matthews and Prothro and by Abney. The second examination — the use of the panel data — sheds considerably more light on the time order of the acquisition of the attitudes in question, even though the panel data themselves will not be able to answer all of the questions concerning this time order.

STABILITY AND CHANGE IN PARTY IDENTIFICATIONS

Although our interest is in changes in party identifications, these changes can be best appreciated in proper perspective. It is clear that changes in identification are relatively few in number. Table 8.1 presents

TABLE 8.1   Cross-Tabulations of Present Party Identification by Past Party Identification, by Year

Present Party Identifica-tion[a]	Past Party Identification[a]							
	D	I[b]	R	Total	D	I[b]	R	Total
		1952				1956		
D	81.6%		21.0%	58.6%	79.7%		14.4%	51.3%
I	2.0	(63)	2.9	6.3	3.6	(97)	2.4	9.0
R	16.4		76.2	35.0	16.7		83.2	39.7
Total	100.0%		100.1%[c]	99.9%[c]	100.0%		100.0%	100.0%
(N)	(964)	(63)	(491)	(1518)	(926)	(97)	(577)	(1600)
		1960				1964		
D	79.0%		22.2	52.3%	86.3%		28.7%	62.0%
I	4.4	(113)	3.9	10.2	1.5	(259)	2.8	7.9
R	16.6		73.9	37.5	12.2		68.5	30.1
Total	100.0%		100.0%	100.0%	100.0%		100.0%	100.0%
(N)	(955)	(113)	(689)	(1797)	(2628)	(259)	(1429)	(4316)
		1968				1972		
D	78.1%		23.0%	55.6%	81.0%	24.6%	14.2%	52.7%
I	4.8	(203)	1.7	10.6	7.2	56.5	5.3	15.7
R	17.0		75.3	33.8	11.9	18.8	80.5	31.6
Total	99.9%[c]		100.0%	100.0%	99.9%[c]	99.9%[c]	100.0%	100.0%
(N)	(1779)	(203)	(882)	(2664)	(573)	(191)	(282)	(1046)

[a]Key: D = Democratic, including Independent Democrats; I = Independent; R = Republican, including Independent Republicans.

[b]Information on past Independents is incomplete except for 1972. See text and note 20.

[c]Column does not total 100.0% due to rounding error.

cross-tabulations of present identification by past identification for each year. The single most impressive fact about these data is the stability in partisan attachments that they display. Since the past attachment of present Independents is not fully probed in the questionnaires, producing the empty cells in Table 8.1, our emphasis throughout this analysis is on present partisans.[20] Among present partisans, in any one of these six surveys, three-quarters or better remember always identifying with the party they presently identify with. Except for 1956, a higher percentage of Democrats than Republicans manifests stable attachments.[21] Since throughout this electoral period, Democrats have outnumbered Republicans, and since stable attachments should be more conducive to party voting, these data indicate one further obstacle the Republican Party has had to overcome in trying to muster an electoral majority.

In any given year the percentage of Democrats recalling their past identifications as Democratic represents the percentage within the entire electorate with stable Democratic attachments. We would expect this figure to remain fairly stable from year to year unless large scale social and political forces should arise to cause realignment. At the same time, to the extent that these figures are reliable, no more than 20% or so of present Democrats, whatever year we are dealing with, remember a different previous identification. Consequently, the increase in the proportion of stable Democrats in 1964 accompanied by the decrease in the proportion of stable Republicans, both to record levels for this period, lend credence to the argument that 1964 was a critical election. Pomper and Campbell have both noted the increase in the proportion of Democratic identifiers in 1964, leading Pomper to expand the traditional classifications of American elections[22] by adding the category of "converting" elections, in which a given majority party alters its electoral base but retains its majority status.[23]

These data reveal a "normal" range of stability against which patterns of change can usefully be compared. We can pursue this comparison by examining more carefully the patterns of change in Table 8.1, which have been removed to Table 8.2 for closer scrutiny. The conversion of former Democrats to present Republicans (row 3 in Table 8.2) is reported at a constant rate of approximately 16 percentage points, with the elections of 1964 and 1972 falling closer to 12 percentage points. For all years except 1956, a higher proportion of present Democrats remembers having been Republican (row 4) than present Republicans remembers having been Democratic (row 3). This is consistent with the data in *The American Voter* that the last known electoral realignment up to 1960 occurred in the 1930s and converted Republicans and potential Republicans to the Democratic Party.[24]

These cross-tabulations are also useful for discussing party decomposition, the loosening bonds between electorate and party. The increasing number of Independents that many scholars have observed is often cited

TABLE 8.2 Stability and Change in Party Identifications, by Year[a]

Party Identification		Year					
Past	Present	1952	1956	1960	1964	1968	1972
Democratic	Democratic	81.6 (964)	79.7 (926)	79.0 (995)	86.3 (2628)	78.1 (1779)	81.0 (573)
Republican	Republican	76.2 (491)	83.2 (577)	73.9 (689)	68.5 (1429)	75.3 (882)	80.5 (282)
Democratic	Republican	16.4 (964)	16.7 (926)	16.6 (995)	12.2 (2628)	17.0 (1779)	11.9 (573)
Republican	Democratic	21.0 (491)	14.4 (577)	22.2 (689)	28.7 (1429)	23.0 (882)	14.2 (282)
Difference		-4.6	+3.3	-5.6	-14.5	-6.0	-2.3
Democratic	Non-Dem.	18.4 (964)	20.3 (926)	21.0 (995)	13.7 (2628)	21.8 (1779)	19.1 (573)
Republican	Non-Rep.	23.9 (491)	16.8 (577)	26.1 (689)	31.5 (1429)	24.7 (882)	19.5 (282)
Difference		-5.5	+3.5	-5.1	-17.8	-2.9	-0.4

[a]Entries are the percent of those with the given past identification who have the given present identification, based on the number of cases (in parentheses) with the given past identification.

as evidence of party decomposition. If decomposition is taking place, then we might expect to encounter smaller proportions of stable partisans within the electorate. The data of Table 8.3 offer mixed evidence about party decomposition.[25] The percentage of Independents has increased throughout this period (serial regression coefficient = 1.003, $p < .05$) with only one figure (for 1964) less than the figure for the preceding Presidential election year. Within this growing group of Independents, the group of stable Independents — present Independents recalling no former partisan identification — has grown fairly steadily and dramatically since 1952, so the group of Independents recalling *some* partisan attachment has shrunk. Finally, the group of stable partisans — stable Democrats and stable Republicans combined — has decreased over this time period. This decrease would seem to suggest the

TABLE 8.3   Stable Components of the American Electorate, 1952-1972

	1952	1956	1960	1964	1968	1972
(1) INDEPENDENTS as % of Electorate (N)[a]	5.9 (1729)	9.2 (1690)	10.1 (1864)	7.9 (4561)	10.8 (3049)	12.4 (1342)
(2) % of INDEPENDENTS Recalling a Previous Party Identification (D or R) (N)[b]	34.4 (96)	32.6 (144)	38.6 (184)	23.6 (339)	33.2 (304)	34.1 (164)
(3) STABLE INDEPENDENTS as % of Electorate: (1) X ((1) - (2))	3.9	6.2	6.2	6.0	7.2	8.2
(4) DEMOCRATS as % of Electorate (N)[a]	58.7 (1729)	51.9 (1690)	52.9 (1864)	61.4 (4561)	55.7 (3049)	52.2 (1342)
(5) % of DEMOCRATS Recalling Past Party Identification = D (N)[b]	88.4 (890)	89.9 (821)	83.7 (939)	84.7 (2677)	87.3 (1593)	84.2 (551)
(6) STABLE DEMOCRATS as % of Electorate: (4) X (5)	51.9	46.6	44.3	52.0	48.6	44.0
(7) REPUBLICANS as % of Electorate (N)[a]	35.4 (1729)	38.9 (1690)	37.0 (1864)	30.7 (4561)	33.5 (3049)	35.5 (1342)
(8) % of REPUBLICANS Recalling Past Party Identification = R (N)[b]	70.3 (532)	75.6 (635)	75.5 (674)	75.3 (1300)	68.7 (967)	68.6 (331)
(9) STABLE REPUBLICANS as % of Electorate: (7) X (8)	24.9	29.4	27.9	23.1	23.0	24.1
(10) STABLE PARTISANS as % of Electorate: (6) + (9)	76.8	76.0	72.2	75.1	71.6	68.1

[a] Based on all respondents assigned to one of the seven categories on the summary party identification scale.
[b] Based on individuals for whom past identification information is available (see Table 8.1).

presence of party decomposition, as would the increase in the proportion of Independents, but the increase in the proportion of stable Independents would not.

Changing patterns in attitudinal data, such as in partisan attachments, may manifest either party decomposition or party realignment (or neither). For instance, if we imagine an individual voter who is about to change his party identification, say from Democratic to Republican, we can predict that the strength of his new Republican attachment will not be as great next year as it will be in 10 years. Strength of partisan attachment is a function of the length of attachment.[26] Consequently, the behavior of this convert to Republicanism may not differ very much next year from that of the nonpartisan. That is, this new Republican identifier may split his ticket, may vote less frequently, and may be more like the Democratic identifiers he is leaving than long-time Republican identifiers are like those Democratic identifiers. But these behavioral traits are the kinds of characteristics frequently mentioned as evidence of the declining impact of party identification, when in fact we see that all they manifest in this hypothetical individual is change in party identification.

Therefore, it may be difficult methodologically to separate the two processes, especially when the evidence is not clear cut. For instance, in Table 8.3 the downward trend in the size of the stable partisan group is broken sharply in 1964, only to start up again in 1968. Here, then, the 1964 election stands out, but deviates from a trend rather than reverses it. Therefore even this distinctiveness is not sufficient evidence of realignment. Furthermore, even if we accept the argument that a "realigning era" is a more useful theoretical concept than that of "realigning election,"[27] we still cannot find positive proof of realignment, since this trend extends across too long a time span even for the concept of "realigning era." Consequently, although these data do not rule out the possibility of realignment within this 20-year period, they do tentatively suggest that party decomposition has occurred. Below we shall encounter evidence of realignment, however.

Despite the possible party decomposition in this period, partisan change has not been great, so the thrust of these data is to reaffirm the stability of party identifications among Americans. Nevertheless, changes in identification have occurred and stability and meaningful change can be reconciled parsimoniously by introducing the concept of party image, to which we now turn.

PARTY IMAGE AND STABILITY AND
CHANGE IN PARTY IDENTIFICATIONS

The stability of party identifications and the changes in identification that do occur are both related to individual party images. When these images reinforce party identification, stability in identification is observed. When images are in conflict with identification, identifications are much more likely to be altered. The data in Table 8.4 document these conclusions.

The table presents the relationship between patterns of party identification stability and change and party image for each of the six Presidential election years under consideration. For any given year, the table presents the percentage of individuals with a given past identification who have the same identification in the present as well as the percentage of past identifiers who have a different identification in the present, by party image. Present Independents have been excluded, so columns often total less than 100%. For instance, in 1952, of those who had had a past Democratic identification, 98.0% of the strongly pro-Democratic party image-holders (DD) had a present Democratic party identification, and 0.4% had a present Republican party identification. Similarly, in 1952, of those who had had a past Republican party identification, 13.6% of the neutral image-holders (N) had a present Democratic party identification, and 72.7% had a present Republican identification.

Among individuals with past Democratic identifications, the more pro-Democratic the party image, the greater the likelihood that present identification will be Democratic. Among individuals with past Republican identification, the more pro-Republican the party image, the greater the likelihood that present identification will be Republican. About 95% of individuals with past Democratic identifications who also have strongly pro-Democratic party images will have present Democratic identifications; about 95% of the individuals with past Republican identifications who have strongly pro-Republican party images will have present Republican identifications. Thus the role of party image in inducing stability of identification can be seen.

When party image is not so strongly directed toward the party one identified with in the past, there is a smaller likelihood that one will retain that past identification. In fact, the more one's party image favors the party one did *not* identify with in the past, the more likely is one to convert to that party in the present. That is, among individuals with *past Democratic identifications with strongly pro-Republican party images,* only one-third or less still identify with the Democratic Party. This is to be compared with the 95% or higher figures of *past Democratic identifiers with strongly pro-Democratic images* who identify in the present with the Democratic Party. (Compare columns 1 and 5 in Table 8.4.) Similarly, among past Republican identifiers who have strongly pro-Democratic party

TABLE 8.4 The Relationship Between Patterns of Party Identification and Party Image, by Year[a]

Year	Present Party Identification[b]	Past Party Identification[b]									
		Democratic					Republican				
		DD[c]	D	N	R	RR	DD	D	N	R	RR
1952	Dem.	98.0	93.0	80.0	60.4	35.6	85.2	58.7	25.0	12.0	5.3
	Rep.	0.4	6.1	16.2	36.8	61.4	14.8	36.5	71.4	84.8	92.5
	(N)	(244)	(345)	(130)	(144)	(101)	(27)	(63)	(56)	(158)	(187)
1956	Dem.	100.0	92.9	73.3	41.7	7.7	86.7	50.7	11.1	4.3	0.0
	Rep.	0.0	4.6	17.0	52.5	90.4	13.3	43.3	84.6	94.3	98.5
	(N)	(223)	(366)	(165)	(120)	(52)	(30)	(67)	(117)	(230)	(133)
1960	Dem.	100.0	92.2	73.8	32.4	29.8	94.9	58.4	13.6	8.6	0.0
	Rep.	0.0	5.7	18.2	56.1	61.7	3.4	31.7	72.7	91.1	100.0
	(N)	(198)	(424)	(187)	(139)	(47)	(59)	(101)	(110)	(269)	(150)
1964	Dem.	98.4	94.5	86.6	57.3	14.3	91.4	67.4	24.8	7.5	2.6
	Rep.	1.6	4.1	11.6	37.6	85.7	8.6	27.5	70.6	90.6	97.4
	(N)	(550)	(1118)	(560)	(295)	(105)	(81)	(316)	(327)	(477)	(228)
1968	Dem.	96.5	96.1	78.9	54.4	25.3	100.0	62.0	26.8	12.0	3.4
	Rep.	1.2	1.9	13.0	38.2	68.0	0.0	34.7	69.5	86.5	96.6
	(N)	(268)	(621)	(399)	(351)	(150)	(37)	(121)	(164)	(326)	(234)
1972	Dem.	98.7	93.5	75.9	55.4	35.3	85.7	62.1	9.8	5.3	2.4
	Rep.	1.3	2.8	8.0	39.1	64.7	14.3	24.1	82.6	91.2	97.6
	(N)	(76)	(214)	(174)	(92)	(17)	(7)	(29)	(92)	(115)	(41)

[a]Entries are the percent of the party image category with present party identification as given. Numbers of cases on which percents are based are in parentheses.

[b]Key: Dem. = Democratic, including Independent Democrats; Rep. = Republican, including Independent Republicans. Past Independents are excluded since information for them is incomplete.

[c]Party Image categories. Key: DD = Strongly pro-Democratic; D = Mildly pro-Democratic; N = Neutral; R = Mildly pro-Republican; RR = Strongly pro-Republican.

187

images, very few identify with the Republican Party in the present — no more than 14.8% (1952) and as few as 0.0% (1968). These figures should be compared with the 92.5% or higher figures of past Republicans with strongly pro-Republican party images who still identify in the present with the Republican Party. (Compare columns 6 and 10.) Thus the role of party image in inducing change in party identification is also seen.

When extreme positive images are projected by the party one identified with in the past, an individual is very likely to retain this past identification. Thus extreme images *consistent* with past identifications are conducive to stable identifications. At the same time, when extreme positive images are projected by the party one did *not* identify with in the past, an individual is very likely to forsake this past identification. Thus extreme positive images *inconsistent* with past identification are conducive to changing identifications.

If we return to the data of Table 8.1, we can "postdict"[28] present party identification from past identification with fairly good success because of the general stability in identifications among Americans. That is, past Democrats are very likely to be present Democrats and past Republicans are very likely to be present Republicans. If we were to predict that present identification would be the same as past identification, the errors we would make are the cases that appear in the nonmodal cells of each column in Table 8.1: among past Democratic identifiers, the present identifications of individuals who actually became present Independents or present Republicans would have been predicted incorrectly; among past Republican identifiers, the identifications of present Independents and present Democratic identifiers would have been predicted incorrectly. The general stability of identifications leads to predictive success, but, despite this success, we can improve on our predictions by considering present party images.

If we ignore past Independents for whom information is incomplete the question becomes whether or not we can better predict present identification with the use of the party image construct in addition to past identification. Within the categories of past identification given in Table 8.4, we have seen that party image is strongly related to present party identification. In Table 8.4, within each category of party image, cases that are in nonmodal present party identification cells constitute errors, as they were when we attempted to predict present identifications. When we use party image categories for these predictions of present party identification, the number of errors is reduced sharply for every year, by as much as 33.2% in 1960, as compared to predictions made only on the basis of party identification.

It is important to realize that we are not comparing directly the ability of past identification and the ability of present party image to predict present identification. Our theoretical thrust, according to Sellers' argument, is to determine whether past identifications change in response to party images. That is, do party images play an intervening role crucial to the transformation of past identifications to present identifications? Consequently, it is appropriate to examine the predictive ability of party image while controlling for past party identification. The data of Table 8.5 let us evaluate the predictive ability of the party image construct.

If we use only past party identification, approximately 20% of our predictions would be wrong (row 3 of Table 8.5). However, if we are given past party identification and present party image, our predictions of present party identification will involve considerably fewer errors, ranging from a high reduction in error of 33.2% to a low of 12.8% in 1960 and 1972 respectively (row 6). In other words, we increase our ability to predict from past party identification to present party identification if we include the apparently intervening variable of party image.[29]

The predictive power of party image in combination with past identification, although consistently greater than past party identification alone, is itself variable. Row (6) in Table 8.5 traces the percent reduction in errors over time; the figures rise to a peak in 1960 and 1964 and then fall. The transition role of party image seems to have been greatest in 1960 and 1964 but has declined sharply since 1964. It is difficult to interpret these data, but if we return to Sellers' argument, we may be able to make sense of them. In the critical role that party image is said to have in transforming party identification, the impact of party image varies over time. Before a realignment begins, party image apparently would have very little impact. In the midst of realignment, its impact would be great. As the forces producing realignment ebb, as realignment ebbs, as the critical issues producing realignment are resolved, the impact of party image would also decline. Consequently, these data are consistent with the argument that an electoral realignment occurred within this 20-year period, and that it occurred around 1964.

This is not to say that these data alone prove that a realignment occurred. Row (6) traces the ability of party image to predict present party identification — the peak in 1960–1964 does not mean that more identification changes took place in this four-year period. However, we

TABLE 8.5   Errors in Predicting Present Party Identification from Past Party Identification, With and Without the Intervening Variable of Party Image, and from Party Image Alone, by Year

	Year					
	1952	1956	1960	1964	1968	1972
(1) Total Predictions: # of Past Democratic and Republican Identifiers	1455	1503	1684	4057	2661	855
(2) # of Errors Predicting Present Identification from Past Identification only	294	285	389	811	607	164
(3) Errors as % of Total Predictions: (2)/(1)	20.2	19.0	23.1	20.0	22.8	19.2
(4) # of Errors Predicting Present Identification from Party Image, Controlling for Past Democratic and Republican Identification	235	202	260	543	473	143
(5) Reduction in Errors: (4)-(2)	59	83	129	268	124	21
(6) % Reduction in Errors: (5)/(2)	20.1	29.1	33.2	33.0	22.1	12.8
(7) Total Predictions: # of Present Democratic and Republican Identifiers[a]	1729	1690	1864	4561	3049	1342
(8) # of Errors Predicting Present Identification from Party Image Only	401	419	471	1118	897	453
(9) Errors as % of Total Predictions: (8)/(7)	23.2	24.8	25.2	24.5	29.4	33.8

[a]Number of usable cases for item (7) is considerably greater than for item (1).

have already encountered evidence relevant to this discussion. We have noted that 1964 marked a high point in Republican to Democratic and in Republican to non-Republican conversions and a low point in Democratic to Republican conversions (see Table 8.2). Furthermore, despite the fact that a high proportion of voters were classified as stable Partisans in 1964 (74.1%), at the same time the proportion of stable Republicans reached a low point (21.1%) for this 20-year period (see Table 8.3).

It is difficult to separate out the idiosyncratic and theoretically less interesting aspects of the 1964 election from those aspects that manifest forces of underlying, durable social and electoral change. Burnham argues that realignment-like phenomena occurred in 1964, producing social groupings that resembled those of 1896.[30] Pomper and Campbell both note the abnormally high conversion rate in 1964 of former Republicans to Democratic identifications.[31] Yet the highly negative personal appeal of the Republican candidate cannot be discounted,[32] and it is difficult to know whether conversions, through party image or otherwise, were more the result of the idiosyncratic candidate factor than of other more interesting theoretical matters. Nevertheless the evidence provides indirect support for the contention that 1964 was a critical election, to complement the argument that party decomposition has occurred.

It is also important to realize that Tables 8.4 and 8.5 display a significant and substantively important interaction between party image and party identification. In predicting present identification from party image, controlling for past identification, we improve our predictive abilities beyond what they would be if we predict present identification on the basis of past identification alone. But we also improve them beyond what they would be if we predict present identification on the basis only of present party image, as Table 8.5 shows. The propensity of strongly pro-Democratic image-holders to be presently identified with the Democratic Party is stronger than the propensity of pro-Republican image-holders, but specifying past party identification serves also to specify this propensity: the propensity of strongly pro-Democratic image-holders to be presently identified with the Democratic Party is greater for past Democratic identifiers than for past Republican identifiers.

PARTY IMAGE AND STABILITY AND CHANGE
IN PARTY IDENTIFICATIONS
AMONG SRC PANEL MEMBERS

Returning to the role of party image in inducing stability or change in party identifications, we note that the data of Table 8.4 would offer better evidence of this role if we were able to demonstrate that present party images had in fact been developed before present party identifications were acquired. Unfortunately, the survey instruments that generated the above data do not ask respondents when they developed their present party images — when they came to like and dislike the parties to the extent that they presently do. It is possible that present identifications in some cases caused individuals to develop the images we have measured. That is, individuals may rationalize present party identifications by adopting images consistent with present identifications.[33] The SRC panel study permits us to measure party identification and party image at three different points in time, so we can better determine whether identification changes induce or respond to party images. Unfortunately, the SRC panel data are somewhat contaminated by period effects including the recession of 1958 and the religious issue in 1960, so that they neither unambiguously nor definitively permit one to unravel the processes of electoral change.

When we examine the ability of party image to induce change in party identification among panel members, we find that this ability is considerably weaker than Table 8.4 would suggest but is nonetheless real. Table 8.6 replicates Table 8.4 for panel members only and provides better (although still not complete) information about the time sequence of attitude development. For instance, among Republican identifiers in 1956, consistent images induced stability in identification; 93.1% of those with strongly pro-Republican images in *1956* retained their Republican identifications in 1958. Among 1956 Republican identifiers, inconsistent images induced change in identification; 38.7% of those with mildly pro-Democratic images became Democratic identifiers by 1958.

Consistency of attitudes is unambiguously associated with stability. Where images and identifications reinforce each other, identifications endure. This finding is not surprising and does little to define the role of party image in the acquisition of identifications. After all, the 1956 identification might still have been rationalized by (i.e., might have preceded) the 1956 image. The crucial test for the role of party image begins by examining its ability to induce change in identification when image and identification are inconsistent at time 1. Table 8.6 reveals that identification is indeed somewhat more likely to change when image and identification at time 1 conflict than when they do not. But the test for the role of party image is complete only when we determine whether individuals whose image and identification conflict at time 1 retain their same image at time 2 while they alter their identification to conform with their stable images. Unless images are stable for individuals who change

TABLE 8.6 The Relationship Between Patterns of Party Identification and Party Image Among SRC Panel Members

	Present Party Identification	Past Party Identification									
		Democratic					Republican				
		Party Image[a]					Party Image[a]				
		DD	D	N	R	RR	DD	D	N	R	RR
1956–1958	Democratic	98.8	95.1	93.3	84.8	100.0	0.0	38.7	27.2	7.2	3.4
	Republican	0.6	2.8	3.3	8.7	0.0	100.0	51.6	65.4	87.2	93.1
	(N)	(165)	(246)	(90)	(46)	(4)	(3)	(31)	(81)	(195)	(116)
1958–1960	Democratic	93.3	91.0	84.5	92.0	100.0	0.0	8.9	9.6	4.9	1.7
	Republican	1.3	4.8	8.6	8.0	0.0	100.0	73.3	84.0	93.0	96.6
	(N)	(150)	(310)	(116)	(25)	(1)	(4)	(45)	(94)	(185)	(58)
1956–1960	Democratic	93.9	93.0	85.7	78.3	100.0	0.0	30.0	18.3	10.8	4.4
	Republican	2.4	3.3	6.6	10.9	0.0	66.7	66.7	69.5	82.0	92.0
	(N)	(164)	(243)	(91)	(46)	(4)	(3)	(30)	(82)	(194)	(113)

[a]For the 1956–1958 party identification data, party images are measured in 1956; for the 1958–1960 party identification data, party images are measured in 1958; for the 1956–1960 party identification data, party images are measured in 1956.

identifications, it is possible that the change in identification is not caused by party image but instead will be rationalized in turn by (i.e., will precede) a change in image.

At this point the evidence becomes much less satisfactory and less convincing. First, one should notice in Table 8.6 the interesting finding that the apparent ability of party image to induce change in party identification is restricted to past Republican identifiers. Of individuals who were Democratic identifiers in 1956 or 1958, those with pro-Republican images in the same year are *not* more likely to become Republican identifiers by the next measurement point. Methodologically this means that there are few converts in Table 8.6 whose conversions seem to have been stimulated by party image, and thus few cases with which to investigate the enduring stability of party image and its role in the conversion of party identifications.

When we investigate the stability of the party images that seem to have induced change in party identification, we find mixed and tenuous results. Table 8.7 presents party identification and party image data for 1960 for those individuals in 1956 with Republican identifications and pro-Democratic party images. We have already seen in Table 8.6 that among 1956 Republican identifiers, the more pro-Democratic the 1956 party image, the more likely the individual would have a Democratic identification in 1958. Too few individuals are found in Table 8.7 to provide much evidence one way or the other about the role of party image. Of the 33 individuals in Table 8.7, 17 have retained stable

TABLE 8.7 Party Identification and Party Image Data for 1960 for SRC Panel Members with Republican Party Identifications in 1956 and with Pro-Democratic Party Images in 1956

1960 Party Identification	1960 Party Image					
	DD	D	N	R	RR	Total
Democratic	1	6	2	0	0	9
Independent	1	0	1	0	0	2
Republican	1	8	4	5	4	22
Total	3	14	7	5	4	N = 33

pro-Democratic images, and these images seem to have induced the change in identification for 8 of the 17. But the 16 others clearly have forsaken the image we hypothesized was responsible for the change in identification. Assuming for the moment that these cases were sufficiently numerous for valid generalization, we would conclude that for some individuals images do in fact seem capable of inducing change in identification. For other individuals, images possibly are rationalizations of change in identification, since change in image *follows* change in identification. More importantly, however, we must note that there are so few cases in the table that not only are these generalizations not statistically valid, but substantively the role of party image in inducing party identification change seems clearly limited.

AN EVALUATION OF THE PANEL
DATA FOR THE STUDY OF PARTY
IMAGE AND PARTY IDENTIFICATION

What do these panel data tell us about the role of party image in inducing change in party identification? We have just argued that they clearly limit the number of individuals whose conversions could reasonably be attributed to party image, even if the data of Table 8.6 suggested such a role. In fact there is stronger evidence that party images in 1956 were related to party identifications in 1958, which we shall encounter shortly, but first some observations are in order about the nature of the panel design.

Data from a 1956–1960 panel are not very useful for secondary analysis of party images. We have seen that party images in the aggregate at least were more volatile after 1960 than before 1960. Significantly, so were party identifications. Consequently, the 1956–1960 panel may reasonably be expected to underestimate the change in these attitudes which might occur in other time periods. Earlier in this chapter we encountered evidence that party identification conversions were more numerous between 1960 and 1964 than between any other two successive measurement points over the 1952–1972 period (even though the ability of party image to predict conversion was greatest in the 1956–1960 period). Thus the weak evidence in Tables 8.6 and 8.7 of the role of party image in transforming party identifications, combined with somewhat stronger evidence we shall encounter below, leaves open the possibility that party images may in fact be able to alter identifications.

But the data from the panel study are useful in alerting us to probable rationalization among many Americans. No doubt data on the role of party image in changing party identifications, which we examined in the aggregate in Table 8.4, overestimated the real impact of party image and reflected a good deal of rationalization. How much rationalization is involved is difficult to determine; the amount depends not only on how real a role party image plays from time to time in the conversion of identifications, but also on what stimuli exist in the political environment which might affect the individual's unconscious need to rationalize change in identification. For instance, among Southern whites it probably was psychologically more difficult to justify a change from Democratic to Republican identification and more necessary to rationalize such a change when so many of one's neighbors were Democratic, but as more and more of one's neighbors became Republican (through their own conversions or through population turnover), it became easier to convert and there was probably less psychological pressure on the individual to justify or rationalize such conversion.[34] And as well-known figures such as Strom Thurmond themselves converted, it would become only that much easier to do so.

Finally, if identification sometimes changes in response to short-term political phenomena, as Brody suggests,[35] it would be interesting to know whether such short-term phenomena first penetrate the individual's party image.

So far, in other words, the data must be interpreted to mean that the proposition that party images can transform party identifications requires further investigation. For some individuals, apparently, the proposition is correct; for others, no doubt it is incorrect. Even the panel data are ambiguous with regard to the very advantage they supposedly possess; there is no way to determine when or how frequently between each measurement point in the study party images changed, and consequently, no way of determining whether such behavior was "reasonable" or "rationalizing." Without more adequate measures of when and not just if images change, the role of party image in inducing change in party identification must remain unresolved.

PATTERNS OF PARTISAN ATTACHMENTS

We can now examine specific patterns of partisan attachments over time. If party image completely determined present party identifications, then all individuals with a given party image score would have the same party identifications, but this is clearly not the case. We argued earlier that it is the interactive pattern of party image with past party identification that produces present identification, and we now examine this interaction.

Matthews and Prothro reported that patterns of stability and change in party identifications from 1960 to 1964 were strongly related to party images among Southerners. By classifying individuals according to pattern of party identification (past-present), Matthews and Prothro showed that Republican to Democratic identification switchers had the most pro-Democratic mean party image score and Democratic to Republican switchers had the most pro-Republican mean party image score, of all identification switchers.[36] But Matthews and Prothro relied on recall data for their measurements of switches in party identification,[37] so their analysis is limited by too little information about the sequence of attitude formation.

We replicate the Matthews and Prothro analysis here in two ways. First, using recall data as they did, we compare changes in party identification to party images, for each of the six election years. Second, we replicate their analysis among members of the SRC/CPS panel, for whom we use actual past party identification rather than recalled party identification in order to more precisely measure change in party identification. We are interested in determining whether party images at time 1 affect change in party identification between times 1 and 2.

Beginning with the recall data, Table 8.8 presents mean party image scores for groups of party identification switchers and standpatters. The stable partisans in Table 8.8 (D→D and R→R) generally have the most extreme mean party image scores. Stable Democratic identifiers have the most pro-Democratic mean party image score and stable Republican identifiers have the most pro-Republican mean party image score. Stability and extreme party images are thus related once again. Among switchers, those who moved further in their identifications (R→D, D→R) have more extreme mean party image scores than others (R→I, D→I).

TABLE 8.8 Mean Party Image Scores by Pattern of Party Identification, by Year[a]

Year	Pattern of Party Identification[b]							Entire Electorate
	D→D	R→D	D→I	I→I	R→I	D→R	R→R	
1952	-2.09	-1.03	+0.32	+0.71	+2.29	+2.67	+3.30	-0.01
(N)	(787)	(103)	(19)	(63)	(14)	(158)	(374)	(1783)
1956	-2.39	-2.21	-0.03	-0.11	+0.85	+2.03	+2.07	-0.41
(N)	(738)	(83)	(33)	(97)	(14)	(155)	(480)	(1759)
1960	-2.15	-2.36	+0.55	-0.66	-0.63	+1.45	+2.33	-0.35
(N)	(786)	(153)	(44)	(113)	(27)	(165)	(509)	(1928)
1964	-1.98	-1.60	+0.23	-0.10	-0.13	+1.76	+1.85	-0.61
(N)	(2267)	(410)	(40)	(259)	(40)	(321)	(979)	(4551)
1968	-1.40	-1.18	+0.58	+0.33	+0.33	+2.59	+2.55	+0.16
(N)	(1390)	(203)	(86)	(203)	(15)	(303)	(664)	(3056)
1972	-1.35	-1.08	-0.02	+0.01	-0.07	+1.43	+1.58	-0.19
(N)	(464)	(40)	(41)	(108)	(15)	(68)	(227)	(1361)

[a]Means are based on the 21-point party image index (13-point in 1972).

[b]Past Party Identification is listed to the left of the arrow, Present Party Identification to the right of the arrow. Key: R = Republican; I = Independent; D = Democratic. Independent Republicans and Independent Democrats are coded as partisans, not as Independents. Past Independents who are present partisans are not included because information is unavailable for them.

Consequently, two general points emerge. First, with regard to mean party image scores, there is a constant rank ordering of five categories into which can be placed the seven patterns of partisan attachment: (1) stable Democrats, (2) converts to Democratic identification, (3) converts to and stable Independents, (4) converts to Republican identification, and (5) stable Republicans. These groups have, respectively, the least pro-Republican to the most pro-Republican mean party image scores. Not surprisingly, the least precision to this rank ordering occurs when assigning a classification to the three groups of category number 3: Democratic converts to Independents (D→I), Republican converts to Independents (R→I), and stable Independents (I→I). The greater volatility of Independents has been well documented[38] and seems to manifest itself again here.

Second, a "strain toward consistency"[39] apparently operates on these two attitudinal dimensions. Mean party image scores are very much in line with *present* party identifications. The two present Democratic identification groups (D→D, R→D) are together at the pro-Democratic party image end of the continuum, the three present Independent groups (D→I, R→I, I→I) are together in the middle, and the present Republican identification groups (D→R, R→R) are together at the pro-Republican end of the continuum. These data reveal the striking relationship between party image and present party identification — the consistency that individuals attain, consciously or not, in party image and present party identification.

Of course party image measurements were made at the same time as respondents were asked to recall whether they had ever had a different party identification, so as with the Matthews and Prothro data, the data of this table leave unanswered the question about the time order of change in party identification and development of party image. Our second analysis thus utilizes panel data and would seem to offer striking evidence of the ability of party images to induce change in party identification. Tables 8.9, 8.10, and 8.11 present mean party image scores for all the possible combinations of party identification at two moments in

TABLE 8.9   Mean 1956 Party Image Scores for Each Combination of 1956 and 1958 Party Identifications

1958 Party Identification	1956 Party Identification						
	SD	WD	ID	I	IR	WR	SR
	Mean 1956 Party Image Scores						
Strong Democrat	-3.25 (179)	-2.50 (84)	-2.62 (13)	-0.67 (6)	-0.33 (3)	+0.33 (3)	+2.20 (5)
Weak Democrat	-2.73 (45)	-1.32 (134)	-1.08 (26)	-0.29 (14)	+0.90 (10)	-0.23 (13)	+2.25 (4)
Independent Democrat	-5.50 (2)	-2.35 (17)	-2.13 (24)	-1.36 (11)	0.00 (10)	+0.67 (3)	-1.00 (1)
Independent	-2.00 (1)	-1.00 (5)	-0.17 (6)	0.00 (37)	+0.93 (15)	+2.13 (8)	+1.00 (1)
Independent Republican	---- (0)	---- (0)	---- (0)	+0.87 (15)	+2.21 (24)	+1.39 (13)	+2.44 (9)
Weak Republican	-1.00 (1)	-1.20 (5)	-0.25 (4)	+0.86 (7)	+1.74 (23)	+1.46 (93)	+2.82 (49)
Strong Republican	-0.50 (4)	---- (0)	0.00 (1)	-1.33 (3)	+2.42 (12)	+2.44 (27)	+3.06 (100)

TABLE 8.10 Mean 1958 Party Image Scores for Each Combination of 1958 and 1960 Party Identifications

1960 Party Identification	1958 Party Identification						
	SD	WD	ID	I	IR	WR	SR
	Mean 1958 Party Image Scores						
Strong	-3.24	-1.72	-2.00	-2.50	----	0.00	+0.50
Democrat	(195)	(61)	(6)	(4)	(0)	(3)	(2)
Weak	-2.68	-1.39	-1.47	-0.75	+0.43	+0.50	+3.50
Democrat	(72)	(143)	(17)	(8)	(7)	(4)	(2)
Independent	-2.20	-1.50	-2.56	-0.80	+1.00	-1.00	----
Democrat	(5)	(20)	(25)	(5)	(4)	(1)	(0)
Independent	-3.57	-1.64	-1.73	-0.35	-0.56	-0.78	+10.00
	(7)	(11)	(11)	(40)	(9)	(9)	(1)
Independent	-3.00	-0.86	-0.86	+0.23	+1.10	+0.73	+1.89
Republican	(2)	(7)	(7)	(13)	(20)	(22)	(9)
Weak	+2.00	-1.25	-7.00	-1.00	+1.00	+0.88	+2.27
Republican	(1)	(8)	(1)	(6)	(14)	(93)	(30)
Strong	0.00	+1.00	----	----	+1.63	+1.50	+2.41
Republican	(1)	(2)	(0)	(0)	(8)	(48)	(100)

TABLE 8.11 Mean 1956 Party Image Scores for Each Combination of 1956 and 1960 Party Identifications

1960 Party Identification	1956 Party Identification						
	SD	WD	ID	I	IR	WR	SR
Strong	-3.12	-1.91	-2.57	-2.25	+1.00	-0.67	+3.20
Democrat	(164)	(75)	(14)	(4)	(4)	(3)	(5)
Weak	-3.02	-1.82	-0.92	+0.14	+1.00	+0.53	+1.33
Democrat	(56)	(124)	(24)	(14)	(12)	(17)	(3)
Independent	-3.33	-1.78	-1.94	-0.43	+0.33	+0.67	----
Democrat	(6)	(18)	(17)	(14)	(3)	(3)	(0)
Independent	-9.00	-1.75	-1.07	+0.06	+1.00	+0.92	+2.50
	(1)	(12)	(14)	(34)	(15)	(13)	(2)
Independent	----	-0.83	-3.00	+0.33	+1.39	+1.00	+3.62
Republican	(0)	(6)	(3)	(15)	(31)	(12)	(13)
Weak	-2.00	-1.17	+1.00	+0.67	+2.17	+1.34	+2.82
Republican	(1)	(6)	(1)	(9)	(24)	(73)	(38)
Strong	0.00	-0.50	0.00	-0.50	+2.71	+2.46	+2.89
Republican	(3)	(2)	(1)	(2)	(7)	(39)	(105)

time among the three-wave panel respondents. Each table is a seven by seven matrix, representing the 49 combinations of the party identification categories over two points in time. The entry in each of these 49 cells is the mean party image score for all individuals with the respective combination of party identifications. If party images in 1956 are associated with change in party identification between 1956 and 1958 or between 1956 and 1960, then reading down any of the columns in Table 8.9 or 8.11 should reveal decreasing mean pro-Democratic images and increasing mean pro-Republican images. At the same time, reading across any row reveals the extent to which party images were related to party identification at time 1, among individuals with a given identification at time 2.

Dealing with the latter topic first, the three tables reveal strong and what should now be unsurprising evidence that the more Republican the party identification at time 1, the more pro-Republican the mean party image at time 1. Whatever the party identification had come to be at time 2, the identification at time 1 clearly was related to party image at time 1.

What is more interesting for our purposes is the finding that party images at time *1* seem to strongly affect party identifications at time *2*. In general, reading down any column in these three tables reveals that the mean party image score becomes decreasingly Democratic and increasingly Republican. Of course the absolute values of the means vary greatly from one column to the next, so there is a clear interaction between past party identification and *past* party image in affecting *present* party identification. For those Democratic identifiers in 1956 who were to become Republican identifiers in 1958, the 1956 mean party image was more pro-Republican than for those 1956 Democratic identifiers who were to remain Democratic identifiers in 1958. Among those 1956 Republican identifiers, those who were to become Democratic identifiers in 1958 had less pro-Republican mean party images in 1956 than those who were to remain Republican identifiers.

The patterns in Tables 8.9, 8.10, and 8.11 are confused somewhat by the low number of cases in many of the cells, but "correcting" these low numbers of cases by averaging them with numbers for adjacent cells only makes the means fit the pattern more strongly.[40] Consequently, this evidence supports the proposition that images can induce change in party identification. Since, however, we have already examined other evidence more ambiguous if not contradictory with regard to this proposition, the conservative position is to maintain at this point only that the proposition requires further examination, and that some preliminary evidence suggests its validity. Again, if party images were more stable between time 1 and time 2, the thrust of Tables 8.9, 8.10, and 8.11 would be all the more striking.

The use of recall data to compare change in identification with party image required the measurement of party image and party identification at time 2, and a recall measurement at time 2 of party identification at time 1 or otherwise (this analysis and that by Matthews and Prothro did not control for the specific time). The data were consistent with the argument that party images can induce change in party identification, but the argument was inconclusive because of the possibility that party images at time 2 followed party identifications at time 2 in some sort of rationalization process. To overcome this problem somewhat we examined the panel data which showed that party images at time *1* were strongly related to party identification at time *2*, and would have been more conclusive about the ability of party image to induce change in party identification if other evidence had not shown that between time 1 and time 2, party images are not necessarily stable.

PARTY IMAGE AND THE VOTE

We have examined the ramifications of party image for partisan stability and change. The final impact of party image can be seen in Table 8.12 in its apparent ability to affect the voting preference of individuals whose party identifications it has converted. With only one exception, individuals whose identifications apparently have been converted by extreme images are more loyal in their voting than party identifiers generally. Individuals who were past Republican identifiers, and who now possess strongly pro-Democratic party images, and who presently identify with the Democratic Party (column 2), are more likely to vote Democratic than all present Democratic identifiers (column 1). Individuals who were past Democratic identifiers, and who now possess strongly pro-Republican party images, and who presently identify with the Republican Party (column 12), are more likely to vote Republican than all present Republican identifiers (column 7). This is all the more remarkable given the high Republican voting rates of Republican identifiers.

Thus party images seem to convert individual identifications when past identifications are inconsistent with present images. In so doing,

TABLE 8.12 The Impact of Party Image on Voting Preferences of Converted Partisan Identifiers, by Year

Year	% Voting Democratic Among ALL Present Democratic Identifiers	% Voting Democratic Among Present Democratic Identifiers with Past Republican Identification, By Party Image[a]					% Voting Republican Among ALL Republican Identifiers	% Voting Republican Among Present Republican Identifiers with Past Democratic Identification, By Party Image[a]				
		DD	D	N	R	RR		DD	D	N	R	RR
1952 (N)	70.5 (654)	100.0 (18)	89.3 (28)	44.0 (9)	0.0 (11)	0.0 (10)	95.7 (460)	0.0 (1)	76.9 (13)	100.0 (16)	95.6 (45)	100.0 (57)
1956 (N)	73.7 (634)	95.8 (24)	77.8 (27)	70.0 (10)	12.5 (8)	100.0 (2)	95.7 (511)	b	92.3 (13)	95.0 (20)	100.0 (55)	100.0 (44)
1960 (N)	81.8 (719)	77.8 (45)	95.0 (40)	57.1 (7)	17.6 (17)	b	92.2 (565)	b	66.7 (15)	100.0 (31)	98.6 (74)	92.0 (25)
1964 (N)	89.3 (1997)	100.0 (74)	98.5 (196)	95.5 (66)	36.4 (33)	50.0 (6)	73.5 (1116)	0.0 (6)	32.6 (46)	42.4 (59)	75.8 (99)	93.1 (87)
1968 (N)	67.2 (1038)	92.0 (25)	66.7 (57)	46.2 (26)	17.2 (29)	100.0 (6)	86.3 (768)	0.0 (1)	60.0 (10)	95.8 (48)	94.1 (102)	95.7 (92)
1972 (N)	57.4 (494)	100.0 (4)	53.3 (15)	0.0 (4)	0.0 (5)	0.0 (1)	97.2 (394)	b	100.0 (4)	91.7 (12)	100.0 (33)	100.0 (11)

a Key: DD = Strongly pro-Democratic; D = Mildly pro-Democratic; N = Neutral; R = Mildly pro-Republican; RR = Strongly pro-Republican.

b No respective identifiers on whom to base a percent.

images seem to create a set of converts whose fidelity cannot be surpassed. (The figures in columns 2 and 12 are close to or equal to 100%.) In other words, we find an example, among extreme image-holders, of individuals about whom we might claim, "there is none so fanatical as the convert." Furthermore, we see that the more extreme the party image of these converts, the greater the likelihood that they will vote for the party they presently identify with (read from column 6 to column 2 or from column 8 to column 12). When individuals change party identification because of strong party images, their fanatical voting support thus distinguishes them not only from present party identifiers generally, but also from changers in general, such as the hypothetical changer discussed earlier, who behaves in a more inconsistent fashion.

Finally, among individuals for whom party images do not reinforce present identifications (columns 5, 6, 8, and 9), voting support for the party one presently identifies with is severely reduced. Thus when party image reinforces present identification, it fortifies voting loyalty; when party image conflicts with present identification it weakens voting loyalty.

There simply are too few panel members whose identification has apparently been converted by party image to probe the impact of such conversion on voting behavior. Table 8.13 presents some relevant data. For instance, among 1958 Democratic identifiers who became Republican identifiers by 1960, the more pro-Republican the 1958 party image, the greater the percent voting Republican in 1960. Voting support does not, however, exceed that of all Republican identifiers.

CONCLUSION

We have been able to present cross-sectional data consistent with Sellers' theory that party images play a crucial role in the transformation of party identifications. When party images reinforce past identifications, identifications are stable. When party images conflict with past identifications, identifications are likely to be altered. Thus there is a systematic pattern to stability and change in identification, and a parsimonious theory — that of the role of party image — seems able to account for such diverse behavior as stable and unstable partisanship. Party images seem also to affect the voting preference of individuals who have experienced change.

TABLE 8.13   The Impact of Party Image on Voting Preferences of Converted Partisan Identifiers, SRC Panel Members Only

Percent Voting Democratic Among All 1960 Democratic Identifiers	Percent Voting Democratic Among 1960 Democratic Identifiers with 1958 Republican Identifications, By Party Image				
	DD	D	N	R	RR
80.5% (452)	---- (0)	66.7% (3)	87.5% (8)	40.0% (5)	100.0% (1)

Percent Voting Republican Among All 1960 Republican Identifiers	Percent Voting Republican Among 1960 Republican Identifiers with 1958 Democratic Identifications, By Party Image				
	DD	D	N	R	RR
93.8% (336)	12.6% (111)	17.3% (220)	22.1% (68)	55.0% (20)	0.0% (1)

Percent Voting Democratic Among All 1960 Democratic Identifiers	Percent Voting Democratic Among 1960 Democratic Identifiers with 1956 Republican Identifications, By Party Image				
	DD	D	N	R	RR
80.5% (452)	---- (0)	71.4% (7)	66.7% (9)	73.3% (15)	25.0% (4)

Percent Voting Republican Among All 1960 Republican Identifiers	Percent Voting Republican Among 1960 Republican Identifiers with 1956 Democratic Identifications, By Party Image				
	DD	D	N	R	RR
93.8% (336)	100.0% (1)	100.0% (5)	100.0% (4)	100.0% (4)	---- (0)

Having claimed so much for the concept of party image, it is important to reiterate that party image interacts with party identification and that the impact of images is clearly affected by past party identification. This interaction enhances the validity of the concept. Attitudinal forces that operate on electoral behavior frequently interact among themselves in a similar fashion.[41] It seems, then, that party images deserve further empirical study to refine their theoretical role.

NOTES

1. This chapter is a revision of my paper "Party Image and Partisan Change, 1952 to 1972," prepared for delivery at the Annual Meeting of the American Political Science Association, Palmer House Hotel, Chicago, Ill., August 29–September 2, 1974; and my "Party Image and Partisan Change," pp. 63–100 in Louis Maisel and Paul M. Sacks, eds., *The Future of Political Parties*, Sage Electoral Studies Yearbook, Vol. 1 (Beverly Hills: Sage Publications, 1975).

2. See Herbert H. Hyman, *Political Socialization* (Glencoe, Ill.: Free Press, 1959) and Fred I. Greenstein, *Children and Politics* (New Haven: Yale University Press, 1965).

3. Angus Campbell, Philip E. Converse, Warren E. Miller, and Donald E. Stokes, *The American Voter* (New York: Wiley, 1960), p. 163. More precisely, ". . . identification is a function of the proportion of a person's life he has been associated with the group." *Ibid.*

4. On the stability of identifications, see Edward C. Dreyer, "Change and Stability in Party Identifications," *Journal of Politics*, **35** (1973), 712–722; Philip E. Converse, "Change in the American Electorate," pp. 263–337 in Angus Campbell and Philip E. Converse, eds., *The Human Meaning of Social Change* (New York: Russell Sage Foundation, 1972); Donald E. Stokes, "Party Loyalty and the Likelihood of Deviating Elections," pp. 125–135 in Angus Campbell, Philip E. Converse, Warren E. Miller, and Donald E. Stokes, *Elections and the Political Order* (New York: Wiley, 1964); Campbell et al., *The American Voter, op. cit.*, pp. 120–167; Richard A. Brody, "Change and Stability in Partisan Identification: A Note of Caution" (unpublished manuscript: Sanford University, 1975); and Douglas Dobson and Douglas St. Angelo, "Party Identification and the Floating Vote: Some Dynamics," *American Political Science Review*, **69** (1975), 481–490.

5. See Campbell et al., *The American Voter, op. cit.*, pp. 453–472; and Seymour Martin Lipset, *Political Man* (New York: Doubleday-Anchor Books, 1960), pp. 267–273.

6. Brody, *op. cit.*

7. Dobson and St. Angelo, *op. cit.*, p. 488.

8. Dreyer, *op. cit.*

9. Brody, *op. cit.*

10. Dobson and St. Angelo, *op. cit.*

11. To ascertain past party identification, Republicans and Democrats were asked, "Was there ever a time when you thought of yourself as a (R) (D) rather than (D) (R)?" Independents leaning toward the Republican or Democratic Party (coded as partisans in this study) were asked, "Was there ever a time when you thought of yourself as closer to the (R) (D) party instead of the (D) (R) party?" Independents were asked, "Was there ever a time when you thought of yourself as a Democrat or Republican? Which party was that?" These items appear as the following variables in the Inter-University Consortium for Political Research Codebooks:

    1952: $v60, v65$
    1956: $v89$
    1960: $v92$
    1964: $v147$
    1968: $v121$
    1972: $v143, v144, v145, v148, v149, v150$

    The 1952 and 1972 studies elicited this information in a slightly more complicated manner, and only the 1972 study permitted the determination of whether present partisans were once Independents. Usually the questionnaire items do not permit one to determine whether present Democratic and Republican identifiers were formerly Independents. Furthermore, past identifications can only be measured imprecisely (Democratic, Republican, or Independent) rather than with the more desirable SRC seven-point summary party identification scale. Consequently, in cross-tabulating present identification against past identification below, there is no point in using the seven-point scale for present identification, and it has been collapsed into Democratic, Independent, and Republican. This strategy is reasonable, moreover, in light of Brody's finding that the three-point, collapsed identification scale is a better measure of stability than is the seven-point scale. See Brody, *op. cit.*

12. Charles Sellers, "The Equilibrium Cycle in Two-Party Politics," *Public Opinion Quarterly*, **29** (1965), 16–38.

13. *Ibid.*, p. 26.

14. *Ibid.*, p. 28.

15. Donald R. Matthews and James W. Prothro, *Negroes and the New Southern Politics* (New York: Harcourt, Brace and World, 1966), Table 13-6, p. 393.

16. "Behavioral standpatters" between any two elections are individuals who have voted for the same party in both elections.

17. Matthews and Prothro, *op. cit.*, Table 13-7, p. 395.

18. F. Glenn Abney, "Partisan Realignment in a One-Party System: The Case of Mississippi," *Journal of Politics*, **31** (1969), p. 1103. These former Democrats became Independents, not Republicans, however.

19. Matthews and Prothro, *op. cit.*, acknowledge as much on page 390.

20. Except in 1972, present identifiers were not asked if they once were Independents. It is possible to determine, however, how many present Independents were also past Independents. Thus the numbers of cases for the top and bottom cells of the Independents columns in Table 8.1 are unknown. Therefore, percents for the column are not computed. The marginals for present party identifiers in the table correspond fairly well to the frequencies for the entire sample, even though the table excludes individuals for whom complete information is not available. In 1972, the proportion of Independents in the table (15.7%) exceeds the proportion within the entire sample (12.4%), which is surprising since data are more complete. In Table 8.3, estimates for the entire population rely on the more complete information in the entire sample, rather than on the data of Table 8.1, whenever possible.

21. Stable identifiers are defined as individuals whose present party identification is the same as recalled past identification (i.e., individuals who report not having changed identifications). Stable partisans are stable Democratic and stable Republican identifiers; stable Independents report never having been closer to either the Democratic or Republican parties. Past-present patterns of identification are represented by two sets of identification symbols (D = Democratic, R = Republican, I = Independent) attached by an arrow. Past identification is always given to the left of the arrow and present identification to the right. The arrow will be used, for convenience, even for stable identifiers. Thus, I→D represents a past Independent presently identifying with the Democratic Party, and R→R represents a stable Republican identifier.

22. Angus Campbell, "A Classification of the Presidential Elections," pp. 63–77 in Campbell et al., *Elections and the Political Order, op. cit.*

23. Gerald M. Pomper, *Elections in America* (New York: Dodd, Mead, 1970), pp. 99–125; and Angus Campbell, "Interpreting the Presidential Victory," pp. 256–282 in Milton C. Cummings, Jr., *The National Election of 1964* (Washington: Brookings, 1966).

24. Campbell et al., *The American Voter, op. cit.*, p. 155.

25. The reader should note that I have coded Independents who acknowledge feeling closer to one of the two parties as partisans, not as Independents.

26. Campbell et al., *The American Voter, op. cit.*, p. 163.

27. Campbell, "A Classification of the Presidential Elections," *op. cit.*, p. 75.

28. Technically, the predictions discussed in the text are after-the-fact, or "postdictions," but they will be referred to as predictions for convenience.

29. The procedures utilized here resemble those underlying some "Proportional Reduction of Error" measures developed by statisticians. See, for instance, Leo A. Goodman and William H. Kruskal, "Measures of Associa-

tion for Cross-Classification," *Journal of the American Statistical Association,* **49** (1954), 732–764.

30. Walter Dean Burnham, "American Voting Behavior and the 1964 Election," *Midwest Journal of Political Science,* **12** (1968), 1–40.

31. Pomper, *Elections in America, op. cit.,* pp. 99–125; Campbell, "Interpreting the Presidential Victory," *op. cit.*

32. Philip E. Converse, Aage R. Clausen, and Warren E. Miller, "Electoral Myth and Reality: The 1964 Election," *American Political Science Review,* **59** (1965), 321–336.

33. On the possibility and occurrence of rationalization, see Bernard Berelson, Paul F. Lazarsfeld, and William N. McPhee, *Voting* (Chicago: University of Chicago Press, 1954); Benjamin I. Page and Richard A. Brody, "Policy Voting and the Electoral Process: the Vietnam War Issue," *American Political Science Review,* **66** (1972), 979–995; David M. Kovenock, Philip L. Beardsley, and James W. Prothro, "Status, Party, Ideology, Issues, and Candidate Choice: a Preliminary Theory-Relevant Analysis of the 1968 American Presidential Election," paper presented at Specialist Meeting B:XI ("New Approaches to the Study of Social Structure and Voting Behavior"), Eighth World Congress of the International Political Science Association, Munich, Germany, August 31–September 5, 1970; and Samuel A. Kirkpatrick, "Political Attitudes and Behavior: Some Consequences of Attitudinal Ordering," *Midwest Journal of Political Science,* **14** (1970), 1–24.

34. The "breakage" or "majority" effect can be interpreted in this fashion also. This concept refers to the phenomenon of individuals predisposed to the minority candidate in a community being inhibited by majority opinion from exercising their inclinations. See for instance Berelson et al., *op. cit.*

35. Brody, *op. cit.*

36. Matthews and Prothro, *op. cit.,* pp. 392–396.

37. *Ibid.,* p. 392.

38. Campbell et al., *The American Voter, op. cit.,* pp. 143–145.

39. Robert E. Lane and David O. Sears, *Public Opinion* (Englewood Cliffs, N.J.: Prentice-Hall, 1964), pp. 44–53; Kirkpatrick, *op. cit.*

40. Certain combinations of party identification over two waves are rare, so many cells have very small n's. Despite the instability of the means in these cells, the data are remarkably consistent with the stated claim. To overcome the problem of instability caused by small n's, n's in adjacent cells were combined and collective means computed. Two such attempts were made, by defining "adjacent" horizontally and vertically. These procedures reduced the numbers of values in these tables, thereby making analysis more difficult. Otherwise, as often as not, the results even more strongly supported the stated claim.

41. Campbell et al., *The American Voter, op. cit.,* pp. 123–145; David E. RePass, "Issue Salience and Party Choice," *American Political Science Review,* **65** (1971), 388–400.

chapter 9

Conclusion — some theoretical considerations for the concept of party image

In this concluding chapter we summarize our principal findings and relate them to a still-developing theory of the role of party image in electoral behavior. We began in Chapter 1 by arguing that party images have considerable relevance for the study of party decomposition, electoral realignment, and issue voting. We proceed here by summarizing the highlights of the study, by discussing the relevance of the concept of party image to each of these three themes, and by speculating about some theoretical questions addressed less directly by the party image data.

SUMMARY OF FINDINGS

Our analysis began with an examination of a generalized, diffuse index of the number of likes and dislikes the individual has for the Democratic and Republican Parties. This particular index behaves in the aggregate in a rather stable fashion, is related both to party identification and to voting, and seems to capture fairly well both the underlying stability of American politics and the responsiveness of voters to short-term stimuli in the political environment. Chapter 3 examined likes and dislikes separately and found that electoral behavior is more responsive to likes than to dislikes and that movement of a part of the electorate contributes a degree of flexibility to the amount of ideological constraint among Americans. At this point, then, we had already encountered substantial evidence of the theoretical worth of the concept of party image. Both stable and changing electoral behavior could be explained somewhat by the concept, and the concept provided a preliminary basis for rethinking the traditional claim that American voting behavior is more likely to respond to negative evaluations than to positive evaluations.

In Chapter 4 the analysis of the substantive concerns of Americans uncovered strong evidence of the imprint of the Depression. While Depression-related themes have defined the Democratic Party since the 1930s, a sense of the dynamics of American politics comes from the realization that such themes are less and less salient to Americans and that images respond quickly and powerfully to potentially critical issues of a contemporary nature. Thus party images not only document the impact of forces that in years past produced the present party system but also the impact of forces of a more contemporary stature that have threatened to transfix that party system.

Yet both Chapters 2 and 3 together revealed that party images were less well defined and less rich than they once had been, so we were inevitably led to ask whether such evidence suggested that parties themselves were less meaningful to Americans. Moreover, the ability of party images to respond to and then quickly ignore the important issues of the day (Vietnam, civil rights) suggested not only something about the perceptiveness of the American voter, about which we say more in a moment, but also something about the difficulties faced by the parties themselves in responding to and articulating positions on those very issues that motivate voters so intensely.

The wealth of issues made it impossible to explore them all in detail, so instead, in Chapters 5, 6, and 7, we concentrated on two sets of highly significant issues. The first deals with class, and we found that differences between the working and middle classes in their images of American parties have been muted since 1952. Several processes have accounted for this effect. Generational replacement has moved out of the electorate individuals with more extreme class differences than those of the individuals who have moved into the electorate. Educational change has moved larger and larger proportions of the electorate into educational categories less concerned with class matters and even likely in recent years to reverse traditional class distinctions. But in addition to these long-term processes whose effects will continue to be felt, the imprint of the Depression itself is simply not so strong among those individuals who experienced it first hand. While the rising level of affluence seems a likely enough explanation of this phenomenon, it is not completely satisfactory, since many individuals who were probably middle class during the Depression nevertheless care less about class matters than they did in 1952.

As class differences have subsided, racial differences have emerged. Here the party image data are particularly enlightening. If data for the working and middle classes reveal the ability of the concept of party image to trace the "normal" dissolution of political themes in America, the data for racial differences reveal the ability of the concept to capture the unusual and the dramatic in American politics. It is perhaps sad testimony to American democracy that the racial issue should have played such a critical role in the political evaluations of Americans in the 1960s, but it is certainly impressive that party image data document both the emergence and disappearance of this issue. Furthermore, both the fast emergence and equally fast disappearance of the issue in party images suggests something about the dynamics of American party politics, about which we speculate below.

In Chapter 8 we began our more direct theoretical explorations and found data consistent with the proposition that party images play an intermediary and crucial role in the transformations of individual party identifications. Clearly the data here are not conclusive, since the panel data reveal that party images are not always stable even among individuals for whom images seem to have changed identifications. The determination of the time sequence of the acquisition of party images and party identifications is unfortunately still somewhat ambiguous.

THE RELEVANCE OF PARTY IMAGE

Party decomposition

How can party image data inform us about the process of party decomposition? If parties mean less to individuals then presumably the symbols, Democratic Party and Republican Party, will stimulate fewer and less complex free associations. We have found evidence that the substantive themes that once so readily appeared among these responses are no longer so common. If traditional themes are not replaced by more contemporary themes, then the disappearance of contemporary themes means that parties are losing any meaning they have. This is not yet the case. While traditional themes are disappearing, they have not completely disappeared and their salience can be temporarily reestablished. Furthermore, some themes, such as the Republican association with foreign policy, are probably no less common than they ever have been (unless events since 1972 make the data analyzed here already obsolete), but are simply volatile in their salience. Furthermore, as contemporary issues arise in American politics, they often appear in the party images of Americans. Their appearance in a sense can be reasonably interpreted as one form of evidence that they have become widespread and important. Issues such as race that temporarily dominate American party images demonstrate first the ability of party images to describe American politics of the moment and second the willingness of Americans to let new issues redefine American parties.

Significantly, however, the issues that appeared so dramatically in the party images of Americans also disappeared equally suddenly and mysteriously. In terms of the process of party decomposition, this has tended to leave parties without contemporary defining themes. Parties mean less to Americans because many traditional themes are less important than they once were while those issues that might have redefined American parties quickly became irrelevant to American political parties. We have argued, with Sundquist,[1] that on issues such as race the parties have failed to take the polarizing stands that could have redefined parties in accordance with the strong sentiments Americans felt. The "ongoing march of party decomposition," of which Burnham speaks,[2] thus includes the growing absence of defining themes and the growing failure of parties to articulate issues or undertake actions that will contribute to the meaning of parties in the eyes of voters. In short, party images reveal that party decomposition has progressed since 1952 and that the decomposition involves the declining salience of class-related themes accompanied by the failure of more contemporary themes to be incorporated (or in the words of Milne and Mackenzie, "annexed")[3] into the definitions Americans have for their parties.

Issue voting

If new substantive themes fail to replace traditional themes in the party images of Americans, does this mean that contemporary political issues are unimportant for electoral behavior? Actually, the party image data seem to suggest just the opposite. It must be pointed out again that we have not directly examined the impact of opinions on issues on the vote. Instead we have only determined whether issues have intruded upon the party images of Americans and whether they have affected voting through these party images. Consequently, the party image data tell us very little about the total salience of issues or about the total influence of issues on voting. Nevertheless, the party image data are rather instructive about the influence of issues.

It is true that some issues have structured the vote less and less over time. It is also true that even salient issues do not necessarily structure the vote. The data of Chapter 4 are clear on these points, and the analyses in Chapters 5 through 7 also reveal that the issues of class and race have not been consistently capable of affecting voting behavior, through party images. It seems, however, that these data are more pertinent to the questions of whether the issues are important at all to the *party images* of Americans. To make judgments about the importance of issues for *voting behavior,* from the party image data alone, we need to consider once again the pattern by which issues emerge in or disappear from these party images.

The data of Chapter 4 convey a sense of the fine perceptiveness on the part of voters. Issues important to voters will influence voting through the images that voters possess so long as, and only so long as, those issues are potentially or manifestly part of the meaning of the parties. That is, to the extent that the meaning of parties influences voting, then issues can influence voting through their contribution to that meaning. But even salient issues cannot influence voting when voters realize that parties do not differ on these issues. There is little doubt that Vietnam was a highly salient issue in the 1960s, but its failure to affect the voting decision of voters was less the result of the voters' inability to engage in issue voting than it was the result of the voters' objectively accurate perceptions that the candidates did not differ on the issue.[4] Similarly, issues operating through the party images of Americans obviously cannot affect voting unless they have become part of those party images, unless they have been "annexed," which can happen only if they distinguish between the parties.[5]

Finally, the data we have considered also suggest that voters are sensitive to issues they consider important. RePass suggested that issues can be expected to affect voting behavior only when they are salient to voters,[6] and the party image data demonstrate quite reasonably that some issues are more salient than other issues. Moreover, even though these data are an indirect measure of the extent of issue voting, the data nevertheless constitute one form of evidence that issues may affect the voting decision.

Electoral realignment

It is more difficult to document the importance of party image in the process of electoral realignment because survey data do not exist from a time about which we can say unambiguously that a realignment occurred. Even if the panel data had been less ambiguous on the role of party image in transforming party identifications, either in more strongly confirming that role *or* in more strongly disconfirming that role, we still could not have been terribly confident about the role of party image in times of electoral realignment. Between 1956 and 1960 there simply were too few permanent changes in party identification for us reasonably to compare that four-year period with a period of electoral realignment.

What can we say then about party images and electoral realignment? First, both the aggregate data and the panel data either support or do not rule out the proposition that party images intervene to transform party identifications, *when images conflict strongly enough with "past" identifications.* Second, the aggregate pattern of frequency of changes in party image suggests that images are more mutable than identifications but more stable than opinions on issues. Finally, the trends in the substantive concerns of Americans and the complementary responsiveness of images to issues of a more contemporary nature further suggest that party images are more enduring than opinions on issues but less enduring than party identifications.

Furthermore, if we accept the micro-level definition of realignment — enduring changes in party identification among massive numbers of individuals[7] — we are forced to ask exactly how identifications are transformed. The lessons of the political socialization literature are that identifications are learned early in life and typically are long lasting. Yet the crises that cause realignment do so by disrupting and eventually overcoming the long-held attachments of many individuals. Sellers' argument that party images are crucial to the transformation of identifications seems all the more plausible given the data we have examined. Issues of a highly salient nature emerge in the party images of Americans. When these images conflict so strongly with identifications, individuals first behave in response to their images. Eventually, if strongly held images persist and continue to conflict with identifications, some individuals will change their identifications. For others, voting behavior will follow the images even while old identifications are retained. When this process has proceded far enough to drastically and permanently alter the coalitional bases of the party system, a realignment has occurred. Throughout the process, individuals perceive parties on opposite sides of the crucial issue or issues.[8]

Party image data on the racial issue reflect such a process, with the significant difference that the process seemingly was aborted. Many Southern whites adopted strongly pro-Republican images in 1964, and some (the vanguard about whom we speculated) even changed their identifications. Most Southern whites who voted Republican did so without changing their identifications. But as the voters perceived that the parties would not polarize around the racial issue, the issue lost its meaning for the parties and stopped affecting the political behavior of voters. Thus the realigning process that may have begun between 1960 and 1964 was aborted, which in turn helps to explain why the 1964 data were so frequently distinctive without ever actually reversing old patterns or establishing new patterns.

Finally, Brody demonstrates that strength of partisan attachment responds to short-term political forces.[9] One wonders whether the impact of short-term forces on identification is felt first in and through the party images of some individuals. If so, to argue that strong party images can cause enduring change in party identifications, and that issues of widespread salience that prompt such strong images can cause massive change, is much more plausible. Certainly the finding of Dobson and St. Angelo, that party identifications may be less stable than scholars once thought,[10] should prompt further examination of potential causes of this instability.

THEORETICAL SPECULATIONS

The implications of the party image data are far reaching. In this section we speculate about some of the more significant possibilities that deal with the nature of the American political party system, its process of change, and the role of the voter in that process.

An intermediary role for party image

It seems reasonable to suppose that if party images can induce change in party identification for one individual, they can cause change in identification for many individuals, and if they translate critical social and economic issues into political terms, then they may even prompt electoral realignment. At any rate, it may be useful to consider party images as constituting a "medium-term" force in electoral behavior, as distinguished from long-term and short-term forces,[11] and as playing an intermediary role that connects identification and opinion on issues. The process of socialization produces party identifications that are very much contentfree, almost entirely affective, and rarely cognitive. Yet in recent years there is strong evidence that identifications and opinions on the issues are coming more into line with each other.[12] Such aggregate correspondence is not evidence that individuals have changed their identifications in response to their opinions on issues, but that over time the aggregate relationship between opinions and identifications has been altered. Pomper suggests that events in the political environment prompted such developments.[13] Were these events incorporated first into the party images? Certainly the critical issues of the 1960s affected party images. It is possible that they did so as part of the process of altering party identifications. That is, changes in party image were intermediary, occurring between the acquisition of past identification and before the adoption of new identification. Furthermore, they were necessary for the transformation of identification.

In addition, party images constitute a medium-term force in electoral behavior because they affect electoral behavior but are less long standing than party identification and more long standing than issues. This is so because they are probably only partially learned through the process of political socialization and reflect the decaying basis of the existing party system. They also incorporate the effects of highly salient contemporary issues.

Party image and the party system

We suggested the possibility in Chapter 1 that party images received earlier attention in Great Britain perhaps because they were more relevant to the nature of the British party system. That is, programmatic parties, especially parties differing in their class base and class appeal, more clearly stand for different things than do the pluralistic, open American political parties. Yet in a fully programmatic, ideological party system, especially one based on class divisions, it matters little whether the scholar chooses to study party identification, attitudes on political issues, party images, or class identification, for all factors would reinforce each other and each factor would lead to the same predictions as every other factor. In this sense, then, party images are more useful in a less ideologically constrained party system. In this latter system, party images can be helpful in explaining why identifications do not necessarily predict voting behavior. Also, party images can explain perhaps why some issues are related to voting and others are not; those issues that the voter sees as defining the parties have greater political relevance for the voter, whatever his or her personal intensity of feeling about the topic. The intrusion of issues into the party images of Americans is a subtle if indirect measure of the "political translation" for the individual of the given issue.[14]

But the party system is itself a dynamic and changing structure. Even while party labels remain constant, for example between 1896 and the present, what the parties stand for clearly may change. Change is particularly sudden and massive in periods of electoral realignment which are created by serious and far-reaching social and economic crises. Our analysis of party image data suggests that party images can trace the process of change in the electoral bases of the party system and can document the transformation of the party system or perhaps even its dissolution. Recent political issues have seemingly had the potential for transforming the party system; their failure to do so, together with the general process of alienation among Americans today, threaten to send the entire party system into oblivion.[15] In Chapter 1 we used the metaphor of the star whose image burned bright in the night light-years after the star itself had disintegrated. If the cataclysm of the Depression created the present Democratic star, or at least the star whose image we have been studying, then the danger for the political system is that the next cataclysm will leave the political sky empty, that the next realignment will fail to produce a set of viable political parties.[16]

The particular difficulty that parties face is that a variety of factors discourages them from articulating highly salient themes and the failure to do so further alienates the public. These factors no doubt include such selfish concerns as the desire to protect the existing organization and set of career channels.[17] More sympathetically, however, we should realize that moral considerations may properly prevent parties from polarizing around socially critical issues such as race. Ironically, the refusal to retreat from a morally upright position incurs citizen distrust. Furthermore, it can be argued that disguised hints at polarization (Southern strategy, refusals to announce support for court probusing decisions) only exacerbate racial tensions. (Perhaps, in fact, explicit polarization by the parties would have been more defensible morally than implied opposition to integration.)

Television and party images

So far we have ignored entirely the process by which images are created or amended, except implicitly to note that they reflect political issues of the past and present. If our arguments so far are reasonable, then party activity in response to these issues determines whether issues will be annexed or not. Vietnam and civil rights did not become part of the party images of either party because both parties refused to take clear and opposite stands on the issue. Economic matters, on the other hand, were strongly debated in the 1932 campaign, and the victorious Democratic administration actively pursued means by which to bring the Depression under control.

In more contemporary America, though, the creation and transmission of images is the activity if not the function of the mass media, especially television. Even in the 1950s Milne and Mackenzie implicitly recognized the importance of television in disseminating party images.[18]

Today scholars and social commentators alike debate the propriety of media campaigns, the political use of imagery, and the techniques of the "new politics."[19] *A perusal of this literature reveals that it rarely discusses the ability or propriety of disseminating PARTY images.* When Burnham and others warn of "the obvious growth of [candidate] image . . . voting,"[20] they lament the transformation of American politics from a quasi-responsible party system to a candidate-oriented (candidate image-oriented), relatively irresponsible form of government.[21]

Contemporary candidate-oriented politics is both cause and effect of party decomposition. The weaker parties become, the less beholden to them candidates want to be. The more independent that candidates become, the less able are parties to influence the behavior of elected officials and to deliver on party platforms, and so the less inclined are voters to put their faith in parties (as well as in candidates since they cannot deliver on their own promises without institutionalized mechanisms such as parties with which to work). The more refined television campaigning has become, the easier it has been for "nonpolitical" candidates, including nonmembers of the parties, to enter the political arena laterally, and the less influential have parties been over elected officials and campaigning candidates. Therefore growing disillusionment with parties is not solely the fault of the parties themselves.[22] Furthermore, the technology of media politics is not necessarily something parties as institutions could have controlled.

However, the growth of media politics can also be seen as a consequence of the parties' failure to reform themselves.[23] The history of American political parties has been a continual struggle between forces seeking to protect the viability of the existing organization and forces trying to make the parties more accessible and responsive to (new) elements in society.[24] Television's recent inroads into politics stem somewhat from the failure of parties to assimilate satisfactorily many of the dissident elements of the 1960s and 1970s.

This process is ironic, for the power of the media no doubt could be invoked in behalf of political parties. If political parties rather than individual candidates controlled the raising and spending of campaign funds, parties would very quickly be invigorated and revitalized. In the meantime, the emphasis on candidate imagery can only detract from party imagery, and the prognosis of healthy political parties in an era of media technology is not encouraging.

Party images in a better-educated electorate

Education has played a crucial role in transforming American politics. Not only are better-educated individuals less concerned with matters of class and more concerned with quality of life issues, but this greater educational attainment has other indirect and important implications for American politics.

Because the present electorate is better educated, better informed, and more able to make decisions, it probably needs the informational activities of parties somewhat less than did the less-educated electorate of the past. Furthermore, educated individuals tend to be media consumers, and to receive political messages from sources other than parties. In addition, the present educated electorate is more ideological than the less-educated electorate of the 1950s.[25] Better-educated individuals undoubtedly demand more of government. In sum, contemporary American citizens are more constrained and less flexible in their political demands and are less easily satisfied. The degree of flexibility that traditionally could be found among the undecided and uninformed[26] must necessarily decrease as this group diminishes in size.

Party images as conveyors of traditional political themes are likely to be less essential to the educated voter. The decaying influence of party image may result from the lessened need of educated voters to rely on party images. Party decomposition may be inevitable among an educated electorate that perceives parties as unwilling or unable to act upon important issues. Yet party images may also become more volatile as an educated electorate forms opinions on issues and anticipates party action on the issues, only to lose interest in the issues *as helping to define the parties* when the parties fail to act on them.

Party images and the reasonable voter

In one important respect the party image data are highly pertinent to the recent debate about the rationality of the American voter. V. O. Key has argued that voters can only echo the voice of the parties; if parties fail to give voters reasonable choices, voters cannot make reasonable choices.[27] This claim is strongly supported by the analysis by Page and Brody, who showed in a mock election that 1968 voters' opinions on the Vietnam War could have caused voters to choose between two candidates who clearly differed in their positions on the war, even though the voters' actual choices between Nixon and Humphrey (who objectively did not differ in their positions) did not reflect the voters' opinions.[28] Similarly Hamilton argues that the presumed irrationality and ignorance of the people results more from parties and their failures to clarify the issues. As issues are clarified, voters do make reasonable choices.[29]

As we have argued before, the party image data on Vietnam and the racial issue reflect this same kind of reasonableness on the part of voters. In terms of defining parties, issues such as Vietnam and race had great potential. They quickly lost it, apparently, as voters accurately perceived that parties would fail to differentiate themselves on these issues.

To argue that voters are or can be reasonable is not to argue that they are or can be rational. Clearly the party image data are insufficient for analyzing voter rationality. In passing, however, it is worth noting that the debate about the rationality of voters is somewhat unfair to them. It is not obvious at all why we should expect them to be rational when the assumption of rationality is an assumption we are unlikely to invoke in almost any human situation. Even administrators who are trained to think systematically and process large amounts of information willingly "satisfice" rather than act completely rationally.[30] The costs of the acquisition of information and the processing of that information are simply too steep for the individual to try to be completely thorough. To assess electoral behavior, then, it seems fairer to the voter to ask whether he satisfices — whether he reasonably uses available information to make a satisfactory if not optimal electoral decision. The party image data on the racial issue especially suggest that information and opinion that can be put to no good use is worthless to the voter, no matter how inherently important the voter once thought it to be. The voter quite reasonably recognizes the lack of worth *for the voting decision* by dropping the issue from his or her party image.[31]

Party image, candidate image, and issue voting

In the Introduction we argued that scholars who combine the party image and candidate image items in attempting to explain the voting decision cannot detect in their combined data the meaning of political parties for Americans. Yet these same scholars successfully identify most of the factors that influence the voting decision and even predict quite accurately from these two sets of likes and dislikes what the individual's vote will be.[32] Their success stems from the obvious fact that party images are neither the sole determinant nor the most important determinant of the voting decision. As the ability of party identification and party image to structure the vote has waned, the ability of candidate image and issues to do so has increased. Furthermore, the viability of political parties is itself threatened as candidate images and issues gain in influence.

To affect voting behavior issues clearly do not have to operate only through party images. In fact, to the extent that issues that structure voting are not annexed by the political parties and do not become part of the images of the parties, then the voter will fail to find an electoral function for parties. As parties fail to perform their electoral function, they will find it more and more difficult to perform their governmental function, since elected officials will be increasingly free of party influence in their personal decision-making processes. Without somewhat consistent and responsible institutions such as parties trying to whip the behavior of elected officials into line, governmental policy making is apt to stagnate or at least become more and more the province of the bureaucracy.[33] Ironically, then, increased issue voting *that is not translated into party voting* is likely to produce frustration with governmental *immobilisme* and diminished representation and accountability.

The importance of candidate image has increased and is likely to continue to increase. The failure of parties to respond to the issues in people's minds, the stagnation of policy making by traditional institutions (parties, Congress, and the Executive), and the growth of the media industry have all promoted the emergence of candidate imagery. In turn, the reliance of voters on candidate imagery for their voting decisions further strips political parties of their electoral function and robs them of their meaning, in the voters' collective eyes.

Longitudinal examinations of survey data reveal that voting decisions depend more and more on candidate imagery and political issues and less and less on party imagery and partisan identifications.[34] Without political parties to structure the votes of the electorate, individual opinions cannot easily or meaningfully be aggregated into governmental policy. Furthermore, the implications for American democracy are not promising, as Pomper has noted:

> Unless parties are revived, the prospects are for a national politics of fits and starts, in which elections are decided by the appeals of transient issues and

passing candidates, in which continuing responsibility is absent, and in which alienation from the political process deepens. The ultimate prospect is substitution of the plebiscite for the party process, and its historical concomitant, the substitution of the domineering leader for the democratic politician.[35]

CONCLUSION

The concept of party image bridges the theories of the dependent voter and the responsive voter.[36] As a relatively long-standing attitudinal component of the vote, party image reveals the voter to be somewhat *dependent* on habitual social and psychological phenomena. As somewhat responsive to short-term issues, party image also reveals the voter to be *responsive* to those same issues. To decide whether the voter is relatively more dependent or more responsive, one might first explore the individual's party images and determine the salience of short-term issues by noting their appearance or absence in the party images, and second measure the impact of dependence factors by noting how important diffuse party images are for electoral behavior.

As voters become more responsive, they no longer need party labels to structure their voting behavior, but presumably because they are more attuned to meaningful distinctions between the parties, they will remain capable of and willing to invoke party images. As meaningful differences between parties become "annexed" by the parties and incorporated into their party images, parties can resurrect their own importance and create party-structured voting even among an electorate of responsive voters. Responsive voters demand more of parties, and television, lack of internal cohesion, and lack of control over campaign funds all threaten to destroy political parties. So the challenge to parties and to the American party system in the 1970s and 1980s is as difficult, perhaps, as any parties have ever faced, and the response to that challenge perhaps will be found in the content and importance of American party images.

NOTES

1. James L. Sundquist, *Dynamics of the Party System* (Washington: Brookings, 1973), pp. 358–366.
2. Walter Dean Burnham, *Critical Elections and the Mainsprings of American Politics* (New York: Norton, 1970).

3. R. S. Milne and H. C. Mackenzie, *Straight Fight* (London: Hansard Society, 1954), p. 137; Milne and Mackenzie, *Marginal Seat, 1955* (London: Hansard Society, 1958), p. 130.

4. Benjamin I. Page and Richard A. Brody, "Policy Voting and the Electoral Process: the Vietnam War Issue," *American Political Science Review,* **66** (1972), 979–995.

5. Milne and Mackenzie make this point; see *Marginal Seat, 1955, op. cit.,* p. 130.

6. David E. RePass, "Issue Salience and Party Choice," *American Political Science Review,* **65** (1971), 388–400.

7. Realignment is defined in terms of changes in party identification by Angus Campbell, "A Classification of Presidential Elections," pp. 63–77 in Angus Campbell, Philip E. Converse, Warren E. Miller, and Donald E. Stokes, *Elections and the Political Order* (New York: Wiley, 1966).

8. The theory of realignment to which the role of party image is applied here has been stated most completely by Sundquist, *op. cit.,* and by Burnham, *op. cit.*

9. Richard A. Brody, "Change and Stability in Partisan Identification: A Note of Caution" (unpublished manuscript: Stanford University, 1975).

10. Douglas Dobson and Douglas St. Angelo, "Party Identification and the Floating Vote: Some Dynamics," *American Political Science Review,* **69** (1975), 481–490.

11. Philip E. Converse, "The Concept of a Normal Vote," pp. 9–39 in Campbell et al., *op. cit.*

12. Gerald M. Pomper, "From Confusion to Clarity: Issues and American Voters," *American Political Science Review,* **66** (1972), 415–428.

13. *Ibid.*

14. On "political translation" see Angus Campbell, Philip E. Converse, Warren E. Miller, and Donald E. Stokes, *The American Voter* (New York: Wiley, 1960), pp. 31–32.

15. See Walter Dean Burnham, "The End of American Party Politics," *Transaction,* **7**:2 (December 1969), 12–22; and Burnham, "American Politics in the 1970s: Beyond Party?" pp. 238–277 in Louis Maisel and Paul M. Sacks, eds., *The Future of Political Parties,* Sage Electoral Studies Yearbook, Vol. 1 (Beverly Hills: Sage Publications, 1975).

16. See, for instance, the column by David S. Broder, "Election Scenarios for 1976," *Washington Post,* June 25, 1975, p. A14.

17. Sundquist, *op. cit.,* pp. 283–285; Burnham, "American Politics in the 1970s," *op. cit.,* p. 265.

18. Milne and Mackenzie, *Marginal Seat, 1955, op. cit.* Also see Kurt Lang and Gladys Engel Lang, "The Mass Media and Voting," pp. 217–235 in Eugene Burdick and Arthur J. Brodbeck, eds., *American Voting Behavior* (Glencoe, Ill.: Free Press, 1959).

19. See, for instance, Ray Hiebert, Robert Jones, Ernest Lotito, and John

Lorenz, eds., *The Political Image Merchants: Strategies in the New Politics* (Washington: Acropolis Books, 1971); Dan Nimmo, *The Political Persuaders* (Englewood Cliffs, N.J.: Prentice-Hall, 1970); Sig Mickelson, *The Electric Mirror: Politics in an Age of Television* (New York: Dodd, Mead, 1972); and Keven P. Phillips, *Mediacracy* (Garden City, N.Y.: Doubleday, 1975).

20. Walter Dean Burnham, "The Changing Shape of the American Political Universe," *American Political Science Review,* **59** (1965), p. 26.

21. See for instance David S. Broder, *The Party's Over* (New York: Harper and Row, 1972).

22. Broder argues that Eisenhower's failure to define politics in partisan terms put in motion the process of party decomposition that we have witnessed for the past 20 years. *Ibid.,* pp. 5–15.

23. For instance, Walter DeVries argues: "The techniques of the new politics have succeeded only because the two traditional parties have failed. The parties have not really reformed the nomination or general election processes, and the voters know it." The techniques of the new politics provide voters with information and make them able "to judge more accurately parties and candidates." See Walter DeVries, "Taking the Voter's Pulse," in Hiebert et al., *op. cit.,* p. 64.

24. For instance, Jacksonian Democrats invented the nominating convention to correct the ills of the closed, elitist "King caucus." Progressives instituted the direct primary to take party control away from closed, corrupt machines. Reform Democrats in the 1960s implemented quota systems in the nominating process to make the process more representative. See William Nisbet Chambers and Walter Dean Burnham, eds., *The American Party Systems* (New York: Oxford University Press, 1967). For a comprehensive history of party reform efforts and a discussion of implications of contemporary reforms, see Austin Ranney, *Curing the Mischiefs of Faction* (Berkeley: University of California Press, 1975).

25. Everett Carll Ladd, Jr. and Charles D. Hadley, *Political Parties and Political Issues: Patterns in Differentiation Since the New Deal,* Sage Professional Papers in American Politics, Series/Number 04-010 (Beverly Hills, Calif.: Sage Publications, 1973), pp. 46–51. See also Norman H. Nie with Kristi Andersen, "Mass Belief Systems Revisited: Political Change and Attitude Change," *Journal of Politics,* **36** (1974), 540–591.

26. Philip E. Converse, "Information Flow and the Stability of Partisan Attitudes," pp. 136–157 in Angus Campbell et al., *Elections and the Political Order, op. cit.*

27. V. O. Key, Jr., *The Responsible Electorate* (Cambridge: Harvard University Press, 1966), especially pp. 1–8.

28. Page and Brody, *op. cit.*

29. Richard F. Hamilton, *Class and Politics in the United States* (New York: Wiley, 1972), p. 93.

30. On "satisficing" see James G. March and Herbert A. Simon, *Organizations* (New York: Wiley, 1958), Ch. 6.

31. The most comprehensive statement on the responsive voter is made by Gerald M. Pomper, *Voters' Choice* (New York: Dodd, Mead, 1975).

32. See for instance Donald E. Stokes, "Some Dynamic Aspects of Contests for the Presidency," *American Political Science Review,* **60** (1966), 19–28; and Stanley Kelley, Jr. and Thad W. Mirer, "The Simple Act of Voting," *American Political Science Review,* **68** (1974), 572–591.

33. Burnham, "American Politics in the 1970s," *op. cit.*

34. See the July, 1975 issue of *American Politics Quarterly* **3**:3, edited by Samuel A. Kirkpatrick.

35. Gerald M. Pomper, "Impacts on the Political System," *American Politics Quarterly,* **3**:3 (July 1975), p. 350.

36. The "portraits" of the dependent voter and the reasonable voter are painted by Pomper, *Voters' Choice, op. cit.,* pp. 5–12.

Index